The Rothschilds

A European Family

Edited by Georg Heuberger

Thorbecke / Boydell & Brewer

The guide and the essay volume are appearing on the occasion of the exhibition »The Rothschilds – A European Family« in the Jewish Museum of the City of Frankfurt am Main, October 11, 1994–February 27, 1995

Published on behalf of the Frankfurt Municipal Office for Culture and Leisure, Department of Science and Art by the Jewish Museum Frankfurt
Editor: Georg Heuberger
Editorial Assistent: Johannes Heil
Translation from German into English:
Dr. Jeremy Gaines and Paul Keast

The exhibition was mounted on the occasion of the 1200th anniversary of the City of Frankfurt am Main and the 250th anniversary of the birth of Meyer Amschel Rothschild in cooperation with Frankfurt Projekte GmbH.

Authors of the Exhibition Guide:
Fritz Backhaus: pp. 1–2, 11–34, 43–46, 149–158
Lisbeth Ehlers: pp. 173–189
Dr. Ernst Karpf: pp. 112–120
Dr. Helga Krohn: pp. 1–2, 50–92, 159–170
Christine Lenger: pp. 121–128, 190–196
Rainer Schlott: pp. 35–42, 47–49, 129–148, 171–172
Dr. Annette Weber: pp 3–10, 93–111, 172

Layout: Norbert Brey

Jüdisches Museum

1200 JAHRE 94
FRANKFURTₑR LEBEN

STADT FRANKFURT AM MAIN

Printed in Germany · ISBN 3-7995-1207-1

First published in 1994

Distribution of the English edition in Great Britain, Ireland, USA, Canada, New Zeeland exclusively by The Boydell Press Woodbridge

ISBN 0 85115 371 2

The Boydell Press is an imprint of Boydell & Brewer Ltd, PO Box 9, Woodbridge, Suffolk IP 12 3DF, UK and of Boydell & Brewer Inc,. PO Box 41025, Rochester, NY 14604-4126. USA

Die Deutsche Bibliothek – CIP-Einheitsaufnahme

The Rothschilds: [anlässlich der Ausstellung »Die Rothschilds – Eine europäische Familie« im Jüdischen Museum der Stadt Frankfurt am Main, 11. Oktober 1994–27. Februar 1995] / hrsg. von Georg Heuberger. [Hrsg. im Auftr. des Dezernats für Kultur und Freizeit, Amt für Wissenschaft und Kunst der Stadt Frankfurt am Main vom Jüdischen Museum der Stadt Frankfurt am Main]. – Sigmaringen: Thorbecke.

ISBN 3-7995-1209-8

NE: Heuberger, Georg [Hrsg.]; Ausstellung Die Rothschilds – Eine europäische Familie <1994–1995, Frankfurt am Main>; Jüdisches Museum <Frankfurt, Main>

Bd. 1. A European Family: [Guide] / Autoren: Fritz Backhaus ...]. – 1994

ISBN 3-7995-1207-1

NE: Backhaus, Fritz

Contents

Preface by the Lord Mayor
Andreas von Schoeler . . . . /8

Preface by Lord Rothschild . . . . . . /10

The Rothschilds – Family History
in the Museum Context by
Museumsdirector Georg Heuberger /12

Acknowledgements . . . . /14

The Rothschilds – Thoughts on
a Remarkable Family History 1

Overture: A Magnificent Ambience . 3
»Goût Rothschild« – The Lifestyle of the
Rothschild Family 4
The Rothschilds as Collectors of Art 7

Meyer Amschel Rothschild – A Life
in the Judengasse 11
A Glance at the Judengasse 12
Life in the Community 14
»Agent to the Noble Court of
Hesse-Hanau« 17
The »Grünes Schild« House 20
On the Road 22

Wars, Princes and Business –
The Career of a Court Jew 23
Supplies to the Army 24
En Route to Kassel 26
The Elector in Exile 30
Rescuing a Fortune 32

Nathan crosses the Channel 35
NM Rothschild, 15 Brown Street,
Manchester 36
The Continental Blockade 39
A Good Match 41
A Banker in London 41

Meyer Amschel Rothschild – Banker
to the Court and Citizen 43
The Struggle for Equal Rights 44
Taking Stock of a Long Life 46

The Five Brothers: New Beginnings
amongst Continued Unity 47
»...at this moment paralysed for want
of money...« – An Army
in Dire Straits 48
»Meyer Amschel Rothschild & Söhne« –
A Family Company With
Clear Principles 51
Rothschild – von Rothschild –
Baron von Rothschild 53

The European Rothschild Bank 55
The Prussian Bond Issue of 1818:
»Only the Rothschilds can handle it« 56
NM Rothschild & Sons, London . . . 59
De Rothschild Frères, Paris 65
M.A. von Rothschild & Söhne,
Frankfurt 70
S.M. von Rothschild, Vienna 76
C.M. de Rothschild e figli, Naples . . 80
What Pigeons Have to Do with
Stock Market Profits 85
The House of Rothschild:
A European Family 90

The Price of Success – Self-Perception, Self-Presentation and Criticisms 93
How to Become a »Rothschild« –
The Self-Perception of the Family . . 94
Portraits – A Rothschild Custom . . . 101
At The Pinnacle of European Society 104
The Rothschilds' »Public« Face 112
Wealth Obliges 121

The Advent of the Age in Industry . . 129
The Steam Railway Comes to Austria 130
Salomon Becomes an Industrialist –
The Witkowitz Ironworks 132
The Rise of Two Competitors:
The Pereires 134
Unequal Partners – Rothschild
and Oppenheim 137
The Transfer of Five Billion Francs . . 139
The Purchase of the Suez Canal 141
Black Gold 142
Worldwide Expansion 144
The End of a Bank Steeped in
Tradition 148

The Rothschilds in the Twentieth Century 149
Propaganda, Persecution and
Relief Work 150
Why There Are Countless Streets
Named Rothschild in Israel:
Edmond de Rothschild and Palestine 159
Beyond the Domain of the Bank . . . 168

The Rothschilds in Frankfurt 173
Rothschilds in Frankfurt? 174
»In terms of money, Rothschild is
still the most distinguished«
(Otto von Bismarck)
Amschel Mayer von Rothschild . . . 174
A Representative of Frankfurt –
Mayer Carl von Rothschild 179
The Family´s Old House 183
The Last Rothschilds in Frankfurt –
Wilhelm Carl von Rothschild 185
The End of the Frankfurt Bank 189
The Name Lives On: The
Goldschmidt-Rothschild Family . . . 190
Foundations for Frankfurt 191

References 197
Bibliography 199
Illustration and photo credits 204
Contributors to the Exhibition 206
Five generations of the Rothschild
family, portrayed graphically 208

Planning and Realization of the Exhibition

Exhibitiondirector: Georg Heuberger
Curators: Dr. Helga Krohn, Fritz Backhaus
Project coordinator: Katharina Rauschenberger
Technical coordinator: Michael Lenarz
Exhibition staff: Fritz Backhaus, Lisbeth Ehlers,
Dr. Ernst Karpf, Dr. Helga Krohn, Christine
Lenger, Rainer Schlott, Dr. Annette Weber.
Research: Avraham Frank, Dr. Felicitas Heimann-
Jelinek, Anna-Luise Knetsch, Carlo Alberto Pal-
miero, Pauline Prevost-Marcilhacy, Hans-Otto
Schembs, Jochen Stollberg, Susanne Urban,
Kerstin Warnke-Dakers
PR, events, guided tours: Johannes Heil, Cilly
Kugelmann
Translation of the exhibition texts: Dr. Jeremy
Gaines, assisted by Paul Keast and Doris Jones
Editorial Assistent: Johannes Heil
Exhibition design: Init Feil und Hahn, Frankfurt
am Main, BSB Architektengemeinschaft Thomas
Bundschuh, Frankfurt am Main
Assistance with installations: Lotte Kroll

Exhibition assembly: Münch + Münch GmbH,
Frankfurt am Main
Photographic work: S & P Schäffer und Peters
GmbH, Mühlheim am Main, Color Fachservice
Edith Zimmer, L & Z Graphisches Atelier, Dirk
Lamprecht, Maria Obermaier, Peter Seidel, Ursu-
la Seitz-Gray, all Frankfurt am Main
Printers: Hanft Siebdruck GmbH, Bietigheim-Bis-
singen
Display cases: Glasbau Hahn GmbH und Co KG,
Frankfurt am Main
Audio-visual production: Arena Agentur für Au-
diovisuelle Kommunikation GmbH, Frankfurt
am Main
Transport: Hasenkamp, Kelsterbach

Scholarly Advisory Council

Chair: Lord Rothschild, London
Prof. Friedrich Battenberg, Darmstadt
Prof. Helmut Böhme, Darmstadt
Dr. Bernward L. Deneke, Bielefeld
Amos Elon, Jerusalem
Prof. Lothar Gall, Frankfurt am Main

Prof. Gerd Hardach, Marburg
Prof. David S. Landes, Cambridge/Mass.
Prof. Manfred Pohl, Frankfurt am Main
Prof. Reinhard Rürup, Berlin
Prof. Moshe J. Zimmermann, Jerusalem

Preface

»Frankfurt – The City of the Rothschilds« was a slogan taken up derogatorily by the Nazis, but is certainly accurate in pinpointing the true significance what was probably Frankfurt's most famous family had for the development of the city in the 19th century. The Rothschilds' houses and garden, the over 30 foundations they set up, and the role of the Rothschild Bank as the leading European private bank had a decisive influence on Frankfurt at a time when the city was changing rapidly. Indeed, only few people today realize that three of the current four large inner city parks were formerly Rothschild property.

The Rothschilds' success is all the more amazing if one bears in mind that the founder of the bank, Meyer Amschel Rothschild, was born 250 years ago in the Jewish ghetto of the then Imperial City of Frankfurt, and spent a large part of his life in the dark and over-crowded Judengasse subject to the numerous constraining regulations imposed by the City Council. Separated from the rest of town by walls, the Judengasse was, however, also the largest Jewish community in the then German-speaking world and one of the intellectual centres of European Jewry. It was here that Meyer Amschel started out professional life as a coin dealer and laid the foundations for the swift expansion of his company, which had soon become the leading bank in Europe. The pinnacle of its success was achieved under the aegis of his five sons, »the five citizens of Frankfurt«, who set up bank branches in London, Naples, Paris and Vienna and in the first half of the 19th century provided financing for most European governments. Ennobled by the (Austrian) Emperor of the day, they built castles and palatial town houses; in fact their lifestyle left their contemporaries open-mouthed with amazement.

In Frankfurt, the family were closely connected with the most glorious epoch in (the city's) Jewish history, when, with the emancipation of the Jews, who were freed from the shackles of the ghetto, the Rothschilds made an enormous contribution to the economic and cultural development of the city. This is not to play down the fact that the path to complete equal rights was by no means an easy one in Frankfurt and encountered sharp resistance from among the ranks of the burghers and the City Council. But the zest of the Jewish bankers and merchants, the scholars and journalists, overcame all the resentment and made Frankfurt certainly the city in Germany which profited most from its Jewish citizens.

The Rothschild Bank in Frankfurt was closed down as early as 1901, to the great regret of everyone in the city. However, the family remained present here. Baroness Adelheid von Rothschild, for example, bequeathed the former bank building in the Fahrgasse to the Jewish Community, making it possible to set up the city's first Jewish Museum. During the Nazi period almost all the Rothschild foundations were dissolved; only the Carolinum Dental Clinic, which had become part of the university, managed to survive as an independent foundation.

The Nazis also regrettably succeeded in almost eradicating the Rothschilds from the public's memory; indeed, even in the post-War period, with the exception of a few street names, hardly anything in Frankfurt brought the family to mind. In this context, I more than welcomed the Jewish Museum's intention to present on the occasion of the City of Frankfurt's 1200th anniversary the first comprehensive exhibition on the history of this European family from Frankfurt - in the city in which it originated.

It was a particular honour for me that, on the 250th anniversary of the birth of Meyer Amschel Rothschild in February of this year, 90 members of the family visited Frankfurt. The visit will go down as one of the glorious occasions in the city's history. We will all remember the tour of the excavations in the Judengasse Museum, the dignified celebration at Meyer Amschel's grave in the Battonnstrasse Cemetery, the visit to the Rothschild graves in the Rat-Beil-Strasse, the presentation given at the Jewish Museum of the exhibition project, the moment when the family signed the City's Golden Book in the Imperial Hall (on the Römer) and finally the marvelous soirée in the Jewish Museum, the musical ambience and setting so skilfully provided by Charlotte de Rothschild, attended by Chancellor Kohl and many leading figures from the worlds of politics, business and society. These were outstanding events and offered many an opportunity for dialogue and mutual understanding. They have echoed well beyond the boundaries of the city and I am sure that, in particular in Frankfurt itself, the awareness of the importance of the Rothschild family history has definitely grown (as a consequence) and will grow still further.

Today, Meyer Amschel Rothschild would perhaps look back with a certain satisfaction on Frankfurt. The fact that the city is now a financial centre in the world's top league and the seat of the European Monetary Institute is the result not least of the achievements of the major Frankfurt bankers in the 18th century, and Meyer Amschel was certainly pre-eminent among them.

The exhibition in the Jewish Museum and present book accompanying it will undoubtedly help shed an inestimable amount of light on the personality and the significance of the House of Rothschild. I have in mind not only those areas which one would not at first sight associate with the history of a famous banking family, such as their pioneering achievements in industry, but also their impact on social work, their art collections and their contributions to art history.

I wish the exhibition the success which is its due and congratulate the family on being able to look back on a many-faceted and proud history.

Andreas von Schoeler, September 1994

Preface

There has been no shortage of books, plays, musicals and films about the Rothschild family but »The Rothschilds – A European Family« is the first exhibition as far as I am aware to be devoted to the subject. It is therefore not only particularly welcome, but it is also appropriate that it should be presented in Frankfurt, birthplace of Meyer Amschel Rothschild, the father of the five sons who went on to create their European dynasty. The exhibition is taking place in the Jewish Museum, the beautiful house which had been acquired by Mayer Carl von Rothschild in 1846 and remained a principal home of the Rothschild family in Frankfurt until 1894 when the house was given over to the Baron Carl von Rothschild Public Library; the management of which was taken on by the City of Frankfurt in 1928.

Lastly, it is a happy coincidence that the year of 1994 celebrates both the 1200th anniversary of the City of Frankfurt and the 250th anniversary of the birth of Meyer Amschel Rothschild.

It should be said at the outset that this exhibition is only taking place because of the imagination, initiative, enthusiasm and perseverance of Mr Georg Heuberger and his colleagues in the Jewish Museum in Frankfurt. But our thanks as a family to them goes far beyond the exhibition itself; the celebration which took place earlier this year together with the exhibition have made 1994 become a truly unforgettable year of celebration and reunion for us.

In February no less than 90 members of the Rothschild family gathered together in the City of Frankfurt to celebrate the an-niversary of the birth of their distinguished forbear. Some of the younger generation had never been to Frankfurt; for some of the generation that had lived through the Second World War it was the first time that they had been back. The welcome we received was extraordinary. The Lord Mayor of Frankfurt, Mr. von Schoeler, addressed us most movingly in the ceremony at the City Hall when we were invited as a family to sign in the Golden Book of Frankfurt. At the ceremony, both the Lord Mayor and I talked about how the City of Frankfurt and the Rothschild family have much more in common than the accident of birth to bind us together: our mutual interests, originally in the field of finance, but later in the fields of the arts and music; our common experience of destruction and revival.

Meyer Amschel would surely have been astonished and delighted by the way in which his anniversary has been celebrated this year and, as far as the present generation is concerned, their letters are perhaps the most moving testament to the impact of the event on our family. I quote from one letter from a cousin of mine aged 14:

I have never had, and probably will never have again the opportunity to learn so much about our ancestors and the history of our family. I have been told many times but I never fully absorbed the information, because, I suspect, of a lack of realisation of its importance and extent.

And from another cousin of mine just a few years younger than myself: When standing behind Arthur Fried reality hit me and I truly felt a real bond between Meyer Amschel and me – walking around the museum I realised that this was not any ordinary »miseoh« but one where Gutle spent most of her life and while I obviously felt very proud of being one of their descendants I also felt an immense debt of gratitude – thanks to them and what they and they alone accomplished I have led a charmed life, being able to move around in any circle I wish and being respected for being a member of the family. I intend for the rest of my life to repay that debt of gratitude in the best ways I will be able to find with integrity and honour.

It is not at all surprising that the older a family becomes the more difficult it becomes to maintain the spirit and cohesion of earlier generations and to feel truly part of a large and diverse family. I believe that the 1994 celebrations in Frankfurt have made a deep and indelible mark on all the members of our family who came together then. In the unequal struggle of trying to make the future of our family live up to its remarkable past, these historic celebrations will be of inestimable and lasting value as a reminder of what we have to try and live up to and the family's gratitude is therefore immeasurable.

The exhibition will trace the history of the family from unemancipated confinement and unimaginable squalor and deprivation in the Jewish Ghetto of Frankfurt at the end of the 18th century through to the »exercise of unparalleled influence throughout Europe« by the end of the first half of the 19th century. From there it attempts to analyse consolidation and aristocracisation in the latter part of the 19th and the early 20th century. Finally, it will give a glimpse of revival and continuity and a different form of Europeanisation as we approach the millennium.

As Chairman of the Academic Advisory Council of the Exhibition, I would like to register my deep appreciation of the generous and distinguished contributions which have been made to the exhibion guide. The book paints an impressive and graphic portrait of the culture and the accomplishments of the Rothschild family. I would also like to express my appreciation to the other members of the Council for their invaluable participation.

I am confident that the exhibition will prove to be a great success and will certainly make a deep and lasting contribution to the history of the Rothschild family, underlining their relationship with Frankfurt and then Europe.

Lord Rothschild, August 1994

The Rothschilds –
Family History in the Museum Context

One of the most striking and inexplicable things in the field of literature is that the House of Rothschild, the most colossal phenomenon in the world of stock exchanges, money and government, currently taking its unique place in world history, and for all its immense influence and eminent world significance has hitherto hardly been taken into account in literature or the public domain and has been completely ignored by historiography.

This astonishment at the lack of historiographical literature on the Rothschild family - the first words of the preface to the first, anonymous publication on the family, which came out in 1857 (Das Haus Rothschild. Seine Geschichte und seine Geschäfte - Aufschlüsse und Enthüllungen zur Geschichte des Jahrhunderts, insbesondere des Staatsfinanz- und Börsenwesen, Prague & Leipzig, 1857. The book was probably written by Fr. Steinmann.) - can be used to preface this volume, if understood to refer to the museum context. There are meanwhile a wealth of publications on the history of the Rothschilds, but to date there has been no comprehensive documentation in the form of an exhibition. This is certainly not the result of the topic not offering enough scope for such an undertaking. On the contrary, the history of the Rothschild family touches on all sorts of aspects of economic, social and cultural history, not to mention involving any number of interesting persons. Perhaps one can assume that such an exhibition project has hitherto been restrained by the family being reserved when it came to seeing its own past put on show in a museum. But

this, too, is not the case. After initial reserve, we have received the whole-hearted support of the family, which has, no doubt, to do with the fact that the time and place of the exhibition (it is taking place to mark the 250th anniversary of Meyer Amschel Rothschild in the former Rothschild palatial townhouse) are both directly bound up with the family history.

The former Rothschild palace, which now houses the Jewish Museum Frankfurt, was bought in 1846 by Mayer Carl von Rothschild, who in turn had extensions added and remodeling work done. Three representative rooms and the glorious stairwell still date from that time. They also lend our museum a special ambience and convey a feel of the Rothschilds' lifestyle and their social significance for Frankfurt. This building is, moreover, the only one of the numerous palatial townhouses the Rothschilds owned to have survived. In former times, these houses helped shape the Frankfurt cityscape of the 19th century and it is their gardens which formed the basis of Frankfurt's most important parks today.

In 1901, with the death of Wilhelm Carl the family closed the Frankfurt bank, a loss which the city sorely lamented at the time. Baroness Edmond de Rothschild, Wilhelm Carl's daughter, bequeathed the bank building on the corner of Fahrgasse and Börnegasse, near Konstablerwache, to the city's Jewish Community. With the support she and her mother Mathilde gave, the Museum of Jewish Antiquities was then set up in the building and generously outfitted by the family. The »Von Rothschild'sche Museum« was part of the new museum: it included the formerly private offices of the brothers Wilhelm Carl and Mayer Carl as well as portraits by Moritz Oppenheim and numerous objects of interest. The former museum, plundered by the Nazis in 1938, was the predecessor of our Museum which was, on its foundation in 1988, consciously placed in the tradition of the earlier museum.

The building in the Fahrgasse was destroyed during the Second World War, as were the family's original home in the former Judengasse, the House Grünes Schild, and other family residences. It was thus also our intention from the outset to make the newly founded Jewish Museum Frankfurt a place where the history of the Rothschilds was revived. With the 1994–5

exhibition, we are, I trust, creating an enduring milestone that will lead to further and hopefully ongoing investigation of the subject. The publications accompanying the exhibition have a special role to play in this context over and above backing up the exhibition itself.

This, the book accompanying the exhibition, the exhibition itself and the essay volume would not have been possible without the lively interest the Rothschild family has shown in the project and the numerous objects it has lent us for the occasion. After what are now several years of intensive cooperation I would like to take this opportunity to thank all the members of Lord Rothschild's family on behalf of all involved in the exhibition project.

Georg Heuberger, August 1994

Acknowledgements

The exhibition would not have been possible without the multi-faceted assistance and support of numerous members of the Rothschild family. We would like to thank the following in particular

Baronin Alain de Rothschild, Charlotte de Rothschild, Baronin Elie de Rothschild, Dr. Miriam Rothschild, The Hon. Amschel Rothschild, Baron David de Rothschild, Mr. Edmund L. de Rothschild, Baron Edmond de Rothschild, Baron Eric de Rothschild, Sir Evelyn de Rothschild, Jacob Lord Rothschild und Lionel de Rothschild.

We would like to thank especially the following for their unflagging help and extraordinary dedication to the project during the two years of preparations

Melanie Aspey und Simone Mace, The Rothschild Archive, London
Dr. Gisela Förschner, Historisches Museum, Münzkabinett, Frankfurt am Main
Victor Gray, Head of Corporate Records and Archives NM Rothschild & Sons Limited, London
Michael Hall, Kurator bei Mr. Edmund L. de Rothschild, London
Yoram Majorek, Direktor der Central Zionist Archives, Jerusalem
Gabriele Teichmann, Sal. Oppenheim jr & Cie, Köln

We would like to thank the following for scholarly advice, encouragement and organizational and material support

Susan Absolon, London
Johannes Adrian, Frankfurt am Main
Air France, Frankfurt am Main
Daniel Alcouffe, Paris
Christoph Andreas, Frankfurt am Main
Martine d'Anglejan, London
Dr. Martin Angerer, Regensburg
Prof. Kurt Apfel, Wien
Archiv der Hansestadt Lübeck
Floriane Azoulay, Paris
Marc Bascou, Paris
Dr. Christian Beaufort, Wien
Frau Becker, Frankfurt am Main
Dipl. Ing. Böhm, Rastatt
Laurence Bougeard, Frankfurt am Main
Pierre Bresson, Villeneuve-Loubet
Danièle Brocheton, Paris
Helga Brown, Abingdon Oxon
Bundesarchiv, Abteilung Potsdam
Dr. Sigrid Canz, München
Prof. Dr. Stanley D. Chapman, Nottingham
Else Claude, Frankfurt am Main
Dr. Thierry Crépin-Leblond, Paris
Beatrice Curty, Genf
Marie Christine d'Allemagne, Paris
Karin Datz, Frankfurt am Main
De Beers Consolidated Mines Ltd, Kimberley
Deutsche Städte-Reklame GmbH, Frankfurt am Main
Deutsches Literaturarchiv Marbach am Neckar
Dr. Rudolf Distelberger, Wien
Dr. Volker Eichler, Wiesbaden
Hans Eisterer, Wien
Erste Donau-Dampfschiffahrts-Gesellschaft, Wien
Peter Femfert, Frankfurt am Main
Frankfurter Bankgesellschaft
Freunde der Zinnfiguren Frankfurt am Main e.V.

Arthur Fried, Jerusalem
Greater London Record Office
Rosamund Griffin, Waddesdon Manor
William L. Gross, Tel Aviv
Frau Großmann-Hofmann, Königstein
The Guildhall Library, London
Valérie Guillaume, Paris
Lilo Günzler, Frankfurt am Main
Michael Hauck, Frankfurt am Main
Volker Harms-Ziegler, Frankfurt am Main
Herr Heidecke, Frankfurt am Main
Jack Hellmann, New York
Rainer von Hessen, Kronberg
Hessischer Rundfunk, Frankfurt am Main
Dr. Hildegard Hoos, Frankfurt am Main
Dr. Jan Hozák, Prag
Mme. Hurel, Paris
Interessengemeinschaft Frankfurter Kredit-
    institute GmbH
Alisa Jaffa, London
Dr. Franziska Jungmann-Stadler, München
Almut Junker, Frankfurt am Main
Michael Jurk, Hamburg
Hans-Dieter Kirchholtes, Frankfurt am Main
Dr. Charles Kirkpatrick, Frankfurt am Main
Stefan Knobloch, Frankfurt am Main
Kölnische Rückversicherungs Gesellschaft
    AG
Achim Korres, Köln
Werner Krebs, Frankfurt am Main
Günter Kroll, Frankfurt am Main
Rudolf Krönke, Königstein
Dr. Peter Kubalek, Wien
Alexis Kugel, Paris
Dr. Helmut Lackner, Wien
Lupold von Lehsten, Bensheim
Prof.Dr. Manfred Leithe-Jasper, Wien
Pierre-Yves Le Pogam, Paris
Schlomit Levin, Mazkereth Batja
Sarah Levitt, London
Jane Loadman, London
Anne Katherine Ludwig, Marburg
Prof. Franz Mailer, Waidhofen
Nadine Mauthner von Bressler, Frankfurt
    am Main
Dr. Eva Mayring, München

Mecklenburgisches Landeshauptarchiv,
    Schwerin
Dr. Anton Merk, Hanau
Judith Meyer-Petit, Paris
Gavin Morgan, London
Moira Mullen, London
Frank Mußmann, Frankfurt am Main
Ernst Neubronner, Frankfurt am Main
Dr. Waltraut Neuwirth, Wien
Elisabeth Ogborn, London
Dr. John Orbell, London
Herr Orlandt, Frankfurt am Main
Prof. Dr. Bernhard Overbeck, München
Prof. Dr. Akos Paulinyi, Darmstadt
Frau Toutchka Pavel
Abraham Paz, Masuot Jizchak
David Pearlman, London
Dr. Klaus Pechstein, Nürnberg
Frau Dr. Pfeiffer, Wien
Elisabeth Pinot de Villechenon, Paris
Dr. Olga Postulkova, Frankfurt am Main
Dr. Powitz, Frankfurt am Main
Marie-Claire Raffenel, Pregny
Dr. Uwe Reher, Kassel
Bernhard Reichel, Frankfurt am Main
Jane Rick, London
Betrand Rondot, Paris-Malmaison
Kurt Roos, Frankfurt am Main
Pierre Rosenberg, Paris
Ora Rosenzweig, Zichron Yaacov
Claudia Rosner, Frankfurt am Main
Royal Archives Windsor Castle
Sächsisches Hauptstaatsarchiv, Dresden
Sächsisches Staatsarchiv, Leipzig
Dr. Reinhold Sänger, Karlsruhe
Luitgard Schader, Hindemith-Institut,
    Frankfurt am Main
Dr. Elisabeth Schmuttermaier, Wien
Ute Schumacher, Frankfurt am Main
Dr. Karl Schütz, Wien
Dr. Lorenz Seelig, München
Dr. Helmut Seling, München
Shell Internationale Petroleum Maatschap-
    pij B.V., Den Haag
Dr. Meinolf Siemer, Eichenzell bei Fulda
W. Simon, Stuttgart

SKG-Bank, Saarbrücken
Jack Spier, Bexhill-on-Sea
Elisabeth Sprenger, Manchester
Stadt Wien
Patricia Stahl, Frankfurt am Main
Dr. Jürgen Steen, Frankfurt am Main
Frau Dr. Sternat, Wien
Erich Stromeyer, Frankfurt am Main
Madeleine de Terris, Paris
Thüringisches Hauptstaatsarchiv, Weimar
Herrn Dipl. Ing. Toncourt, Düsseldorf
Franz Toth, Bingen
Vitkovice AG, Ostrava
Christina Voigt, Frankfurt am Main

Mme. Wallet, Cannes
Dr. Susanne Walther, Wien
Karl-Hermann Wegner, Kassel
Erika Weidemann, Frankfurt am Main
Frau Elli Wendt, Frankfurt am Main
Dr. Kurt Wettengel, Frankfurt am Mainl
Prof. Dr. Dieter Windecker, Bad Nauheim
Dr. Witt-Döring, Wien
Dieter Wolf, Butzbach
Dr. Hans-Joachim Ziemke, Frankfurt am
   Main
Rainer Zietz, London
Mordechai Zucker, London

The Rothschilds

Thoughts on a Remarkable Family History

When, in the Eighties, a home was being sought for the City of Frankfurt's Jewish Museum, the choice finally fell on the »Rothschildpalais«, one of the 19th century town houses that had belonged to the Rothschild family. The building is not only one of the last surviving representative house owned by Jews, but it also reminds us of the most brilliant Jewish epoch in the city's history. In order to acquaint a broader public with the historical background to the »Rothschildpalais«, the idea arose of presenting for the first time a comprehensive history of the Rothschilds, the banking family which originated in Frankfurt's Judengasse.

»The Rothschilds« – a name that almost everyone knows and which today still prompts associations with wealth, power and luxury. However, on closer investigation it soon transpires that there is little or no public awareness any longer of the history of the family. There are admittedly a series of popular publications that attract readers owing to the fascination exerted to this day by the Rothschilds' success, their rapid ascent up the social ladder and out of the ghetto and their elaborate lifestyle. In historical research, however, the Rothschilds have always remained a marginal topic. They are singled out in the context of certain episodes in the Napoleonic age or of the sale of Suez canal shares to the British government. But the family company as a phenomenon in its own right has hitherto not met with a commensurate appraisal.

There are a number of reasons for this.

Political history as a rule does not focus on complex economic transactions such as those conducted by the Rothschilds. Social and economic history concentrated for many years more on the structural side to questions such as industrialization and its social consequences than on the history of individual banks.

The most important reason, however, is the fact that historiography continues to be geared towards nation states. A phenomenon such as the Rothschilds, who, via their branch offices in Frankfurt, London, Paris, Vienna and Naples, acted on a pan-European basis, the source of their success, all too frequently fails to attract researchers whose work stops at the borders of a particular country or national economy.

As a consequence, the exhibition and the presentation of its themes in this book are structured in terms of two different perspectives: The main body of the exhibition presents the Rothschilds as a family enterprise; the emergence of that company as one of the world's most important banks and the emergence of the family as one of the best known families in the 19th century are discussed in terms of their being a European phenomenon. In a special section, the stress is on a detailed portrayal of the Rothschilds' significance as a Frankfurt family.

The presentation begins in Frankfurt's Judengasse and attempts in a first major section to explain the surprisingly rapid ascent of Meyer Amschel Rothschild and his five sons, given their origins in the Frankfurt ghetto.

In a second section, an analysis is offered of their branches in five important European cities as well as a discussion of the question of how, under the conditions of the day, European-wide cooperation was at all possible.

The third section discusses the family's view of itself and the elaborate lengths the Rothschilds took in building up their image as the leading Jewish aristocratic family; this is contrasted with the press' perception of them, as is reflected in countless newspaper reports and caricatures.

In the fourth section, important aspects of the Rothschilds' business activities in the second half of the 19th century are investigated, i.e. at a time when increasing industrialization, the foundation of large joint stock banks and the stronger penetration of national economies posed new challenges for a European private bank.

Only those themes of the family's 20th century history are addressed as refer to the family as a whole: the Nazis' defamatory propaganda and persecution of the Rothschilds, on the one hand, and the family's commitment to the Jewish settlement of Palestine and the State of Israel, on the other.

The final section brings us back to Frankfurt and emphasizes the substantial contribution the family made to the development of the city during the 19th century.

The exhibition commences with a glorious overture in three rooms of the Rothschild Palace, rooms that are still in their original mid-19th century state. The furnishings include such precious furniture, paintings and collected items that the viewer is immediately transported into the world of the Rothschilds - and at the same time back to the zenith of their history.

Overture:
A Magnificent Ambience

Historical room in the style of Louis XIV with a bay ceiling in the Rothschildpalais on the Untermainkai

»Goût Rothschild« – The Lifestyle of the Rothschild Family

Of the original interior of the Rothschild-palais on Untermainkai in Frankfurt, apart from sections of ornamental plasterwork on some of the walls and ceilings, and the magnificent staircase, three historical rooms on the ground floor have survived. They were designed in the mid-19th century by Friedrich Rumpf, the architect, in the style of historicism. Their decor reflects three successive styles of French palace interior design from the late Baroque of the late 17th century to the early Classicism that preceded the French Revolution. For the purposes of this exhibition, two of these rooms have been arranged with furniture and collectors' objects which document the lifestyle and artistic taste that was specific to the Rothschilds.

The first room of the exhibition shows the style of Louis XVI (last quarter of the 18th century), with simple wooden panels and an elaborately pargetted cavetto in pseudo-Classical forms. The next room has panellings with stucco in white and gold, a reference to the style of Louis XV (mid-18th century). It originally served as a music room. Its furnishings reflect the family's characteristically ostentatious lifestyle, as expressed in the elaborately worked furniture, valuable paintings and priceless showcase objects in French Rococo style. The last room of the three, with its magnificently carved panelled ceiling and its mirrors, evokes the age of the »Roi Soleil«, Louis XIV (last quarter of the 17th century and first quarter of the 18th century). It is furnished as a collectors study and shows a selection from the Rothschilds' collection of metalwork, sumptuously inlaid furniture and Old Master paintings.

The succession of these styles of decoration in the three rooms is neither coincidental, nor was it left to the architects who carried out the work. It was deliberately stipulated by the family, and was typical of many of their residences. In this respect, the Rothschilds were following the taste of their day, which regarded these three styles as the height of luxurious interior design.

Through the elaborateness of their interiors, the Rothschilds manifested not only their lifestyle and social status, but also gave palpable expression to their fabulous wealth, which in the eyes of many of their contemporaries had reached mythical proportions.

In contrast to the stuccowork of the residence's walls and ceilings, many of which were imitations, the furnishings and ornaments were frequently originals. Their immense value was just as unusual as their

Three snuff boxes, gold, partly enamelled and set with diamonds, France, mid-18th century

Vase de forme
Medicis, ca. 1755, por-
celain manufactured
in Vincennes, later
called Sèvres

Vase grec à festons,
ca. 1765,
Sèvres porcelain

outward appearance and prestigious origins. Many of the items of furniture acquired by the family were among the crowning achievements of the French Rococo, made by famous craftsmen and decorated with precious inlays and ormolu. The chairs and sofas were out of carved gilt-wood and elaborately upholstered using Beauvais tapestrywork.

Almost all of the members of the family had a particular liking for two kinds of objects; they can be said to epitomise the refined luxury of the period in that they combine the greatest skill of the craftsman with the use of the most expensive materials:

Snuff boxes made of gold or precious stones, and porcelain from the royal factory in Sèvres.

Some of the porcelain in the Rothschilds' collection was originally owned by the royal mistresses Madame Pompadour and Madame Dubarry as well as Queen Ma-

rie Antoinette. In accordance with their predilection for interiors in the style of the French Rococo, the Rothschilds were among the first art collectors to systematically acquire all kinds of objects from the Queen Marie Antoinette period. It was their passion for collecting which created a general awareness of this period, today considered the apogee of French interior decoration.

It was probably James de Rothschild who began to acquire objects from this period after settling in Paris in 1812. In 1818, one of the first paintings he bought was *La Laitière* (The Milkmaid), which today is in the Louvre.

It is the *chef d'oeuvre* of the French painter Jean Baptiste Greuze (1725–1805). Greuze was one of the most sought-after painters of the French late Rococo. His peasants and genre scenes were sentimental

»La Laitière« (The Milk-
maid), oil on canvas,
ca. 1785,
Jean Baptiste Greuze
(1725–1805)

find incomplete sets, James had craftsmen make imitations of the missing pieces. His aim was an aesthetically homogenous reproduction of a period, in which originals and copies stood side by side on an equal terms. A representation room designed in this manner not only testified to the high social standing of its owner, but also identified him as an educated, cultivated person, a connoisseur of art.

Initially, then, the collecting of paintings, furniture and valuable ornaments was not an aim in itself for the Rothschild family, but a consequence of the need to acquire and display social rank as a means of promoting the family business. Since this aim was common to all members of the family during the 19th century, it is hardly surprising that the composition of their art collections and interior styles remained similar for over three generations; what evolved was the »goût Rothschild«, modelled on the opulent lifestyle of glorious periods such as the French Baroque or Rococo.

and frolic but nevertheless offered a coun-tertype of life to the frivolous amusements at the court of Versailles. Out of the same reason Greuzes portrayals of ›innocent‹ girls became popular subjects for the court aristocracy.

In acquiring such a painting, James de Rothschild was asserting his claim to social rank on a par with the aristocracy of the An-cien Régime who were such keen collectors of Greuze. By the 19th century, that aristocracy had lost virtually all of its politi-cal power, yet still set the tone of Paris so-ciety. At first, this society turned its back on James de Rothschild, the Jewish upstart. However, by cultivating a lifestyle that was more expensive and more elegant than anyone else's, he was finally able to gain acceptance.

Perfect planning and a vast amount of money went into creating his household. If he was unable to obtain matching furni-ture, such as chairs or bureaus, or could only

Drinking horn. Ivory,
silver gilt mounting
set with precious
stones,
Aix la Chapelle,
c. 1875, Reinhold
Vasters (1827–1909)

The Rothschilds as Collectors of Art

Following the death of Mayer Carl von Rothschild in 1886, one fifth of his collection of gold, the so-called »Goldschatz« (gold treasure), was put on show to a paying public in the ground floor rooms of the Rothschildpalais on Frankfurt's Untermainkai. It took Mayer Carl more than 40 years to collect his »treasure store«, comprising over 5,000 precious items of metalwork dating from the late Gothic to the Baroque period. Among them was the so-called »Merkelsche Tafelaufsatz« (Merkel Centrepiece), the most important piece of German goldsmith's art to emerge during the Renaissance. Another prized object was the huge ivory horn in a silver-gilt mounting, which was once considered to be the climax of Gothic metalwork but was in fact a brilliant forgery, made as late as 1875 by Reinhold Vasters, the goldsmith who restored the Aachen cathedral treasures. Today it is regarded as one of the main works of historicist metalwork.

Goblet of the Hanau City Council, silver gilt, Hanau, before 1625. Hannss Rappolt (master goldsmith in Nuremberg, lived 1610–1625 in Augsburg)

The Rothschilds were among the first collectors of arts and crafts in the 19th century. Given that virtually no scientific criteria for determining authenticity had yet been developed at that time, it was not unknown for forged objects to find their way into the collections.

Mayer Carl von Rothschild and other members of the family deliberately based their collections on the »Kunst- and Wunderkammer« established by the Renaissance princes: Apart from artistic works of Renaissance and Baroque metalwork, they collected stone-cut objects, mechanical instruments, furniture with precious inlays, ivory carvings, Limoges enamels antique glass, majolica and Renaissance jewellery.

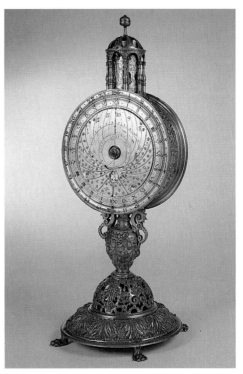

St. George Fighting
the Dragon.
Table centrepiece,
silver gilt, set with
precious stones,

Augsburg, c. 1615.
Jakob I. Miller (master
goldsmith,
1583–1618).

Table clock in the
form of an ostensory,
ormolu and brass,
probably Nuremberg,
ca. 1580

Ewer and basin of
Johann Count of
Nassau-Siegen, silver
gilt, Nuremberg,
first quarter of
the 17th century,
The Waddesdon
Bequest

The most famous art collection was that of the Habsburgs, and it appears to be no coincidence that the members of the Rothschild family did their best to find pieces for their collections which resembled those belonging to the Habsburgs. An expression of this link can be seen in the painting by David Teniers which depicts the House of Habsburg's most outstanding collector of paintings, Archduke Leopold Wilhelm. This work was part of Alphonse de Rothschild's collection in Vienna.

The family's collecting activities can be traced back to the acquisition of Greuze's *La Laitière* in 1818.

Yet there is reason to believe that their interest in collecting and in acquiring valuable objects goes back even further. Meyer Amschel, founder of Rothschild banking business, not only dealt in rare coins, but also in antiques and precious objects, including jewels and indeed snuff boxes, the latter of which were later to be one of the family's favourite objects for collection. Antiques, coins and precious objects were also the main contents of a princes' »Kunstkammer« and it happened to be the Landgrave of Hesse with whom Meyer Amschel did such important business who owned a reknown »Kunstkammer«. It therefore seems reasonable to assume that the five brothers' passion for collecting was first aroused by their father and that they became knowledgeable on the subject at an early age. This is suggested by Nathaniel de Rothschild's remarks on how his Uncle James, while convalescing in Heinrichsbad in 1839, himself went hunting for art and antiques.

In their endeavours to expand their collections, the five brothers and their sons not only went out searching themselves, but also employed the services of a number of agents, many of whom, like the painter Moritz Daniel Oppenheim, were based in Frankfurt. Oppenheim also served as the family's portrait painter. In the latter part of

Archduke Leopold
William
in his Galleries in
Brussels,
oil on canvas, 1653,
David Teniers the
Younger (1610–90)

the 19th century, all the leading art dealers in Frankfurt – the Löwenstein Brothers, Selig Goldschmidt, Jacob Rosenbaum and Zacharias Hackenbroch – worked for the Rothschilds in an advisory capacity. So it was that Frankfurt became an international centre for the trade in objets d'art.

Just how extensively and methodically the Rothschilds went about collecting objets d'art is reflected above all in the fact that they systematically bought up treasures from monasteries and guilds that were liquidating their assets, or from the estates of princes.

What was the purpose of these collections, which, like the styles of their house interiors, all resembled each other?

Above all to own precious objects and valuable works of art was by far the most impressive manifestation of wealth. It is surely no coincidence that a number of the more spectacular art purchases, such as the »Merkel'sche Tafelaufsatz«, were reported in the press, thus helping to turn the Rothschilds' art collections into a synonym for their fabulous wealth, the scale of which was astronomical according to the rumours circulating at the time.

Collecting was closely linked with business, as is documented by numerous letters between members of the family. During the course of the 19th century, collecting became a family foible which was by no means confined to the world of art. The incredible diversity of the collections even extended to botany and zoology, and was an excellent means of demonstrating to the general public the family's outstanding status. By the same token, the social significance of collecting determined the kind of objects and in particular the kind of artworks that were collected.

Besides expressing wealth and social prestige, the collections conveyed another value that was quintessential to 19th century society: they were proof of membership of a highly educated, highly cultured elite.

If on the one hand the Rothschild family was following the aristocracy and the princes in their tradition of collecting, the perfectionism and the quasi-scientific expertise with which these collections were assembled were an expression of the bourgeois passion for education and culture. The manner in which the Rothschilds went about the business of collecting was based on bourgeois educational and cultural ideals. This new form of collecting emerged during the 19th century, and was characterized by the fact that almost as much importance was attached to the quest for knowledge and the research work itself as was given to the material acquisition of objects. Collecting was a manifestation of intellectual and material substance as well as bourgeois education and culture as if they were a kind of capital that could be owned. These two pillars of the bourgeois value system were key factors in determining social prestige in the 19th century, and the Rothschilds embodied these values to a substantial degree.

When collecting became a task for the bourgeois public sphere, great importance was attached to recording and presenting the objects and to opening up new categories of collectible items and new areas of knowledge. Here the Rothschild family played a pioneering role in two respects. Firstly, they published comprehensive catalogues of their own collections which bore witness to their specialist knowledge that was on a par with that of the public museums. Secondly, by collecting arts and crafts, they aroused public interest in this field, as is reflected in the founding of an arts and crafts museum in Frankfurt, which was established in Frankfurt following the death of Mayer Carl von Rothschild.

Meyer Amschel Rothschild

A Life
in the Judengasse

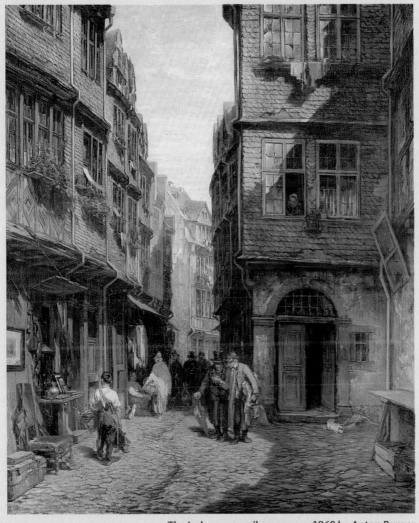

The Judengasse, oil on canvas, 1860 by Anton Burger

The sumptuous lifestyle of the Rothschild family in the 19th century and their proverbial wealth prompted admiration, amazement and criticism among their contemporaries. The family's origins in the Frankfurt ghetto formed the background to both the favourable and unfavourable reactions. The noticeable contrast between the confined living conditions of Meyer Amschel Rothschild, who founded the bank, and the elaborate palaces in which his sons and grandsons lived, continue to this day to influence all appraisals of the family's history.

Thus, any attempt to analyze the rise of the Rothschilds starts with a description of life in the Judengasse. It was here that Meyer Amschel was born in 1743 or 1744, it was here that he married Gutle Schnapper in 1770, and it was here that he initially lived with his fast growing family in his parents' house, until he was able to afford a larger house on the Judengasse in 1786. He died in 1812, shortly after the ghetto had been dissolved and he himself had become a citizen of Frankfurt. Despite his highly successful career, he never left the Judengasse. It shaped his outlook, his professional opportunities and the overarching conditions of his life.

A Glance at the Judengasse

In the 18th century, approximately 3,000 to 4,000 people, or more than 10 percent of the city's population lived in Frankfurt's Judengasse, a ghetto separated off from the rest of the town. Frankfurt was thus one of the centres of Jewish life in Europe. Nevertheless, we know what the Judengasse looked like physically and many aspects of everyday life there only from reports on it from people from outside. In the 18th century, the densely populated lane exerted a ghastly attraction on travellers; yet in the 19th century, painters such as Anton Burger felt the heavily built-up ghetto to be romantic.

The municipal authorities regarded the Jewish population with great distrust. Since the 15th century they had been trying via repeated censuses and regulations to collect data on and control the Jewish population.

A bird's-eye view of the Judengasse, detail of an engraving by Matthaeus Merian

1

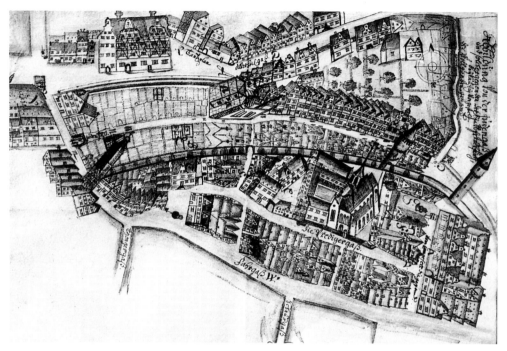

If you approached the walled ghetto from the outside, the first thing you noticed were the gates. They were closed at nights and on Sundays and holidays. The Jews were not allowed to leave the lane or the city at these times. Behind the gates was a narrow, approx. 300 metre long lane with high, sombre houses on both sides. In the north, a second row of houses lay concealed behind them, crowded in close to the ghetto walls.

The lanes was always densely populated, not only by the numerous inhabitants, but also by clients who purchased goods from the major and minor merchants. Travelogues of the day, often laden with resentments against the Jews, repeatedly emphasize the hustle and bustle, the noise, the poverty of many of the inhabitants and the stench from the partielley open sewage channels.

The first member of the Rothschild family, of whom there are records in Frankfurt, was Isaak Elchanan, who lived there in the 16th century. In 1567 he built the House »Rotes Schild« (from which the family drew its name; the German means »Red Shield«) in the southern part of the lane. There were various branches of the family, of which one remained until the early 18th century in the house Rotes Schild. As early as 1634, Meyer Amschel Rothschild's forebears had moved to »House Hinterpfann«. This building in a backyard in the northern section of the lane was inhabited until 1796 by five generations of the Rothschilds.

According to the censusses the municipal authorities repeatedly carried out, as a rule several families lived in the house simultaneously. Meyer Amschel Rothschild shared it, for example, with his two brothers

Rear courtyard buildings in the Judengasse. Watercolour by Carl Theodor Reiffenstein, 1849

and lived there together with his wife Gutle and their four children, his brother Moses and the latter's family as well as his brother Kalmann, who was single: a total of roughly 14 persons in other words. The municipal records usually refer to the Rothschilds as merchants and money exchangers. To the extent that records were kept of their assets in the 17th and 18th centuries, they belonged to the lower middle class of Frankfurt's Jewish community.

Like all the houses in the Judengasse, house Hinterpfann contained not only residential premises, but also storage and sales rooms for the brothers' trading activities. The house itself was directly adjacent to the eastern ghetto wall and could only be reached via a corridor through the Pfanne building in front of it. The backyard buildings in the Judengasse were allowed to be one storey higher than those in front of them, so, given an average of 3.5 x 10 metres per floor, the Hinterpfann building probably had about 120 square metres total space.

Life in the Community

Meyer Amschel Rothschild was born in either 1743 or 1744 in House Hinterpfann. Like almost all the boys in the Judengasse, he first attended primary school (»heder«), where he was taught by a schoolmaster – the latter were, as a rule, very poor and taught the boys at home. It was in such a home that he learned in Bible study to read and write Hebrew. Even at a later date he still wrote the lion's share of his correspondence in German, but using Hebrew characters. The only picture of such a »heder« in the Judengasse was produced by the Frankfurt painter J. B. Nothnagel. The picture shows a teacher, recognizable by his stick, practicing reading out loud from the Hebrew bible with his pupils and keeping them in order with his stick. Nothnagel's painting is also a typical example of the way outsiders saw the Judengasse and emphasizes how Christian citizens of Frankfurt viewed life in the Jewish community as somehow strange and exotic.

As Meyer Amschel, unlike his ancestors and brothers, was presumably meant to become not a merchant but a rabbi, he subsequently went to Fuerth, where he attended a Jewish secondary school. Yet he soon had to leave this »Yeshivah« as his parents died at an early age in 1755–6. However, Bible and Talmud study continued to play an important part in his life. At least, the obituaries describe him as having listened to a rabbi's sermon every day and having devoted the Sabbath and holidays to study and the discussion of religious questions with his guests.

The school system is an example of just how much the Judengasse in Frankfurt constituted a closed and largely autonomous world of its own, shaped by the instruction laid down in the Torah and the Talmud, by local customs and the rabbis' decisions. And the community was also independent in numerous areas in a political and legal sense. The Community's Board of Leaders, recruited from among the members of its upper class, had comprehensive powers over everyone and was able to pass down substantial punishments. The community's most important institutions included the two burial brotherhoods which were responsible for burial of the dead and administration of the cemetery. Their honorary members were highly respected and belonged to the leading circle of the Jewish community. The names and house signs of the annual chairmen of the »Hevra kaddisha« from 1776 to 1806 are engraved on the sides of a precious jug, which is one of the few remaining pieces bearing testimony to the brotherhood. Amongst them are those of Meyer Amschel and his elder brother Moses.

The fact that they were accepted into the ranks of one of the two »Hevra kaddisha« is not only a sign of the Rothschild brothers' professional success and high social standing. It also testifies to their strong roots in the traditional world of the Judengasse, in which devoutness and the fulfillment of the religious commandments

Primary school in the
Judengasse.
Oil painting by
J. A. B. Nothnagel
(1747–1804). Undated

Jug of the Frankfurt Jewish burial brotherhood. Silver, Frankfurt on Main, 1773

Moses Rothschild's tombstone in the Jewish cemetery at Battonnstrasse. Visible is his house sign, the »Pfanne« or pan

determined the individual's place in the community just as much as did wealth and family connections. The Rothschilds' lives were therefore shaped by charity work (and the especially highly esteemed personal service on behalf of the deceased) to a far greater extent than existing records suggest, for the latter focus predominantly on their business activities.

We can only guess what importance his elder brother had for Meyer Amschel's life in the Judengasse after the death of his parents. Moses Rothschild undoubtedly ensured that Meyer Amschel had an easier road to travel, for Moses was a successful businessman and was highly respected within the community. He was not only a member and chairman of the burial brotherhood, but in 1790 had also been elected Leader of the community. For many years thereafter he was in charge of the poor box. This was particularly important, as the community was obliged by law to provide shelter and food at least for one night for the large swarm of impoverished Jews of no fixed abode who travelled from town to town. Meyer Amschel was also to follow in his brother's footsteps in this regard, too.

On the jug Moses and Meyer Amschel are both represented with the signs of their houses. House signs generally played a key role in the way the individual families presented themselves and were displayed on the houses themselves, on gravestones, on jewellery and on other objects. Like the Rothschilds, many families derived their names from their houses. There are no other Rothschild portraits available of the Judengasse. Portraits have not survived and were hardly ever made for religious reasons.

»Agent to the Noble Court of Hesse-Hanau«

About 1764, at the tender age of 20, Meyer Amschel Rothschild set up his own business as a dealer in coins and bills in Frankfurt. Before that he had spent some years in Hanover working for the Oppenheimer bank and trading house. The deliveries he made to the minor court of the Landgrave William of Hanau gave him the opportunity in 1769 to try and acquire the title of Court Agent to said court. In his petition he pointed out that he had proven his reliability and that he now hoped »to make his fortune in Frankfurt«. It is difficult to assess how important this title was. It certainly did not give Meyer Amschel a position equivalent to that of the court Jews in Berlin and Vienna. As civil servants, the latter enjoyed direct access to their respective prince, were granted substantial privileges which marked them off from the rest of the Jewish community and, with their extensive family and social connections, comprised an aristocratic upper class within the Jewish community. The court Jews fulfilled an important function at the absolutist courts at a time when considerable sums of money were needed to cover the upkeep of the elaborate courts and the standing armies - a function which, given the growing demands made of them, the traditional civil service was not able to fulfil. Jewish merchants offered a way out of this dilemma; their family contacts enabled them to tap pan-European loans and to put up the necessary money required at short notice. In order to secure their services in the long term, they were incorporated into the ranks of the respective prince's civil service by being appointed as court agents. State income or business monopolies were placed in their hands, they became head of the mints appointed as regular supplier to the respective army. The leading families in the Frankfurt Jewish community were also members of this Jewish upper class.

The example of Meyer Amschel shows that the ranks of those who were court agents was much larger and included a whole number of Jewish merchants who had acquired the titles owing to the supplies they delivered to the various courts without being members of the leading families of court Jews, who were interconnected by marriage and by financial transactions. The title of Court Agent to the Court of Hanau

Last page of Meyer Amschel's 1783 coin catalogue

Es hat Innhaber dieses, ohne diese Münzen auch eine Anzahl Medaillen um billige Preiße zu verkaufen.

Adresse

Mayer Amschel Rothschild,
Hoch-Fürstl. Hessen-Hanauischer Hof-Factor, wohnhaft in Frankfurt am Mayn.

1783.

did not bring any special rights with it and was probably no more than a useful reference Meyer Amschel could give his clients. His status within the Jewish community remained unaffected by his being granted this title.

Shortly after being awarded the title of Agent to the Court of Hesse-Hanau Meyer Amschel married Gutle Schnapper, whose dowry was quite considerable. Together, the couple moved into Meyer's father's house, the »Hinterpfann« house, where both his brothers already resided. Meyer Amschel engaged in a wide variety of activities at this time. Alongside trading in coins, antique artwork and goods of all types, he also bought bills of exchange and worked as an agent procuring loans. In the Judengasse there was no one else than Meyer Amschel, specialized in the coin and medals trade. Between 1770 and 1790 he published, presumably annually, a catalogue of the coins and medals he had to offer. The majority of them were thalers from the 16th to 18th centuries, the value of which, unlike the bills of exchange business, did not just depend on their precious metal content but also and in particular on their historical value. This he had to establish with the help of the numismatic manual that had just appeared, in which Priest Samuel Maddai extensively described each item in his large collection of thalers. Using the classification system put forward by Maddai, clients were able to pin-point the exact value of the coins offered in Meyer Amschel's catalogues.

Alongside commemorative thalers and medals, Meyer Amschel also offered for sale antique gold and silver coins. As, unlike for the thalers, there was no manual available for these, Meyer Amschel Rothschild had himself to provide quite careful descriptions of these coins. These descriptions required a quite profound knowledge of history and art history, which he had had to teach himself.

In 1789 Meyer Amschel sold a series of coins to the Coin Exhibition Rooms of Elector Karl Theodor of Bavaria. We can reconstruct from the invoice the exact steps involved in the sale. Meyer Amschel had sent a larger selection of coins to Munich. The

Title page of Meyer Amschel Rothschild's coin catalogue, c. 1785

Thalers and medals
Meyer Amschel
Rothschild supplied
to the Bavarian Court
in 1789

coins the client then wished to purchase were then sold to the Elector's Collection, presumably after written negotiations, at a price reduced by between 30 and 50 percent. The items the Elector did not desire were returned at cost to Meyer Amschel. No doubt the Coin Exhibition Rooms chose the coins that were first despatched to them in the first place by using a catalogue.

What the invoice clearly shows is that Meyer Amschel had set up his coin trade on a mail order basis. Alongside this, he himself also held auctions - probably during the Spring and Autumn fairs. He purchased the coins individually or from collectors who sold their collections en bloc. His clients included not only courts, but also aristocratic and middle-class collectors. The collections of the day, such as that gradually established by Landgrave William of Hanau, were no longer mere curio exhibitions, but were increasingly structured according to numismatic criteria and managed by

specialists. The Hanau Collection, for example, was organized chronologically and the underlying organizational principles presented to the public in a scholarly article by the librarian responsible. In order to curry favour with this circle of clients, Meyer Amschel had to accumulate a substantial knowledge of the subject, something for which his traditional Jewish education had not readily equipped him. His achievements are all the more astonishing if one bears in mind that the surviving letters he wrote show that he had difficulties writing in German.

The coin trade was of great significance for him, as it opened doors that could be important for other avenues of business. Thus, The Librarian Wegener, who was in charge of the Hanau Coin Collection, later became director of the Hanau County Treasury, the most important financial body in the county. It sold bills of exchange issued by the English government and redeemable in London. These bills were the payment for troops from Hanau that fought on the English side during the American War of Independence. They were sold to the highest bidder and could be redeemed by the purchaser or his partners in London.

Contact with the men in charge of the Court's Coin Collection thus afforded Meyer Amschel the opportunity to acquire bills from the Hanau County Treasury and resell them for redemption in London. This trade in bills was highly profitable.

The »Grünes Schild« House

Between 1784 and 1786 Meyer Amschel Rothschild purchased the »Grünes Schild« House for more than 11,000 guilders, one of the largest houses in the Judengasse. He sold his three-eighths' stake in »Hinterpfann« to his brother Moses for 3,300 guilders. The purchase of this very expensive house shows just how successful his business activities as a coin dealer and dealer in bills had been. In 1787 he moved into the house, with his wife and six children. A further four children saw the light of day there by 1792.

As the house remained intact as a museum until the Second World War, we have a clearer idea of what the interior looked like than we do of other houses in the Judengasse: numerous photos and drawings exist of it. On entering Grünes Schild, one encountered a stairwell and a wash basin that was supplied with water via a pump from the private well in the cellars. Originally, as with most houses in the Judengasse, the kitchen and stove were also located in the entrance area.

Meyer Amschel's business activities centered on his office on the first floor. A felony committed in 1796 gives us an idea of how the office was organized. Meyer Amschel's servant Hersch Liebmann had been stealing from him for years. The protocol of the cross-examination that it was above all the chaotic state of the office that had made

The »Grünes Schild« House, after 1874. The photo was taken after the western row of houses in the Judengasse had been torn down.
The three windows on the left were part of the neighbouring »Schiff« House, which shared part of the gable roof of »Grünes Schild«

Office in the Rothschild house, drawing by Richard Enders, 1927

this possible. Large sums of money from bills business (and, at the time, also from money supplies to the Emperor's army) were kept relatively openly in a cupboard and a chest. Numerous clients could make their way into the room, approximately 10 square metres large, where the books, business correspondence, bonds, medals and precious coins were also held. Despite the large sums of money that came in every day, no regular book was kept of incoming and outgoing payments for the day. Meyer Amschel was thus not able to specify exactly what sums had been stolen from him.

Alongside the office, the cellar and other parts of the house contained storerooms, so that little actual space remained for residential quarters. All the younger children probably slept in one room. Not only the sons helped out in the business as soon as they were 13 or 14, but also the daughters and, at a later date, the daughters-in-law. The Rothschilds did not employ servants until the 1790s. The first, Hersch Liebmann, later couvieted of theft, was the son of poor parents from Bocken-

heim and became Meyer Amschel's servant at the age of 20. He accompanied him on journeys, delivered money and goods, but also had to cut wood and carry water. Later, a second servant was appointed to carry out these menial tasks. Hersch Liebmann was not allowed to sleep at Grünes Schild, but instead shared a room with four others in a hostel in the Judengasse. He paid roughly a third of his wages for the lodgings (12 out of 30 guilders a year). But he received free meals and tips. He stole approximately 2,000 guilders, or 70 times his annual wages.

Meyer Amschel did not employ a bookkeeper until expanding his trade in English cloth and groceries in 1795. Presumably he also required someone who could conduct foreign-language correspondence on his behalf.

On the Road

From the very beginning, Meyer Amschel Rothschild travelled extensively, as many of his clients in particular in the coin business lived outside Frankfurt. When travelling he had to contest with numerous hurdles. The Frankfurt Jews were not allowed to leave the Judengasse on Sundays and Christian holidays and at many customs barriers the Jews had to pay a special Jews' levy. Some court agents in Frankfurt were, however, on the request of their aristocratic employers, granted the right to travel in and out of that city on such days. In his capacity as Agent to the Court of Hesse-Hanau Meyer Amschel received such a pass in 1783, as the Hanau County Treasury required his assistance in business in English bills.

In 1787 seven Frankfurt-based court agents, and Meyer Amschel was among them, complained to the Town Council about the new regulations regarding their passes for Sundays and holidays. The passes, which were each valid for a group of agents, were now to be changed to contain descriptions of the persons entitled to use them. This meant that only one court agent could travel at a time and that they had to fear harassment at the town gates. They wrote:

»Every Jew has, as a human being, the same rights as the others;... Unfortunately the lower classes are still too used to the prejudices of their fathers to be able to not doubt that the Jew is a being like themselves. They allow themselves to mistreat the latter in all sorts of ways and some old men enjoy the fact that their sons annoy Jews. Even the guards on occasion indulge in such punishable tyranny. Would they not take such a signal as the occasion for countless acts of irritation? Even the smallest difference in clothing, hair, beards and the like would be taken by them as an excuse for the most stringent examination at the town gate; it would enable them to arrest the Jew for the slightest deviation from the description, as if he were a common thief, and take him to the main guardhouse.«

What is interesting here is not only the way in which the numerous limitations on freedom of movement for Jews impacted on their everyday lives. The reasons given for the petition show that Meyer Amschel's world was starting to change. Under the influence of the Enlightenment, the ghetto and the proscriptions associated with it were increasingly regarded as scandalous. Even the Frankfurt Jews, who, compared with those in Berlin, were still very traditional, were seized by the ideas of the time, which, in the wake of the French Revolution, were soon to have an effect on German society as well. They afforded Meyer Amschel Rothschild and his sons new unexpected opportunities. Yet it was the wars unleashed by the French Revolution which first had direct consequences for the Rothschilds, offering profitable opportunities in a traditional area of business conducted by court agents: namely supplying the army.

Wars, Princes and Business

The Career of a Court Jew

A parade of Austrian hussars on the Fischerfeld in front of the gates of Frankfurt, 1797

Supplies to the Army

In 1792 Austria and other countries attacked France, setting a war in motion that was to devastate Europe for 20 years. At the outset of the war Meyer Amschel succeeded, together with two business partners from the Judengasse, Wolf Loeb Schott and Beer Nehm Rindskopf, in concluding a contract with the Imperial Army. They provided the money to pay the soldiers as well as grain and equipment for the army during its operations in the Rhine/Main region against the French. The supplies of coins thus required were so extensive that Meyer Amschel's servant was able for two full years to steal large sums without this being noticed. The profits were also evidently so considerable that between 1792 and 1795 Meyer Amschel moved up from the lower middle class to the highest class of tax payer in the tax estimates of the Jewish community: instead of 2,000 guilders he now had to pay tax on assets totalling 15,000 guilders. However, this says little about his actual net worth, as for taxation within the Jewish community there was a tax ceiling and assets over the 15,000 guilder mark were no longer stated in the tax return.

From now on Meyer Amschel's three eldest sons, Amschel, Salomon and Nathan, were also active in his business, and clearly they played a good part in the business upturn in the years in question.

Extensive organizational tasks and unforeseen problems had to be overcome in the context of supplying the army. In October 1795, Meyer Amschel and his partners were contracted, for example, to deliver 15,000 pecks of oats to the Imperial Army's storerooms in Heidelberg. They employed subcontractors in Heidelberg and the Rhineland-Palatinate, who supplied the grain on time. As the Army had, however, already moved on, the storeroom administrators refused to take receipt of the delivery. The suppliers were thus left sitting on their goods and demanded that Meyer Amschel Rothschild and his partners pay them. They in turn refused and were first forced to do so by court order.

The successful organization of deliveries to the Imperial Army led to Meyer Amschel and his son Amschel both being awarded the title of Agent to the Imperial Court. The business also expanded the family's creditworthiness. Thus, Johann Friedrich Städel, Frankfurt merchant and patron of a large art collection, invested over 70,000 guilders in Meyer Amschel's business from 1795-9. And he was no doubt not the only person to invest money in the Rothschilds' operations at this time. Meyer Amschel in turn invested these sums in trade in English cloth and groceries, which he evidently sold in particular to the armies. He attempted at the same time to gain a foothold in the highly profitable trade in state bonds, which had first emerged in the 1780s. As of 1798 Meyer Amschel focussed increasingly on procuring bonds on behalf of clients.

In these years of incessant activity, involving countless trips to Berlin, Hamburg, Kassel, Munich and Vienna, Meyer Amschel Rothschild acquired further Court Agent titles for himself and his eldest son. Alongside the links to Landgrave William of Hesse that had been established back in 1769, he also became court agent to the Emperor, agent to the Order of St. John and the Prince of Thurn und Taxis. He also applied in vain to another court in Bavaria. The application was turned down because at that time the whole law on Jews was being reformed in Bavaria. The links with the household of Thurn und Taxis arose from bills business which Meyer Amschel and his sons had conducted from about 1780

At the request of Meyer Amschel Rothschild, Karl Anselm von Thurn und Taxis appoints the former's son, Amschel, to the position of Court Agent, January 17, 1804

onwards via the Thurn und Taxis postal office in Frankfurt. And, finally, the Rothschilds became agents to the Order of St. John, as one of the first government bonds they themselves floated in 1803 was conducted on behalf of the Order.

The practical benefits the title of Court Agent could have can be seen from an episode in 1801, when Meyer Amschel Rothschild was to be prosecuted for a »customs offence«. When travelling to Kassel and Berlin he was stopped at the Hesse-Darmstadt Customs Office in Butzbach and, on presentation of his certification as Agent to the Imperial Court and that of Hesse-Kassel, was freed from having to pay the obligatory Jews' Levy. However, this transpired to be a mistake on the part of the customs officer, so that the Hesse-Darmstadt authorities tried to reclaim the levy retroactively.

The astonishing collection of titles of Court Agent and the trade supplying the army, which, after long years of gradual growth in Meyer Amschel's business, enabled him to take the decisive step forward, show that his career followed the tradi-

tional pattern of the court Jews. By 1800 he was well on his way to getting a foothold in the door of the uppermost class of court Jews. However, as the rejection of his application in Bavaria shows, the era of the court Jews was in legal terms coming to an end anyway. The business in government bonds, which became ever more important for the Rothschilds, marked a further step along the path to their becoming modern bankers. What counted were no longer just contacts to a local prince, but a knowledge of the capital markets and the ability to work them successfully. Meyer Amschel's breakthrough into the banking business still occurred in traditional terrain, however, for he followed his lord, Landgrave William, when the latter moved from Hanau to take up residence in Kassel.

The peer's immense wealth was reflected, above all, in his large building projects in Kassel. In 1786 work commenced on the Wilhelmshoehe Castle he had commissioned, the grounds of which he had transformed into one of the most famous English landscaped gardens of the day: it even included artificial ruins. The city itself became renowned as one of the most beautiful and modern German royal residences.

To manage and increase his wealth, the Landgrave and his financial advisers used the services of the Kassel court Jews and the large Frankfurt banks. As no distinction was made at the time between public and private coffers, the Landgrave had sole right to decide on how these large sums of money were used, and he concerned himself closely with the area of finance. In 1789 Meyer Amschel Rothschild attempted to participate in this lucrative business with the Landgrave's Treasury. Despite his connections from his work for the Landgrave's agencies in Hanau, it took him over ten years before he was successful.

As of 1800 he started procuring government bonds on a wide scale for the Elector's War Treasury Office. Until that time the surplusses in the Kassel War Treasury had been simply lent out as loans. As the Elector always had to take political considerations into account when making loans, an anonymous investment of the money in the new form of »partial bonds« was less problematic politically speaking and also contained less risks. This new in-

En Route to Kassel

After the death of his father Frederick II, William IX became Landgrave of Hesse-Kassel. Hitherto he had only ruled over the small county of Hanau-Muenzenberg, north east of Frankfurt. In 1803 he succeeded in acquiring the additional title of Elector. Despite ruling over an impoverished county, Landgrave William IX. was one of the richest peers of the day, as his predecessors had already pursued the policy of hiring out their well-armed and well-trained army to allied powers for a considerable fee. The most famous operation was when troops from Hesse and Hanau fought on the English side in the American War of Independence, something that was sharply criticized in the papers of the day, where headlines spoke of »sold soldiers«.

Friedrichsplatz
in Kassel in 1789,
in a colored engraving
by Johann
Werner Kobold

vestment instrument had been introduced by the Gebr. Bethmann Bank in Frankfurt in 1778 to cover the credit requirements of the prince for whom they worked. They did not, as had been customary, grant one large credit tranche, which was a highly risk-laden approach. Instead they attempted to package the capital resources of numerous smaller owners of capital and themselves only worked as agents for the bond issue. For example, the Austrian Emperor made a main bond for the total debt, say 200,000 guilders, available to the bank. The bank then sliced it up into tranches of 1,000 guilders, »partial bonds« which the buyers could then subscribe to purchase. These »partial bonds« could then be sold to others. This new form of investment was a great success and turned Frankfurt into an important European capital market. Above all, it was thus easier to cover the large credit needs of countless German princes and states. In the process, the bankers stood to make a profit in two respects. Firstly, they received a commission for floating the bond and were also able to reap profits from sales of the bonds.

As of the 1790s, Landgrave William preferred this investment instrument and placed all his money in »partial bonds«. As these purchases had to be effected via bankers, the Landgrave himself remained discreetly in the background and, unlike in the case of direct loans, was now able to make investment decisions purely on economic grounds. His most important business partner in Frankfurt was, alongside the Bethmann Bank, the Rüppel & Harnier Trading Company and Bank, which had close contacts with Kassel. Simon Rüppel was the Senior Postmaster of Hesse in Frankfurt, his partner Louis Harnier was the son and nephew of two important civil servants in the Kassel War Treasury Office. When working as the go-between for »partial bonds« placed with the Court in Kassel, the Frankfurt banks frequently worked together with Kassel court Jews.

Despite the competition from the Kassel court Jews, Meyer Amschel gradually succeeded in gaining a foothold in Kassel, initially as acting in cooperation with the Bethmann Bank and the Rüppel & Harnier company. His success was evidently closely bound up with the career of Karl Buderus, to whom he had established closer contacts during the latter's time in Hanau. Buderus, himself of humble origins, had been appointed Senior Collector to the County Treasury. In 1792 he was posted from Hanau to Kassel, where he took up the position of War Paymaster, probably as he was considered an expert in government bonds. In 1795 he was appointed War Councillor and in 1802 War Paymaster General. He was soon Landgrave William's most important financial advisor, one of the few civil servants the latter consulted when deciding on how best to investment his formidable wealth. After several of Meyer Amschel's business proposals had been rejected, as of 1798 he sold numerous »partial bonds« to the Kassel Court, always through the agency of Karl Buderus.

The breakthrough for Meyer Amschel came in 1803, when he succeeded for the first time in floating a bond for the State of Denmark and sold it in its entirety to Elector William. With Buderus acting as go-between, Meyer Amschel Rothschild had established business connections with the Hamburg banker Lawätz, who, unnoticed by the competition, had established direct links to Danish civil servants. Danish bonds

had hitherto only been floated by the Bethmann and Rüppel & Harnier banks, and it was into their domain that Meyer Amschel broke with his own issue. For this transaction, for which the Landgrave granted Rothschild highly favourable conditions, he was rewarded with the title of Higher Agent to the Court of Hesse. From then onwards, a bitter competitive battle broke out, with the two main players, Meyer Amschel Rothschild and Rüppel & Harnier seeking support from important civil servants in the financial administration in Kassel. They intrigued against one another with all the means at their disposal. Buderus on occasion had letters sent by his competitors opened.

Landgrave William exploited the conflict, in order to keep his officials in check and to get the best terms in agreements with the various bankers. The first successful bond launch was followed in 1806 by further bonds for Denmark. Despite the fact that he still had only a meagre capital base, Meyer Amschel nevertheless did not risk much with these transactions, as he was able to arrange to sell all »partial bonds« to the Landgrave in advance. And that was the real advantage of his business contacts to the Landgrave.

The close contacts to the Landgrave's Court led to Meyer Amschel spending considerable time in Kassel and managing his business from there. In 1802, the Kassel Jews complained of the competition the Rothschilds posed for them. In order to not endanger the Kassel end of his operations, Meyer Amschel applied in 1803 for his son to be given a letter of safe-conduct, i.e. to be granted the right to take up a fixed abode in Kassel. He wrote: »Your Excellency... My trading house does not insignificant business in bills in northern Germany and this causes me to wish that your Excellency the Elector mercifully grant me safe-conduct for one of my sons in the town in which you reside. Your merciful granting of this humble wish would not impair the activities of the local merchants in any way and those who conduct business in bills will rather profit from this, as such transactions always benefit from large competition. I remain in awe and deepest respect the humblest servant of your Highest Excellency.«

He was granted his wish as probably the argument that competition was good for business caught the Landgrave's attention. It was, however, not until 1805 that the letter of safe-conduct was issued, for, as Meyer Amschel wrote sometime after making the petition, his eldest son Amschel planned to join operations with his brother in England. He therefore requested that the letter of safe-conduct be specifically issued in the latter's name. However, as he could not always be personally present during the tax audits conducted by the Jewish community, he asked for special dispensation and that he be simply taxed in line with the level paid by the highest payer in the Kassel Jewish community. This met with opposition among the Kassel Jews, so that eventually Amschel Mayer, the eldest son, formally took up residence in Kassel.

Kassel thus became the Rothschilds' first branch office on the continent. However, it had to be disbanded only a year later as the Rothschild's most important business partner, the Elector, was driven out of that city.

Meyer Amschel Rothschild petitions Elector William I that the latter issue one of his sons a letter of safe-conduct for the City of Kassel, August 1, 1803

The Elector in Exile

In 1806, following the defeat of Prussia at Jena and Auerstedt, French troops also occupied the Electorate of Hesse. Landgrave William had admittedly had signs put up at the border points saying »Neutral Territory«, but Napoleon treated him as if he were an ally of Prussia. The Elector had to flee and Kassel became the capital city of the new state: the Kingdom of Westphalia, which was ruled by Napoleon's brother Jérôme.

Prior to fleeing, William and some of his most faithful civil servants managed to hide a total of 119 chests containing the large part of his fortune in his castles. Some of them were admittedly discovered, above all the prince's silver treasures and his coin collection, but the chests containing title deeds and the documents on state bonds were smuggled out of the country by bribing the French governor Lagrange. The Rothschilds played only a minor part in this, even if at a later date a legend arose, promoted by members of the family, that the Rothschilds had been largely responsible for saving the Elector's treasure. The Elector – who initially went into exile in Holstein, which belonged to Denmark, and then, as of 1807, in Prague – was immensely

Map of the route the Elector took from Itzehoe to Carlsbad. 1807.
The route was chosen with a view to circumnavigating French territory wherever possible

Some of the questions to be decided in connection with the damage to the capital funds in Kassel owing to coupons being in the hands of certain parties, to be answered speedily by Privy Electoral Councillor Buderus von Carlshausen«, Castle Gottorf in Holstein, December 5, 1806

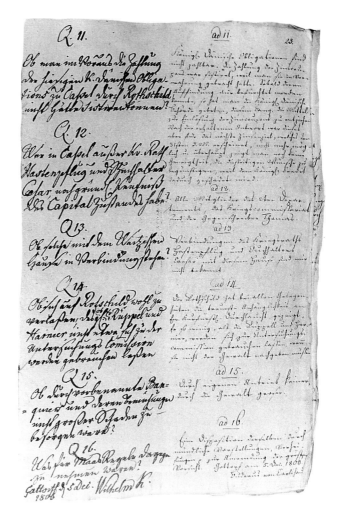

wealthy. Managing and safekeeping this wealth was, however, very difficult, as the French authorities continued to hunt for it.

Together with Karl Buderus, the Elector tried to find a way of managing his assets, which although he had rescued them for the time being, were still in danger of confiscation. To do so, he compiled a questionnaire containing 16 questions, that Buderus then answered. The central question with respect to the future course events were to take was: »Whether we can trust Rotschild, and Rüppel & Harnier for that matter, not to allow himself to be used

by the investigating Commission« Buderus' answer was clear: »To date, Rothschild has on all occasions shown the greatest loyalty to your Excellency the Elector. He, as little as Rüppel & Harnier, will not allow himself to be used by the (French) investigating Commission, unless they have to give in to violence.« This paved the way for these banks. The Rothschilds, however, still had Rüppel & Harnier to contend with.

Rescuing a Fortune

The Elector's assets which were saved, and they still totalled some 16 million guilders, consisted for the main of bonds. The particular situation enabled Buderus to squeeze all the bankers competing with the Rothschilds and all the Elector's financial civil servants who were competing with him out of the picture. War Councillor Lennep, the most important contact Rüppel & Harnier had, fell into the forever mistrustful Elector's disfavour, as some documents among those rescued by him in the chests of bonds and interest coupons failed to turn up. Buderus endeavoured, moreover, to work on the Elector, sowing seeds of discontent with Rüppel & Harnier. In this manner he succeeded in settling the fierce competition since 1802 between the various banks and the various groups of civil servants clearly in favour of the Rothschilds; as of 1809 he was a dormant partner in their company.

Buderus took up residence in his home town of Hanau, which, although still occupied by the French, was close to the Rothschilds in Frankfurt. Here, he kept the books, monitored payments and reinvestment of interest due to the Elector and providing the Elector with money. The books Buderus kept show that as of 1807 only the Rothschilds received income from the Elector. Buderus was watched over by a mistrustful French secret police force, on occasion even arrested, but the contacts the Rothschilds had to Karl Theodor von Dalberg, the Primate of the Rhenish Alliance, ensured that he was soon released again. The Elector made him a peer for his efforts.

Buderus' invoices, 1806–12.
This page, dating from 1811, clearly shows that only the Rothschilds still collected funds due to the Elector

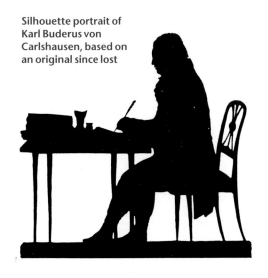

Silhouette portrait of Karl Buderus von Carlshausen, based on an original since lost

The most important means of contact between Buderus, the Rothschilds and the Elector were letters, which were either handed over by a messenger or entrusted to the regular post. As the French secret police kept an eye on the Rothschilds and Karl Buderus, the letters were all the more frequently sent under false names. Meyer Amschel thus became Peter Arnoldi, War Councillor Knaatz, who was in charge of the Elector's finance office in Prague, became Johannes Weber, Buderus Mr. Waldschmidt and the Elector himself Mr. Goldschmidt. The Rothschilds also took care of forwarding the Elector's political mail, who was trying to regain his state and was, therefore, informed of plans of insurrection against the French in Hesse. In order to write the letters in code, Meyer Amschel or his son translated them into Hebrew and then translated them back again.

Although all matters financial went through Buderus' hands, Elector William endeavoured to make sure that he kept a careful eye on his wealth himself and thus desired to take personal receipt of the chests with government bonds. Thus, a series of handwritten notes exist from his time in exile in which he wrote down the size and scope of his assets. He finally succeeded in having all his bonds brought to Prague.

The Rothschilds collected the interest due to the Elector from the bonds and, in consultation with Buderus and the Elector invested it anew or transferred funds to the Elector in Prague, on whose behalf they also sold bonds. Thus, for his account they reacquired his coin collection, which had fallen into the hands of the French, but also sent him jugs of Selters mineral water from Frankfurt. One of the Rothschild sons, usually Kalmann, but on occasion also Salomon or Amschel, was constantly in Prague, or else on the road somewhere between Prague, Frankfurt and Hanau, where Buderus was located. They had had a secret compartment built into their coach in order to enable them to ferry conspiratorial post, bonds and coupons back and forth.

Envelope of a letter from Meyer Amschel Rothschild to War Councillor Knaatz using the pseudonym »Johannes Weber«

The lion's share of the Elector's wealth consisted of English government bonds. The annual interest on this was disbursed in London and it was thus difficult to transfer it to the Elector in Prague given the war and the Continental Blockade. As of 1809 Meyer Amschel's son Nathan, who had moved to England in 1798, was instructed to reinvest these immense sums. He thus had considerable capital at his disposal, capital resources that the Elector could only with the greatest difficulty make sure were invested as he wanted. In order to allay the Elector's fears in this regard, Buderus repeatedly described to him why it took months to get the invoices for the purchase of English bonds to Prague.

The fact that the Elector had to go into exile was thus a stroke of luck for the Rothschilds. After Buderus had dealt with the competition, they acted as sole bank servicing the massive amount of capital the Elector possessed. It was, in particular, Nathan in London who thus received extensive financial scope and it was he who laid the basis for the further boom in the family's fortunes.

Nathan Crosses the Channel

»A View from the Royal Exchange« (Nathan Rothschild)
Drawing by Richard Dighton, 1817

To become Court Agent to a rich noble was the highest objective a Jewish merchant could aspire to in the Age of Absolutism. Meyer Amschel managed to acquire such a position at a time when the importance of Court Agents was receding and was an office only upheld by a few small states. The nascent modern state required different financial institutions. A banking sector gradually emerged that met these changed requirements. The personal relation of a Court Agent to a monarch was replaced by anonymous banking structures.

Meyer Amschel was well aware that the times were changing, but it was his sons who first started the move away from the traditional lines of business. What was decisive for the reorientation of business was Nathan Rothschild's move to England. Meyer Amschel's third son thus took up residence in a country that was well ahead of the backward small German princedoms. The world's industrial and trade centre offered a substantially more modern economic framework and called for a completely different strategy if Nathan wanted to be successful. However, the decision to move to England was prompted by the needs of his father's firm, which, quite traditionally, conducted merchant business alongside its banking activities.

»N. M. Rothschild, 15 Brown Street, Manchester«

As is known from the files of a legal action, the Rothschilds had been trading with goods from England since 1795. They imported above all goods from the colonies, such as indigo and arak, but predominantly cloth. England led the world in the production of cotton textiles, obtaining the cotton from its colony India and from its former colonies in America. Spinning and weaving were already machine-based in England's cotton hubs. These two factors caused the cotton industry to be by far the most developed in the world and English textiles were sought after in all of Europe.

In 1799 we find Nathan in England. In an after-dinner speech 36 years later he explained why he went there: »There was not room enough for all us in Frankfurt. I dealt in English goods. One great trader came there who had the market to himself: he was quite the great man, and did us a favour if he sold us goods. Somehow I offended him, and he refused tho show me his patterns. This was on a Tuesday; 'I said to my father I will go to England.' I could speak nothing but German. On the Thursday I started«.

The real reason for his departure was quite different. The Napoleonic Wars made the import of textiles difficult and expensive and the family hoped that by a member of the family moving to England they

Nathan Rothschild's
business card,
c. 1800

Manchester, seen from Kersal Moor, from an engraving by E. Goodall after a painting by W. Wyld, c. 1840

would secure supplies for his father's company. Nathan's move was also most certainly not so spontaneous. Instead he had probably carefully discussed with his father and brothers what was best for business in view of the difficulties facing textile imports from England.

Nathan was only just 21 when he decided to go to England. He went first to London, taking up his father's business contacts there and, moreover, receiving a credit line from him. Following a short apprenticeship with a business associate of his father's in London, he moved to Manchester, the centre of the English cotton trade. Here he set up a cloth wholesaling business, mainly supplying customers in Europe.

In the 1790s Manchester had become an industrial city. Scores of agricultural workers flocked to the city to find work. Numerous foreign merchants were also attracted by the spurt in the city's growth. In 1799, the city already had 90,000 inhabi-

tants – and was thus the second-largest city in the kingdom. The early stages of the industrial revolution had caused the population to triple within the space of only 25 years. The majority of the people, including many children, worked in the cotton industry. By 1810, the large spinning mills already dominated the city's skyline, whereas weaving was mainly still carried out as a cottage industry.

Nathan set up his business initially in order to secure cloth supplies to his father's company, yet at the same time Nathan built up his own network of customers, above all in Europe. He sold goods to Amsterdam, Frankfurt, Geneva, Hamburg, Paris and even Moscow, and yet he also had a client base in London itself. Nathan not only sold the fabrics, but also organised their dyeing

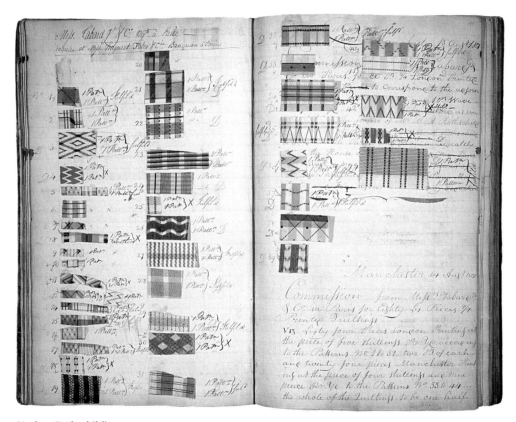

Nathan Rothschild's
Cotton Book,
c. 1800

and printing. He often bought the raw cloth in small quantities from the numerous weavers on the local market, but also from distant cities such as Leeds and Glasgow. He sent his customers samples to choose from in terms of quality and design, or he asked them to send him samples. Depending on the orders he received, he would send the selected fabrics to the printer's or dyer's for the finished goods to be produced. He also traded in indigo, a dye, which he sold to dyers. The finished goods were transported by ship or by the costly method of carting to Hull, whence they were forwarded to addresses overseas.

What the samples, which were so important for communication between the merchants, looked like is to be seen from a book of samples preserved for posterity in the Rothschild Archive, London. It was found among Nathan's numerous business books, which he kept for all areas of the business: the sale of cloth, print orders, incoming and outgoing bills. This »book of samples« was meant for internal use, keeping a chronological record of orders, together with remarks on prices and payment schedules. Nathan pasted a sample of the respective cloth next to every entry. This made it easier to deal with repeat orders.

The Napoleonic Wars made regular trade relations between England and the Continent difficult. Other German cloth merchants consequently also decided to set up branch offices in England. Nathan was the first of a whole series of Frankfurt Jews who, as active cloth merchants, moved to England in subsequent years. It is striking that they included relatives of Nathan: his brothers-in-law Worms and Sichel, the brother of his sister-in-law Hanau and his cousin Rindskopf. All of them set up their own businesses in England but maintained contact with their mother companies. It was probably Nathan who encouraged them to make the move, because it enabled him to rely soon thereafter on a business network of relatives in England.

Nathan followed an aggressive business strategy. But this also got him into difficulties. For example, he drew a bill on a Hamburg trading partner for a sum well in excess of the agreed limit and this was »protested«, which damaged his reputation. In a similar case, Meyer Amschel had to intervene and ensure that the bill was paid.

Nathan called his firm »Rothschild Brothers«, because he envisaged his brothers also settling in Manchester. At various times the family also considered setting up a further cloth business in Paris. Both plans, however, came to nothing. Nathan decided nevertheless to stay in England. In 1804 he became naturalized.

The Continental Blockade

Nathan's main trading partner was his father's company, which took care of organising the subsequent sale or at least the forwarding of the goods he supplied. Owing to the uncertainties of war time, Nathan's brother Carl resided in Dunkirk, where he took receipt of the cloth deliveries and forwarded them to his father's company. Meyer Amschel's cloth business had reached such proportions that he had to rent a storage room in Frankfurt's Schnurgasse, exploiting the fact that the ban hitherto on Jews renting houses outside the Judengasse was no longer enforced.

In order to damage England as a trading nation, Napoleon issued a decree in 1806 forbidding any trade or correspondence between states under French rule and Britain. Traders got around this so-called »Continental Blockade« either by bribing the French officials or using false marks of origin. Nathan was involved in these smuggling activities, and lost some goods through confiscation, but also made sizable profits. As a consequence of the shortage created by this decree, those merchants who nevertheless succeeded in obtaining goods from England recorded increased sales and profits. In a letter to his son written in English in 1807 Meyer Amschel stated: »You cant make you an idea how goods are demanded in our marked, I sold all Comon Cambrics left to me since 3 years ago all Thickset in Generally all fustian goods I had.«

The Rothschilds found ways of keeping deliveries going in the years thereafter. When the blockade was tightened in 1810, however, their situation became more difficult. The regulations were now enforced far more stringently. On Napoleon's orders, confiscated English goods were publicly burned in numerous

English goods being burned on the Fischerfeld near Frankfurt on Main. Johann Carl Wilck, oil on canvas, 1810

German cities. In October 1810 French troops marched into Frankfurt and at their instruction, storage rooms and houses belonging to merchants were scoured for English goods, with fines totalling over 10 million francs being imposed, not to mention the large sums paid in bribes to French officials. Part of the goods were burned under French military supervision on Frankfurt's Fischerfeld.

Meyer Amschel Rothschild was ordered to pay a modest fine of 19,381 francs. This was by no means in keeping with his extensive trade in English goods, but we do not know exactly why he only had to pay such a low figure. The French had achieved their goal of deterring merchants from further trade. Meyer Amschel also abandoned trade in English goods forthwith.

A Good Match

In 1806 Nathan married Hannah Cohen, daughter of the prominent London merchant, Levy Barent Cohen. Until well into the 19th century, marriage for a merchant still had the important function of consolidating his existing business relationships. Cohen was one of Meyer Amschel's business acquaintances and someone he had contacted and visited on first arriving in England. Cohen stayed in contact with his later son-in-law after Nathan had moved to Manchester, for he, too, predominantly traded in cloth. The marriage afforded Nathan access to the Jewish financial elite of the City. When Hannah's father died two years later, her inheritance enabled the couple to establish themselves permanently in London.

Nathan's father-in-law was the centre of a kinship network linking the most important Jewish families in London's financial sector. This included the Montefiores, the Mocattas and the Goldsmids. The Mocattas were among the richest traders in London, while the Goldsmid brothers dominated the English bond market up until 1810. Members of the Cohen and Montefiore families were stockbrokers, and therefore among Nathan's business associates.

A Banker in London

In London, Nathan devoted himself to banking and set up a company there, while, in the interim, one of his employees continued to run the Manchester business.

At around the turn of the century, London had over 1 million inhabitants and was thus the largest city in the world. Goods from all the British colonies were transhipped in London; it was also the centre of European trade, and, at the latest with the French occupation of Amsterdam, the undisputed main financial centre. England not only kept opposition to Napoleon going with its troops but above all with its subsidies. Political decisions were taken in London that had an impact on the whole Continent. The City was the suitable place for Nathan to fulfil his ambitions and in the course of the following years the hub of Rothschild trading activities shifted from Frankfurt to London.

Nathan laid the foundations for this by opening a bank. As early as 1805 Nathan had set up a small office in London where he dealt mainly in bills of exchange. Bills of exchange were promissory notes to pay a certain sum at a specific date in the future. The bill of exchange was a means of payment and a credit note at one and the same time, for the bill stated a payment date several weeks or months after its date of issue. Bills were of great importance, in particular in long-distance trade, because they could be used to avoid the physical transport of large quantities of money over great distances. In order to supply merchants with cash, banks bought bills, after deducting a »discount«. As Nathan predominantly traded with clients on the Continent, he was forced to accept numerous bills, to sell them on, and to issue them himself.

Nathan's switch from trading into banking was nothing unusual, as the two sectors were closely linked; until well into the 19th century, banks themselves engaged in trading and a large number of bankers, the so-called »Merchant Bankers«, had themselves started out as wholesalers.

In the course of time Nathan intensified the banking and stock exchange side to his business. For example, the Elector of Hesse had had the interest payable on his securities paid into an account held with the Bank of England. In 1809 Nathan began investing large amounts of capital belonging to the Elector of Hesse in British government securities. As Nathan had to wait until a price was reached at which the Elector had instructed him to buy the securities, he initially used the funds for his own devices. For this privilege he paid the Elector a relatively low rate of interest. The Continental Blockade impaired communication between Prague, where the Elector was in exile, and London, so that Nathan had plenty of room for manoeuvre. Using this money, the origins of which were unknown to anyone else, Nathan was able to play the role of a respected businessman. He borrowed money from other sources and was able to conclude large-scale transactions.

For some years Nathan's banking and cloth trading business existed in tandem. However, with the intensification of the Continental Blockade in 1810 it became much more difficult for cloth manufacturers and traders to sell their goods. The crisis in the sector was accentuated by unrest among the weavers in Manchester and the surrounding region, because the Blockade had led to unemployment and higher food prices. Nathan therefore decided to continue the banking business, which seemed to have a better future, and to discontinue the Manchester side of the business. He had chosen a favourable time to go into banking. The unforeseeable risks of the war years had shaken the foundations of the capital markets. In 1810 the head of the leading Goldschmid bank had shot himself out of fear of the shamefulness of having to go into liquidation. Nathan was soon to fill the vacuum this left behind in the London banking world.

Meyer Amschel Rothschild
Banker to the Court and Citizen

Judengasse and synagogue, watercolour by Carl Theodor Reiffenstein, 1845

Nathan Rothschild's success in London would not have happened without his ongoing links to his father. Meyer Amschel was not only one of his main trading partners on the Continent, but it was the latter to whom he was indebted for access to the enormous funds the Elector of Hesse held in London, funds with which he laid the foundations of his future career. While Nathan entered into new areas of business in London, Meyer Amschel would appear to have led a fulfilled life in a traditional frame. He was Court Agent to numerous princes and had acquired a monopoly on managing the Elector's finances. However, in the closing years of his life he came to play an unusual political role in Frankfurt.

Baron Karl Theodor
Anton von Dalberg
(1744–1817). Portait
by an unknown artist,
undated

The Struggle for Equal Rights

As of 1806, Baron Karl Theodor Anton von Dalberg (1744-1819), previously Archbishop of Mainz, was appointed Prince-Primate of the Rhenish Confederation established by Napoleon and thus governed Frankfurt. In 1810 he was made Grand Duke of Frankfurt. Meyer Amschel Rothschild maintained close business contacts with him and granted him several largish loans. In return, Dalberg made him Banker to the Court.

Once Frankfurt had fallen under the sway of Napoleon's France, the Jews in the city hoped that they would, following the French example, be accorded civil rights. Their hopes were dashed by Dalberg, who in 1807 renewed the old restrictions; this meant they were again compelled to live in the ghetto. The Jews protested against this both in newspapers and by petitioning Napoleon. In 1811, against payment of 440,000 guilders, they were in fact given full civil rights. Meyer Amschel Rothschild played a key role in the negotiations with Dalberg. Although in the years leading up to this event he had on numerous occasions on grounds of ill health successfully ensured that he had not had to stand for the position of Chairman of the Jewish Community, in the context of the negotiations he did not turn down an appointment as one of the Community's five legal representatives. And it was not only his close links to Dalberg which helped the negotiations to be brought to a successful conclusion, for he also advanced the Community 100,000 guilders towards paying the fee.

When difficulties arose in connection with the payment, Dalberg addressed the letter in which he reduced the sum the Jewish Community owed him to none other than Rothschild. He started by saying: »Most Honoured Court Agent, You are a trusted and upright man and have with all possible fervour spoken on behalf of your Community from the bottom of your heart...«

The 1812 entry in the Community's Memorbuch clearly attests to the high esteem in which the Jewish Community held him:

»Incomparable are his achievements and successes on behalf of our Community and the freedom it has gained, both for the current generation and for future generations...«

Poignant expression of Meyer Amschel's advance from the ghetto into the upper echelons of society was the fact that in June 1812, shortly before his death, he was elected a member of the Département of Frankfurt's Electoral College, which was made up of the five most venerable members of the city.

Taking Stock of a Long Life

Meyer Amschel Rothschild's life was characterized by success in business and his reaching the top of the social ladder. His professional success was hard earned and can be put in precise figures. In 1770 his taxed income was 20,000 guilders; by contrast, on his death he left behind an estate of 190,000 guilders, with the capital of his family business already totalling 800,000 guilders.

However, it is not easy to paint a clear picture of Meyer Amschel's personality. We cannot rely on a portrait of him, as he had none painted, probably for religious reasons. The obituaries and the few anecdotes about him that have survived tend to stress his traditional Jewish piety and way of life in an age transformed by rapid modernization. His professional career took place against the backdrop of regular attendance in the synagogue, the study and discussion of religious questions at home and with guests on holidays, membership of the burial brotherhood and administration of the poor box. He did not confine himself to traditional charity, however, but instead also supported reform projects such as the »Philanthropin«, the newly-founded Jewish school, as he was undoubtedly aware of the limitations of his own exclusively Jewish education and knew that a modern secular education was now an imperative. A comparable undertaking had been banned a few years earlier by the rabbi, which the latter had then to rescind at the instruction of the Council. And his professional career also moved between the twin poles of traditional examples he followed and the incalculable risks of the new age. His social and professional aims were undoubtedly formulated with traditional Court Jews in mind. The fact that he collected corresponding titles, engaged in the traditional business of a Court Agent and concluded the

Gravestone of Meyer Amschel Rothschild. Jewish Cemetery, Battonnstrasse, Frankfurt

right marriages for his eldest children shows that he was en route to becoming a member of that Jewish upper class established during the Age of Absolutism.

However, his success occurred while society was in upheaval, when Jewish emancipation was on the agenda and comprehensive social reforms followed in the wake of the French Revolution, rendering Court Jews obsolete as an institution. Bourgeois society afforded new hitherto uncountenanced possibilities for social success, and the nascent capital market offered unprecedented opportunities for business and profits. The final years of Meyer Amschel's life were shaped by an awareness of this fact, even if he never abandoned the traditional world of the Judengasse and the Absolutist courts in his personal life. He left it to his sons to turn their backs on the ghetto and establish a European bank.

The Five Brothers:
New Beginnings amongst
Continued Unity

The baronial coat-of-arms approved in 1822 and still valid to this day

Meyer Amschel's death did not create a caesura in the activities of the family company, as in 1810 he had already officially taken his sons on board as partners in the company. The further development of the company therefore depended both on whether the joint business transactions, which were highly risky at the time, were successful and on the brothers' ability to maintain the family and legal ties.

»… at this moment paralysed for want of money…« An Army in Dire Straits

The very first major piece of business conducted by the Rothschild brothers after their father's death, namely the support they provided for Wellington in Spain, shows that they embarked on new areas of business and no longer geared all their efforts toward the activities their father had conducted as Court Agent.

In order to understand the approach they took it is worthwhile shedding a glance at the situation prior to that famous major transaction:

During the Continental Blockade, like many other bankers, Nathan engaged in highly profitable smuggling: he had cash illicitly imported into France. Waiting at the French coast, his brother James took receipt of the cash and used it to buy bills drawn on London that were on the market far below nominal value owing to the trade embargo. Nathan then redeemed them in London at their face value. The French government approved of this operation in the hope that it would lead to a money shortage in England. The official French passes the Rothschilds needed for these activities they procured from Grand Duke Dalberg, who thus showed his appreciation for the service the Rothschilds had done him. The French government's position was essentially ambivalent. They furthered the brothers' activities on the one hand and yet, on the other, at the same time completely distrusted them and had them watched by the secret police. After all, it was a well-known fact that the Rothschilds had worked on behalf of the Elector of Hesse during his exile.

In the Archives Nationales in Paris numerous police reports on the brothers have survived to this day. One of the police agents gives a characteristic assessment of things: »The Rothschild brothers, who I visited today, are very clever, very careful and well versed in the art of making friends. Nevertheless, the police underestimated the brothers' resourcefulness. For, once what had started as a piece of private business had become support for the enemy's army under Wellington's command the French officials did not succeed in seeing through what was going on.

Wellington headed the army fighting Napoleon in Spain. As it was not possible to supply him with sufficient cash from the English government, he was forced to issue bills drawn on the English treasury. These bills were then sold at the nearest financial hub at a great loss. The perpetual lack of money threatened to prevent Wellington's advance. And the Treasury was also looking for a way out of the situation, as honouring the bills was costing a lot of money. The shortage of funds the Treasury faced did not go unnoticed by traders in bills, as bills issued by the English commander started cropping up in ever greater numbers on the market. Nathan quickly recognised the difficulties Wellington and the English treasury were in. Wellington, having crossed the Spanish border into France now needed French cash or bills drawn on banks in Southern France. Nathan decided to place his smuggling activities in the service of the British government. His plan for supplying money to Wellington was carried out under the strictest secrecy.

From then onwards, the English army was supplied with money by various means. Firstly, the Rothschilds continued making cash deliveries to France, with James buying bills drawn on Paris. There, he exchanged them for bills drawn on a French bank in geographical proximity to Wellington's army and which Wellington could redeem at a much higher rate. Secondly, the Treasury minted coins, for which Nathan provided the gold, and sent them to France. Thirdly, French cash was secretly hoarded in Northern France, in the Netherlands and in Germany, paid for by bills drawn on the Frankfurt Rothschild Bank. The money was then forwarded to the Dutch port of Hellevoetsluis and taken from there by English warships which awaited its delivery to Southern France, where Wellington took receipt of it.

Wellington was able to resume his advance. The Rothschilds made relatively slender profits considering the risks and the outlays involved. However, the link thus forged with the British government was to pay off for the Rothschilds: for the most part, they were entrusted with the payment of subsidies destined for the British allies. At the same time, the Rothschilds turned to numerous German governments who received English subsidies and managed to persuade some of them to have the funds transferred via the Rothschild Bank. They also participated in the transfer of contributions made by states to the French government to help cover the costs of the French occupying forces.

For the Rothschilds, Nathan's branch of the bank in London and that of James in Paris proved to be highly advantageous in this context. In their letters to the respective governments the brothers emphasize that when transferring subsidies they were »cheaper than any other company, because we have our own branch in Paris and are already effecting such payments for most Courts.« They offered to issue bills for any location desired and in any currency. These transfers promised risk-free commission and often entailed profits on exchange rate difference to the extent that the officials who negotiated the conditions did not know the ins and outs of financial transactions. The Rothschild took on transfers for Austria, Russia and Prussia (all three were major powers) and for smaller states such as Schaumburg-Lippe and Mecklenburg-Schwerin. These money transfers mark the transformation of the former Rothschild merchant trading company into a bank.

Amschel Mayer von
Rothschild,
1773–1855, head of
Bankhaus M.A. Roth-
schild & Söhne,
Frankfurt. The five oil
paintings are
attributed to Moritz
Daniel Oppenheim

Nathan Mayer
Rothschild,
1777–1836, head of
the London bank
N. M. Rothschild &
Sons

Salomon Mayer von
Rothschild, 1774–1855,
head of the Vienna
branch of M.A.
Rothschild & Söhne

Callmann, known as
Carl Mayer von Roth-
schild, 1788–1855,
head of the Naples
branch of M.A. Roth-
schild & Söhne

Jakob, known as James
Mayer de Rothschild,
1792–1868, head of
De Rothschild Frères,
Paris

»Meyer Amschel Rothschild & Söhne« – A Family Company With Clear Principles

After Meyer Amschel's trade in money and bills had developed well and his five sons had proven themselves to be able staff members, he decided to prevent the firm being split up in any way. In 1810 he set out the family company's principles and maintained that only if the brothers remained united would the company continue to be successful. On September 28, 1810 he conveyed to his business friends that he had made all of his sons partners in his trading company, which had then been in existence for a full forty years. Shortly beforehand he had concluded a contract with his sons who had reached maturity, namely Amschel Mayer, Salomon Mayer and Carl Mayer, all of whom had been working in the company for some years. This partnership agreement guaranteed that the firm would continue to be a family company named »Mayer Amschel Rothschild & Söhne« for the next decade. In so doing, Meyer Amschel concentrated the family's assets in the company, strengthened unity among the brothers and prevented any split into separate companies.

Although only three sons signed the contract, it was valid for all five. Jakob Mayer (James), who was already active in the company but had not yet come of age, was specified as a future partner. Being based in London, Nathan Mayer could not be included for political reasons: in 1810 Frankfurt was occupied by the French, and France and England were still at war.

The most important clauses in the contract were:
– The trading company could not be dissolved for ten years.
– The share capital of 800,000 guilders was divided up between the partners, with Nathan's share being covertly allocated to his father. All the capital had to be kept in the company; the partners received annual interest and money for their household needs.
– No partner was allowed to conduct a piece of business without the approval of the others.
– In the case of death, the inheritors were not permitted to withdraw money from the company. It was forbidden for members of the family to see the company's books and to contest the conditions governing inheritance.

In his last will and testament, which he drew up two years later in 1812, Meyer Amschel stipulated that as a matter of principle only his sons were to be eligible as partners of the company and his daughters and daughters-in-law were to be excluded from the company's management. He

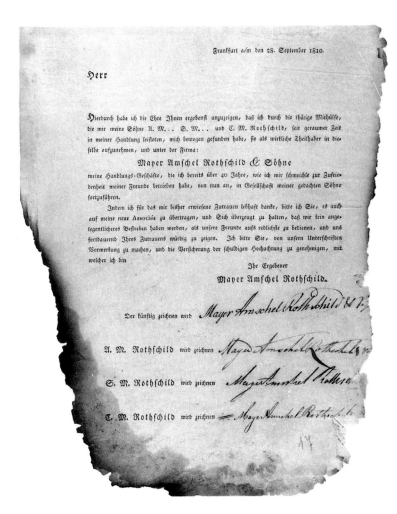

Frankfurt a/m den 28. September 1810.

Herr

Hierdurch habe ich die Ehre Ihnen ergebenst anzuzeigen, daß ich durch die thätige Mithülfe, die mir meine Söhne A. M... S. M... und C. M. Rothschild, seit geraumer Zeit in meiner Handlung leisteten, mich bewogen gefunden habe, sie als wirkliche Theilhaber in dieselbe aufzunehmen, und unter der Firma:

Mayer Amschel Rothschild & Söhne

meine Handlungs-Geschäfte, die ich bereits über 40 Jahre, wie ich mir schmeichle zur Zufriedenheit meiner Freunde betrieben habe, von nun an, in Gesellschaft meiner gedachten Söhne fortzuführen.

Indem ich für das mir bisher erwiesene Zutrauen lebhaft danke, bitte ich Sie, es auch auf meine neue Associés zu übertragen, und Sich überzeugt zu halten, daß wir kein angelegentlicheres Bestreben haben werden, als unsere Freunde aufs redlichste zu bedienen, und uns fortdauernd Ihres Zutrauens würdig zu zeigen. Ich bitte Sie, von unsern Unterschriften Vormerkung zu machen, und die Versicherung der schuldigen Hochachtung zu genehmigen, mit welcher ich bin

Ihr Ergebener
Mayer Amschel Rothschild.

Der künftig zeichnen wird

A. M. Rothschild wird zeichnen

S. M. Rothschild wird zeichnen

C. M. Rothschild wird zeichnen

Meyer Amschel Rothschild notifies his business associates that he had taken on his sons as partners in the business that would henceforth be called M.A. Rothschild & Söhne.
Copy found after the destruction of the Rothschild Museum in the Fahrgasse in 1938

stated: »I hereby decree and therefore wish that my daughters and daughters-in-law and their successors have no part in the actions undertaken by the firm »Mayer Amschel Rothschild & Söhne« and even less that they are able or are permitted to make a claim against it for whatever reason. Rather, such actions shall exclusively be and belong to the domain of my sons. None of my daughters, daughter-in-laws or their successors are therefore entitled to demand that such actions or the books or notes be revealed to them, or to demand to see securities, seals or stock lists pp. In that none of my daughters of their successors have a right nor claim to such actions, and I would never be able to forgive it should, against my will as father, my sons be disturbed in the calm possession of such actions.«

Meyer Amschel concluded by calling on the sons to remain united: »Finally I recommend to all my children that they confront each other with ever growing mutual love and friendship and that they obey these instructions of their well-meaning and conscientious father as children should.« These principles were directed initially at his five daughters, but they remain valid to this day.

In the future, the partners met every three years, drew up the accounts and distributed the profits. Letters repeatedly attest to disputes on the distribution of the shares of the assets and capital, which formed the basis for financial activities by the individual family members.

The partnership contracts were renewed until 1905, with all sons who had reached the age of majority being made partners on marrying. Until the 20th century no Rothschild had been denied entrance into the bank. Daughters-in-law and daughters continue to be excluded from management to this day, even if their expert knowledge and contacts were often put to good use in the company. Until 1960 there was no partner who was not directly descended from the company's founder.

The principles of the family tradition were adhered to rigorously in order to keep the number of decision-makers manageable and to secure clear indisputable succession. The disadvantages of this tradition first emerged in the second half of the 19th century, when, on the one hand, some Rothschild sons became interested in other areas and, on the other, capable bank employees moved to other banks or went independent. Initially, however, the advantages outweighed the disadvantages: the company was able to tap the private wealth of the family members and the five brothers and their sons sufficed in number to conquer the European financial markets.

Rothschild – von Rothschild – Baron von Rothschild

It was not unusual to ask a King or Prince as reward for services rendered by making one a member of an order or granting one a special title. However, when, after having completed the first major financial transaction for Austria (disbursement of English subsidy payments after the battles against Napoleon) the Rothschild brothers petitioned the Austrian Emperor Franz I for a further public distinction, this was unprecedented. Amschel Mayer had since 1808 borne the title of Imperial Court Agent, but what the brothers now wanted, without stating this in the petition, was to be made peers.

At the time, Austria was the only country in which Jews could hope of being given a peerage, and being made a noble meant far more than just receiving the Emperor's acknowledgement and proof of his mercy - it freed you from constraints and ostracization: being made a peer was a decisive step toward becoming a member of the ruling class.

The statements made by the Austrian officials, who were predominantly nobles themselves, contain numerous reservations against approving the Rothschilds' request: »The trader undertakes business for profit. But he does not claim to render any service where no profit is.« And: »The special consideration comes to bear here that the Rothschild brothers are Israelites.«

On the other hand, there were good reasons to try and obtain the loyalty of the bank for the future, which is what the Minister of Finance proposed: »The bank in question possesses great net worth, and even greater credit and can even conduct business which may seem quite out of the question for a private person on the Continent but which it is enabled to perform by virtue of the fact that the Government of Great Britain uses it for extensive operations and therefore furnishes it with the requisite funds.« This financial clout eventually won the day and in 1816 the Emperor decided in to make the Rothschild brothers simple patrimonial nobles, entitling them to place the word »von« in front of their surname.

On being made nobles the Rothschilds were authorized to have a coat of arms. The brothers thereupon submitted a crest for approval that symbolized the ascent of the House of Rothschild: The lion from the crest of the Elector of Hesse represented him; the leopard/lion from the English crest stood for England; half an eagle from the Imperial Austrian crest represented Austria. In the middle of the coat of arms is a red shield referring back to the sign of the former family house in Frankfurt's Judengasse. The five arrows held in a fist represent the brothers' unity. The crest is borne aloft by a hunting hound, symbol of loyalty, and a stork, symbol of devoutness and good fortune.

The Austrian heraldic office rejected this proposed coat of arms because it involved symbols of the high aristocracy and foreign governments. A simpler crest was approved, in which the hand holds four arrows, as only four of the brothers were made nobles.

In 1817 certifications of nobility were issued for Amschel, Salomon, Carl and James. When initially only those two brothers stood to be made nobles who had conducted the business with Austria, Salomon made sure that Carl and James were included as well. The object was not for individuals but for the family to receive a place among the peers. Nathan could not be one of the number, however, as he was already an English citizen.

When, five years later, the brothers sought to be made barons, their economic and social situation had changed completely. They were now the leading bank in Europe, conducting business in bonds and money with all the European princes and states. They now had such close links with the Austrian government that they financed the latter's campaign in the field against Naples. Nathan and James were representatives of the Austrian state, namely its consuls in London and Paris.

As a consequence, all five brothers were made barons. And they were allowed to take as their coat of arms the crest that is still the family's today. It contains a crown as a sign of the baronetage with the usual embellishments. It is held by a lion, symbol of strength, and a unicorn, symbol of purity. On a shield divided into four the lion of Hesse and the Austrian eagle are to be seen. Two quarters contain the fist with the five arrows symbolizing the brothers' unity. Again, the red shield is in the middle, now bearing a boss, the sign of sincerity and strength. Beneath the crest is a motto bearing the words »Concordia, Integritas, Industria,« concord, integrity and diligence. This links the significance of the peerage as the still dominant social class with the notions of performance nurtured by a middle class rapidly gaining power and influence.

The twofold presentation of the hand with the five arrows in this crest, which became the family coat of arms as of 1822, lent expression to the brothers' final decision to stay united in one company even if at the time bank branches existed in five different cities.

The European Rothschild Bank

The Five Brothers, lithograph by Hermann Raunheim after
a portrait by Moritz Daniel Oppenheim, Paris, 1852

When, in 1810, M. A. Rothschild & Söhne was founded in Frankfurt, the N. M. Rothschild bank already existed in London. A good decade later, the brothers James, Salomon and Carl had set up branches in Paris, Vienna and Naples, respectively. The brothers' mobility was an advantageous factor that definitely fostered the success of the company. Just as important was their ability and tenacity in ensuring they were involved in all the important financial transactions conducted by the leading European states. The development that led to the Rothschild bank being the foremost bank in Europe was, however, only possible because the brothers and soon thereafter their children, too, cooperated smoothly and in a quite unique manner, despite the company's decentralized branch structure.

The Prussian Bond Issue of 1818: »Only the Rothschilds can handle it«

(Letter from Nathan to Rother, a Prussian financial official, May 19, 1818)

In the years following the conclusion of peace on the Continent in 1815 the brothers did especially profitable business in government bonds. The almost twenty years of war had left numerous states heavily in debt and, moreover, funds were required in many quarters in order to build roads and found companies. The only way states had of meeting the urgent financial obligations was to take up loans. To this end, governments negotiated with renowned banks headquartered near the major stock exchanges in London, Amsterdam and Frankfurt.

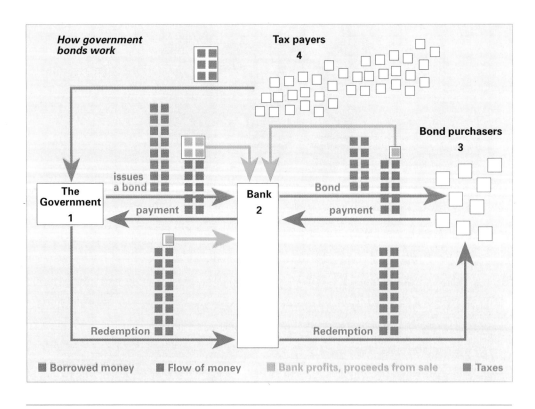

How government bonds work

Tax payers
4

Bond purchasers
3

issues a bond

The Government
1

payment

Bank
2

Bond

payment

Redemption

Redemption

■ Borrowed money ■ Flow of money ■ Bank profits, proceeds from sale ■ Taxes

The competition among the leading European banks when it came to placing government bonds was immense, although only few of them were in a position to float large bonds on their own. The Rothschilds sensed that bonds were going to be good business in the future. However, in 1815 they simply did not have access to the governments and courts of Austria, France and Prussia, the major continental powers.

During 1815-8 the Rothschild brothers worked exceptionally hard and had to run numerous risks. The brothers reported to each other in almost daily letters on business deals concluded, transactions that had not come off and stock prices. They conducted numerous transactions at once and now and again they simply did not know what their net worth was. Frequently, large amounts of money, even six figure sums, accrued. And yet again, suddenly they had cash flow difficulties. The brothers argued with one another about the degree of risk to be borne and by no means held back in mutual accusations or objecting to certain activities or missed business opportunities.

The brothers were, however, unanimous in their desire to land a really important piece of business in order to gain the attention of various governments. The negotiations on the Prussian bond were the first major bond negotiations the Rothschilds conducted. They were intended to gain the Rothschilds access to further government business and, as a consequence, all the members of the family were expected to make a great effort.

The Prussian state had been in financial difficulties for years. At the beginning of 1814 the national debt had risen to 70 million thalers. Interest of up to 24 percent had to be paid on the short-term liabilities it could not honour. After the end of the war, small bonds were floated to alleviate the situation, amongst others one handled by the Rothschild Bank in Frankfurt. However, this by no means sufficed to ease the enormous debt burden. The King and government therefore decided in November 1817 to float a large bond.

They immediately started searching for a bank that would offer them the best terms possible. Enquiries were made on credit opportunities not only in Berlin, the main Prussian banking centre, but also in London. London was the most important market for securities because England, owing to its preeminent position in industry and trade, had great wealth at its disposal.

The Rothschilds immediately showed an interest in the project. Nathan had an offer submitted for a bond issue of 10 million thaler and an issue price of 70 percent. That was in line with the price at the time for French bonds and was approved by the Prussian government.

However, before the deal was finalized, it became known that Austria, France, and Russia also wanted to float bonds. This meant that Prussia's chances of placing its bond on the market worsened. On January 13, 1818, the Rothschilds made a far more

---

State Bonds: An Example

A bond totalling for 20 million thalers, issued at 70 percent, at five percent interest and four percent commission:
Given an issue price of 70 percent, the state receives 14 million thalers.

It has to pay:

Repayment	(= 100 %)	20 million thalers
Interest	(= 5 %)	1 million thalers
Commission	(= 4 %)	0.8 million thalers
Total		**21.8 million thalers**

unfavourable offer of a total bond issue of 12 million thalers at an issue price of 60 percent. Although this bond was very expensive, the Prussian emissary to London, Wilhelm von Humboldt, was for continuing negotiations with Nathan: »If the bond is to be a success here, then, to my mind only if Rothschild handles it, unless, that is, we manage to get another equally large bank interested, which is always very difficult. Rothschild is simply the most enterprising businessman here. Through his brothers he is closely acquainted with the situation of the Prussian state and therefore has high interest to obtain the favour of our Court ... Rothschild the banker is also a reliable man with whom the government here does much business, in which context he is, as far as I know him, fair, upright and understanding.

I must, however, add, on the other hand, that were one to place the business in his hands one would have to more or less follow his ideas...« (Wilhelm von Humboldt to Count Hardenberg, Prussian State Chancellor, January 1818).

After efforts to raise money in Amsterdam failed, Rother, a Prussian financial official, negotiated with Salomon Rothschild in Coblenz and Berlin. He did not succeed in obtaining improved terms. However, the Berlin banks now submitted an offer: they proposed a bond issue totalling 15 million thalers, then one of 20 million thalers. Thereupon Nathan raised the bond sum he offered to 30 million thalers at 65 percent. The Prussian State Ministry decided to accept the London bond issue.

Rother travelled to London and held seven days of negotiations with Nathan. On March 31, 1818 both signed a contract: the Prussian State received 30 million thalers: 15 million thalers at 70 percent, 7.5 million thalers at 72 percent and 7.5 million thalers at 75 percent with a maximum 28-year repayment period. At the very last moment Nathan had dropped his demand that he be awarded four percent commission or 1.2 million thalers. On April 1, 1818 he sent one million pounds sterling (worth 6 million thalers) by ship via Hamburg to Berlin.

The demand for the bonds was exceptionally large. It was launched on the exchanges in Amsterdam, Berlin, Frankfurt, Hamburg and London.

Pleased with the conclusion of the deal, James wrote to his brothers Nathan and Salomon on March 30, 1818: »It would be impossible to describe to you the plaisir caused by your two couriers of the 27th and 28th. I see that you were lucky... to conclude the Prussian loan. Prussia must be very satisfied, because ... you gave them very good prices and it is (satisfactory) to us, too...«

The Rothschilds had thus got a foot in the door of the extensive bonds business. They did not stand to make a large profit on the Prussian bond, but the risks were slight.

N M Rothschild & Sons, London

»It requires a great deal of boldness and a great deal of caution to make a great fortune ...«

Within a space of a few years Nathan Rothschild had, thanks to his energy and exceptional talents, established an unassailable position in the English financial marketplace. Unlike many other bankers, he gave up commodity trading and concentrated solely on banking. The most important business he conducted was thenceforth issuing bonds, although his everyday work involved all sorts of other activities. He granted traders loans, accepted bills of exchange and provided credit notes for travellers. Coin minting and trading in money metals was another important area of business. In 1824 he set up a life insurance company and a ship insurance company together with his brother-in-law Moses Montefiore.

In 1810 Nathan had opened up business in the heart of the City, only a few steps away from the Royal Stock Exchange and the Bank of England. He rented a house at St. Swithin's Lane which was part of a complex called New Court, a typical three-storey merchant trader's house. The family, already five persons strong, lived in the upper floors, and the business premises were on the ground floor: one room in which Nathan and his closest employees sat, another in which letters were written and copied as well as storage rooms for gold, silver, coins and goods.

N M Rothschild & Sons Limited continues to be domiciled at New Court, St. Swithin's Lane and for some years New Court was the centre of world finance.

Alongside his office, Nathan's other important place of work was the stock

Silk cloth, printed 1836, in memory of Nathan Mayer, following his sudden death. It shows the famous silhouette of him in front of the pillar in the Royal Exchange

exchange. During trading time from 3.30 to 4.30 p.m. he always stood at the same column in the south eastern corner of the exchange, where he negotiated with other businessmen and gave his instructions. He bought and sold stocks, for example for the English government and he continued to do so for the Elector of Hesse.

Nathan's silhouette in front of a column became a symbol of his exceptional position in the financial markets. In 1817 Richard Dighton completed his »A View from the Royal Exchange«, which shows the relatively small Nathan with a round belly; with one hand in his pocket, in the other he holds a bill. Nathan did not enthuse about this first caricature. However, his brother Salomon wrote to him on October 23, 1817: »I hope our children, my Anselm and your Lionel, are also the butt of such caricatures, if, with God's help, they achieve a respected position in society.«

Dighton's portrayal was taken as the basis for numerous other caricatures of Nathan. Thus, the image of »Nathan at the column« was also at the centre of a printed silk scarf. In the corners the major government bonds are to be seen which Nathan floated between 1814 and 1835. At the edges the following text appears in four languages: »Equally distinguished for his commercial skill and enterprises for his charitable and benevolent disposition«. After his sudden death on July 28, 1836, the City took its leave of Nathan by commissioning the picture »The Shadow of a Great Man«: At the column the shadow of a great man remained, holding in his hand four keys as the sign of his four brothers or four sons.

»... and when you have got it, it requires ten times as much wit to keep it.«
Nathan M. Rothschild

Nathan changed his simple lifestyle only hesitantly and carefully. The wealth he had quickly accumulated and his influence on the financial markets were in themselves potential sources of mistrust and animosity. And he did not wish to leave any other flanks exposed. This was at the back of his mind when he wrote on January 2, 1816 in a letter to his brothers, which like all their letters to one another were written in Hebrew characters: »I read your letters not once, but perhaps hundreds of times... since I have nothing to do after supper, do not read books and do not play cards, do not go to the theatre, and my only pleasure is my business... Amschel asks me if he should buy a house. I asked Herries... He advised me not to indulge in luxuries, otherwise the newspapers might start to write stories against me.. He advises me to live on a small and modest scale for twelve months.«

Nathan's wife Hannah, who came from a respected Anglo-Jewish family, was, unlike Nathan, very interested in acquiring titles and honours and pressed him to adopt a lifestyle commensurate with his wealth and rewards. The painter William Armfield Hobday probably took the occasion of Nathan's appointment as Austrian Consul General as the occasion in 1821 to produce a three-and-a-half by three metre large painting of Nathan and his family and to put it on public exhibit. He painted the family members in the stance and clothing of upper class or noble families and inserted the requisite background. It was probably not until many years later that the family really did lead such a lifestyle. Nathan albeit soon only used New Court as a bank and moved with his family to another town house, but it was not until 1835 that he decided to buy a country manor in

Nathan with his family. After an oil painting by William Armfield Hobday, 1821.

The painting shows, from left to right: Nathan Mayer with his youngest son Mayer Amschel, his wife Hannah carrying their daughter Louise, and the children Charlotte, Lionel, Anthony and Hannah Meyer sitting on the ground

Gunnersbury near London. There, his wife Hannah and his son Lionel developed a decidedly luxurious style of living.

As in all aspiring families, the Rothschild brothers attached great importance to the education and training of their children. The brothers themselves had little general education: tutors had imparted the absolute minimum to them before, between the ages of 13 and 14, they had gone into their father's company. Several contemporaries remarked on Nathan in a manner similar to that of Wilhelm von Humboldt, who wrote from London to his wife on September 22, 1818: »Yesterday Rothschild took supper here; he is a quite un-couth and completely uneducated person, but has a sharp mind and is a real genius with money.«

Nathan's sons attended a Jewish boarding school. They subsequently completed university studies in Goettingen and Strasbourg and the youngest son, Mayer, like all later sons of the English Rothschilds, went up to Cambridge. After general studies they underwent many years of bank training in the Rothschild banks in Frankfurt, Paris and Vienna or with agents, for example in Madrid or Constantinople. Like but few youths of the day, the Rothschild sons had the opportunity to familiarize themselves with many European banking cities, to become acquainted with politicians and diplomats as well as being assured entry into the respective society.

While Nathan was not able to write a letter in English or German without the assistance of a secretary, his sons spoke fluent English, French and German. Nathan lived solely for his business. His sons became sound bankers who had to shoulder great responsibility at any early age after the untimely death of their father. But the focus of their interests shifted. They busied themselves with expanding their standing in society, became politically active, built country houses and set about laying the foundations of art collections. To them, sports and hunting were as important as financial transactions. Their life-style contradicted the widespread prejudice that Jews could not be real gentlemen. In 1836 Lionel made sure that he was entitled to bear the title of an Austrian baron and henceforth called himself Baron Lionel.

The First Jew in Parliament: A Rothschild

In 1828 the English Jews started their final battle for equal civil rights. They demanded, above all, that they be allowed to take up public office. Hannah and her sons consequently first took the side of the Whigs. They supported a programme that called for the abolition of all differences in terms of birth and origin as well as the recognition of property and achievements, free trade and unhindered economic growth. Nathan had already taken part in an unsuccessful attempt by the Jewish community to achieve the legal abolition of all obstacles, but distanced himself from the Whigs.

As no majority was to be found for legally enforcing equal rights, solutions

Baron Lionel de Rothschild, by Alfred de Dreux, 1838

were sought for individual problems. As a consequence in the 1847 elections, the Whigs stood Lionel de Rothschild (City of London), Mayer Nathan Rothschild (in Kent) and David Salomon (in Greenwich) as Jewish candidates for Parliament. There was no law prohibiting Jews from becoming Members of Parliament, but a Jew was hardly in a position to take the oath »in the true faith of a Christian«. The Whigs hoped that the election of Jews would enable them to force through a change in the oath.

Of the three Jewish candidates, only Lionel won. The amendment Lord Russell tabled, which involved different possible oaths, was passed by a slender majority in the House of Commons but defeated in the House of Lords. Lionel refused to take his seat, but stood at the next election again and won. For eleven years his parliamentary seat remained empty, because he always won the election but was never able to take up his seat owing to the oath. It was not un-

til 1858 that the Lords agreed to a compromise, according to which each of the two houses could decide on its oaths itself, thus opening the door for Lionel's entry into the House of Commons.

In his fight for the seat, Lionel had relied not only on the support of the Whigs and the Jewish community in England but also on that of the Rothschild family.

Thus, his Uncle Salomon in Vienna wrote him on August 4, 1857: »No news could quite literally have brought more joy to my heart than to hear of your election as a Member of Parliament ... May you be the beginning of the long desired impetus for the betterment of our brethren in the faith,

for then your election would be truly victorious.«

Convinced that he should be awarded the highest English distinction, a peerage, Lionel was not satisfied with winning his seat in the House of Commons. He turned down the knighthood he was offered, but as a Jew and as a banker he was refused a peerage.

In 1885 Queen Victoria made his son Nathaniel a lord. The last hurdle separating Jews from truly equal rights had thus been removed.

It was customary to change one's name when made a peer. Nathaniel, however, demonstratively stuck with »Lord Rothschild«.

De Rothschild Frères, Paris

»I never doubted we shall become the richest men in Europe.«

A mere 22 years old, well educated and full of entrepreneurial verve, the youngest of the five Rothschild brothers settled in Paris. Jacob Mayer, who called himself James in France, had received his training in finance less in his father's company than from the financial transactions during the war against Napoleon.

Despite the Restoration, post-revolutionary French society formed the ideal backdrop for a capable and ambitious newcomer. The traditional groupings, namely the aristocracy and the military, had lost in influence. Titles and religion, origin and inheritance now counted less than did one's abilities, money and success.

Nathan helped James start up by sending him his share of the transfer of English subsidies and French reparation payments and helping him be appointed to

manage the assets of those returning from exile, such as Louis XVIII, who had been instated by the victorious powers. There was fierce competition among the banks active in Paris. Moreover, James had worked for France's enemies during the war against Napoleon and conservative ministers such as Richelieu were not willing to cooperate with a Rothschild.

James was consequently only given a very small cut of the first bonds issued. During a crisis of 1818, which threatened the large banks, James, together with other bankers, kept prices from falling further by buying into the market and thus succeeded in stabilizing things. Henceforth he was one of the most prominent Parisian bankers and was given a sizable slice of future bonds business. In March, 1818 he wrote to his brothers: »I have never doubted that, if we continue this way, we shall become the richest men in Europe.«

Judging from the admittedly very incomplete balance sheets of the Rothschild banks, the company capital suddenly shot up: Whereas in 1815 the capital of the company as a whole amounted to £ 136,000, by 1818 it was £ 1.7 million, by 1825 £ 4 million and by 1828 £ 4.3 million. This capital was divided up among the brothers. Nathan received the largest share, James the smallest. Nathan therefore kept his head start, but after 1818 James was on a par with the other brothers.

James was finally established as banker to the government in 1823. France had been instructed by the Holy Alliance to put down the revolution of the Liberals in Spain. James made the financing of the war possible by issuing a bond and negotiated a bond with Spain.

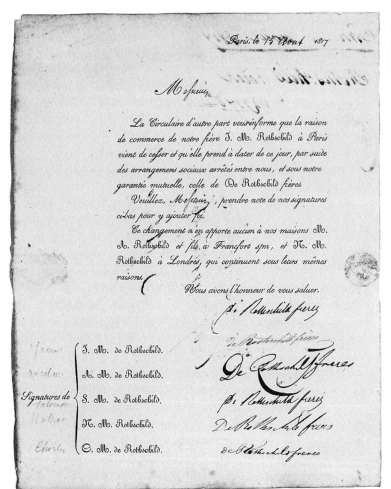

In 1817 James founded the bank »De Rothschild Frères«, in which all the brothers were partners

1830 – »Rothschild Does Not Provide Money For War«

Despite his close ties with France's reactionary government, after the revolutionary upheaval of 1830 James swiftly succeeded in switching to the side of the Liberals. The latter wished to prevent the spread of the popular uprising and the foundation of a republic and made Louis Philippe king. They demanded in return that he recognize the constitution, grant the upper middle class political rights and complete economic freedom.

In 1830 James was greatly interested in the peace being kept. From the perspective of a bank acting on behalf of all governments, a European war involved unforeseeable risks. James used his connections and his influence to prevent an armed conflict between the major powers, for example in Italy and in Belgium. He succeeded in being leaked information from the new French government. And, via couriers, he provided his brothers with certain information for Metternich. »Dear brothers,« he wrote on March 9, 1831, »I am sending you a courier, because bonds have risen; we stayed at 3 perc. 53.20, because it is general opinion that Périer will enter the ministry … he doesn't want a war; I told him that I am truly convinced that the foreign powers are not for a minute thinking of attacking France and that our good Count is doing his utmost in the cause of Peace.«

Four days later, he reported to Salomon: »… I went to the King and told him all my wealth and family is in France and I will consequently certainly not mislead your Majesty and thus lull Your Highness into believing, that the foreign powers do not want war, if they have plans to make war …« He provided comprehensive information on developments in Paris and called on his brother: »I beg you now, dear Salomon, urgently, do not cease to pester the Prince in which to strengthen the ministry here and beseech him to maintain the peace, that all of Europe so desperately needs, as the Count alone has the power to keep Peace …« Salomon left Metternich in no doubts as to the fact that the Rothschilds would not provide any money for a war against the revolutions. As early as December 1830 an Austrian diplomat, Baron von Prokesch, had noted in his diary: »Everything depends now more on the funds, and Rothschild's word is all the more important therefore, but he does not provide money for war.«

At the Pinnacle of Success

Peace was maintained and the Rothschilds sustained manageable financial losses. 1830 marks a turning point in the Rothschilds' financial strategy. Henceforth the banks in London and Paris formed an axis which no longer supported the reactionary policies of the Holy Alliance but instead the more liberal thrust of English and French policies.

A visible sign of this realignment was the sizable bond which the Rothschilds issued on behalf of the new state of Belgium, created out of the revolution, for the purpose of industrializing the country. Belgium inaugurated the spread of railways on the Continent and decided to adopt the world's first state-owned railway system. The Rothschilds floated bonds to finance the railway construction and the industrialization of the country (see pp. 130 sqq.).

Developments in France brought James to the pinnacle of his power and influence. Alongside other bankers, he was among the those who promoted the rapid growth of industry and the expansion of the railway network. The »bourgeois king« Louis Philippe allowed the finance magnates and industrialists a considerable say in political affairs.

James enjoyed power, wealth and the aristocratic lifestyle of the haute bourgeoisie. In 1824 he had married. Several years earlier his brothers had already urged him to marry. But it was not easy to find a woman of the right station. The Rothschilds were not only rich and had great influence, but in 1822 they had also become barons. James could not follow Nathan's example, as there were no Jewish families in all of France at the time into which he could have married. And marriage to a non-Jew was out of the question. In 1824 he decided to marry his brother Salomon's daughter Betty, who was then only 19 years old. By marrying within the family, James began a tradition which was to continue for over 40 years.

Betty had no difficulty in maintaining a grand salon. Her balls and dinner parties surpassed anything that Paris had ever seen before. The royal family, ministers, diplomats, bankers and industrialists, writers,

Betty de Rothschild,
née Rothschild,
1805–1886.
Oil painting,
anonymous, probably
1824, on the occasion
of her wedding

musicians and painters were regular visitors to her house on Rue Laffitte. It was one of the few in Paris in which persons of different political opinions and social status could mix.

Admiration and Criticism

»Would it not be the greatest blessing for the world if all kings were to be deposed and the Rothschilds were to take the throne?« asked Ludwig Börne, an exile in Paris, in 1832, alluding to James' influence and the role of money. Like him, numerous journalists, writers and social theorists remarked on the dominance of the moneyed bourgeoisie, be it approvingly, in criticism, bitterly or ironically, humourously or

seriously. They all also commented on the Rothschilds, who increasingly came to be regarded as the epitome of dominance and exploitation. Heinrich Heine was one of the most outspoken critics of the French grande bourgeoisie and the Rothschilds. But he admired Betty, occasionally had the opportunity to attend one of her dinners, and corresponded regularly with her. Several times he sent her his manuscripts, showing no qualms about mentioning his criticisms of the Rothschilds. He thus wrote to her on June 1, 1840: »Dear Lady Baroness. As promised I am sending you enclosed the beginning of my novel 'The Passover Festival' and the beginning of my 'Ludwig Börne'... Precisely those pages which I am sending you contain the sharp passages on the House of Rothschild. Here you have in your hands the corpus delicti that so frightens me. May I ever again appear before you. I ask...«

When Nathan Rothschild died in 1836, James took over the running of the House of Rothschild, which remained in his hands until his death in 1868. He opened up new perspectives for the firm that went beyond bond business. Rapid industrialization had generated substantial tax revenues for

Letter from Heinrich
Heine to Betty
de Rothschild,
Paris, June 1, 1840

governments, which led to a decline in public-sector borrowing. James therefore shifted his attention to new lines of business, such as the financing of rawmaterials trading, railway construction and – to a certain extent – manufacturing industry.

He was the only one of the five brothers who not only experienced permanent expansion. He was still alive to witness the challenge posed to the monopoly of the House of Rothschild by the emergence of new banking organizations.

– In the Bank –

»In order to come to an end with the description of the famous banker, i.e. to continue, to show him in his office, I must by no means forget to mention that an ear-shattering incessant noise prevailed there, the crash from the continual slamming of doors, the coming and going of employees bringing despatches or wanting signatures. The employees' obsession with bill and stock brokers who came to ask for orders also contributed to the tumult which brought the office of 'Msr. le Baron' the reputation of being a tower of Babel. All languages were spoken there, including Hebrew. People of all three sexes, men, women and beggars, were continuously on the lookout for something new and took one another's place all day long. They included jewel dealers who spread out their wares before the sick eyes of the Baron; dealers in porcelain vases and paintings, offering their rare objects; young women who manage to find their way into everything and want information – or something else. And, at the other end of the queue, incessantly and mercilessly, while the brain of the millionaire kept working, into the middle of the heaps of numbers and the battalions of calculations plunged his youngest daughter, a fattish, chubby-cheeked girl – I still see it in my mind's eye - who sometimes came running in, riding on her father's walking stick and blowing a trumpet like an angel in the valley of Jehoshaphat. And the poor Baron did not complain, did not even raise his eyebrows.

However much people envied Baron de Rothschild, it was never accepted that he should sleep or eat in peace. From five in the morning in summer and in winter people thronged around his door, seeking news or requiring such. With a twinkle in their eye, the Baron's valets led them in one after the other, smiling with pity. If business called for it, he ate with his whole family in a small room next to the office and the stock exchange prices he read were the spice of his meals, for the queue of stock brokers moved impatiently and mercilessly round his table. One of the evil habits of this cunning old man, who was no doubt tormented by this procession, was not to say a word, not even to lift his eyes to look at the person addressing him and to leave them standing there, downcast by his behaviour, hat in hand or standing on one foot, while he passed the stock prices to one member of the family after another, without these showing more interest than had the Baron himself previously.«

(Ernest Aymé Feydau, Mémoires d'un Coulissier, Paris, 1873, pp. 133-4)

Sketched portraits of Lionel, Carl and Gutle by Moritz Daniel Oppenheim

Centre of the Family

Following the death of the firm's founder in 1812, his eldest son Amschel Mayer took over management of the Frankfurt branch of the Rothschild Bank. His partners, brothers Salomon and Carl, were perpetually on the move. They travelled from court to court and from congress to congress, trying to make connections and negotiate contracts. Even after Salomon had set up a branch in Vienna and Carl had gone to Naples, the two continued to conduct major bond transactions on behalf of M. A. Rothschild & Söhne of Frankfurt. At a later date, Carl managed the Naples branch from his home in Frankfurt and after they had completed their training, Carl's sons Mayer Carl and Wilhelm Carl lived in Frankfurt. Amschel, who remained childless, regarded

M. A. von Rothschild & Söhne, Frankfurt

»Amschel von Rothschild is regularly at the stock exchange at lunch time«

After 1815 the citizens of Frankfurt regained control of the affairs of state of what was now a Free City. The dominant spirit of the day was conservative: civil rights remained closely bound to income and the Christian faith; freedom to engage in trade was rejected. Nonetheless, generous town planning and extensive construction works led to Frankfurt's much admired modernization.

Frankfurt's significance as a centre of trade and banking remained closely linked to its central location at the nodal point of intersecting trade routes. As the seat of the German Diet, it was also regarded as the unofficial capital of Germany.

Gutle Rothschild, by Moritz Daniel Oppenheim, 1849. Photograph of a painting since lost.

Anselm Salomon and Charlotte with their eldest children, Nathaniel Mayer und Caroline Julie (in the arms of a nanny), Charlotte von Rothschild, 1838

Charlotte took drawing lessons from M. D. Oppenheim. This picture shows her working on a portrait of her husband.

these two nephews as his heirs. He made his nephew Anselm Salomon a partner as early as in 1825. Anselm conducted the firm's business in Berlin, Copenhagen and Brussels until taking over the Vienna branch in 1849.

Gutle, the »matriarch of the family«, lived to be 96 years old. Until her death she lived in the small house on the Judengasse, while her sons had long since moved to palatial town houses. She did not travel, but had the family reunions take place in Frankfurt, and frequently invited her sons, daughters-in-law and sons-in-law, and grandchildren to visit her. It was she who instilled in them an awareness of the family's origins in the Judengasse and an interest in the family's roots. She closely followed

her sons' success. Numerous anecdotes contain her sayings. For example, in 1830 she is said to have remarked during the Revolution: »It won't come to war; my sons won't provide money for it.«

As long as Gutle was alive, Frankfurt remained the centre of the steadily growing Rothschild family.

Frankfurt's Leading Bank

Since Bankhaus Gebrüder Bethmann introduced the public bond in the form of a partial option in 1779, Frankfurt had developed into Germany's most important stock market. After a brief high, the city's importance as a trading hub receded gradually and its position as a banking centre and capital market increased rapidly. More and more commodity traders and wholesalers began to specialise in the continually expanding, crisis-proof trade in government bonds. Soon government securities from all over Europe were exchanging hands in Frankfurt. In 1848 44 government bonds were being traded on the Frankfurt exchange, compared with 25 in Berlin, nine in Hamburg, eight in Leipzig and five in Vienna.

For the most part, it was the Rothschilds who introduced them to the stock exchange, and many of them were bonds that had been issued via one of the other Rothschild houses. Even in later years, the Frankfurt stock exchange concentrated on government bonds. Industrial stock was hardly traded at all, Frankfurt traders preferring to leave that kind of paper to the Berlin stock exchange, which at the time was still only of secondary importance.

In financial affairs, Amschel Mayer was the most cautious of the five brothers. In the first two decades of his work, he attempted to brake the European-wide activities of the bank and sparked off a controversy among the brothers. He was forever concerned about liquidity, avoided risks and preferred to conclude safe deals. His main activity was to continue the work of a Court Agent, in which capacity he issued bonds on behalf of numerous German states. At the same time, he managed the assets of the German Confederation and a small number of high-ranking individuals - such as the Elector of Hesse, for whom the Rothschilds continued to do business.

After 1815 the Rothschilds had taken the lead in the bond business, leaving the Bethmanns and their other Frankfurt competitors to play no more than a subordinate role. Between 1820 and 1830 almost all the

Session of the Stock Exchange in Haus Braunfels
Anonymous, c. 1830

Stock market reports,
Frankfurt, 1835

»This happiness would make an epoch in my life...«
(Amschel Mayer)

Although M. A. Rothschild & Söhne was a sought after and respected bank, it remained difficult for the Rothschilds as a Jewish family to attain a commensurate position in Frankfurt's upper class.

On November 3, 1821, after the House of Rothschild had already conducted extremely extensive business with Austria and had been ennobled by Kaiser Franz, Amschel sent this straightforward letter to the State Chancellor, Prince Metternich: »Your Serene Highness, Gracious Prince and Master, I hope that Your Highness shall not take it amiss and consider it impertinent of me when I make so bold as to request that Your Highness do me the great honour of taking soup with me this noon. This happiness would make an epoch in my life...«

Metternich, who was stopping over in Frankfurt, accepted the invitation. Instead of merely offering soup, Amschel in fact laid on a magnificent banquet at his house on the Zeil.

The leading south German newspaper, the Allgemeine Zeitung, of Augsburg reported: »The Count took lunch at Msr. von Rothschild, who had made the greatest preparations. The stairs leading to the banquetting room were laid out with red carpet, and decorated with garlands of flowers and plants from the Orangery. Several of the most distinguished emissaries to the German Diet, as well as foreign ministers present here, enjoyed this guest luncheon prepared with no expense spared.«

A few days later, the newspaper emphasized in a retrospective of Metternich's visit that Madame von Rothschild was permitted to take part in a diplomatic recep-

middle-sized and minor German states were indebted to Amschel. The minor states had a great interest in having a famous bank launch their bonds, because this meant the obligations were more likely to find a ready market.

These operations led to the capital of the Frankfurt bank burgeoning, but it soon lagged far behind the strongly expanded London and Paris branches. Even during Amschel's lifetime, business in Frankfurt was beginning to show signs of stagnating, despite his short-lived attempt after 1835 to engage in financing railway construction.

Although, immediately after being made peers, the brothers started signing their letters with »von Rothschild«, the company name »M. A. Rothschild & Söhne« was not changed into »M. A. von Rothschild & Söhne« until 1828.

tion for the first time: »Hitherto one had seen this lady neither in local diplomatic circles, nor at the social gatherings of the Christian merchant class.«

Despite Metternich's demonstrative gesture, it was a long time before prejudices in Frankfurt against Jews were abandoned and societies and associations opened their doors to Jews.

Several caricatures during 1848, the year of the Revolution, focussed on the Rothschilds' role in the two decades before in the interplay of politics, business and society.

One of the depictions showed Bethmann as an honourable Frankfurt burgher: in elegant, fashionable clothes, confidently driving a carriage. Amschel Mayer, by contrast, looks like a Jewish second-hand dealer. He is dressed shabbily in old-fashioned clothes, and his face is slightly distorted into a grimace. He is standing on a money-chest, secured with two padlocks, being pulled by the Austrian double-eagle. This is probably the way some Frankfurt citizens perceived the Rothschilds. Aliens among the burghers, dominated by a foreign power, their wealth furtively locked away.

There is a close link between the ostracization which the Rothschilds suffered in Frankfurt and their exceptionally strong interest in honours and titles, as these were seen as a public sign of their close association with kings and princes. Titles such as »Court Agent« or »Commercial Councillor« were bestowed on them by German princes such as the King of Hanover, the King of Prussia and the Grand Duke of Hesse. These titles were awarded in direct connection with the business conducted by the Frankfurt Rothschilds, yet numerous appointments were no longer coupled with business or legal advantages. The honours were bestowed on them predominantly in

Baron Moritz von Bethmann, Baron Amschel von Rothschild. Ernst Schalk, Philip Herrlich. Caricature, Frankfurt, 1848

recognition of their work on bond issues, for example by the Kingdom of the Two Sicilies, by the Kings of Spain and Denmark, or by the Grand Duke of Hesse. Such honours were prompted by emissaries suggesting them, or the Rothschilds themselves requesting them.

After completing the launch of the Prussian bond in May 1818, Nathan wrote to Rother, the Prussian financial official: »My brother Carl writes me that you wish to persuade your Government to bestow an honour upon me, for which I thank you. However, here in London I have no use for such a thing and would therefore ask you most strongly whether you could procure a beautiful decoration for my brother Salomon, who loves ribbons and is a Baron who intends to live in Paris, where one can decorate oneself with such things...«

Lobbying for Equal Rights for Jews

The newspaper report on the reception Amschel Mayer gave for Metternich also stressed that the two mayors of Frankfurt refused to attend. The background to this was the legal dispute between the Jewish Community and the City of Frankfurt on the recognition of equal rights for Jews, as decreed during the Dalberg era. After Napoleon's fall and the dissolution of the Grand Duchy of Frankfurt, the reinstated municipal authorities of what was now a Free City were of the opinion that the Law on Equal Rights of 1811 was null and void.

The name Rothschild is closely associated with this dispute. Every protest letter from the Jewish Community against the suspension of equal rights bears Amschel Mayer's signature as does every petition sent to the German Diet asking for equal rights to be granted. His brothers used their connections to see to it that Metternich,

von Hardenberg, the Prussian Prime Minister, and other princes put pressure on the Frankfurt Senate and the City parliament. Successful business transactions provided an occasion to ask for a statement to be made in favour of according Frankfurt Jews equal rights. Without the efforts of the Rothschilds, the compromise of 1824, according to which Jews were eligible to become »Israelite citizens«, would never have been reached. This at least gave them rights equal to those of the other burghers under private law, even if they continued to be refused political rights until 1864.

Bucking the trend of the day, Amschel and his family resisted assimilation and remained strictly orthodox Jews who conscientiously adhered to all the religious laws and customs. They did not work on the Sabbath and did not eat any non-kosher food at dinner parties. Maria Belli Gontard, a female member of the highest echelon of society, wrote in her memoirs: »Baron Amschel von Rothschild, who lived next door to us, accepted invitations to join us, but he was highly religious and took no food with us or anyone else; even at the major diplomatic luncheons he held, he always only ate what his cook had prepared for him...«

In his business life Amschel did not allow anyone to pressurize him. When, in 1844, a new set of rules on bills trading was decreed, ordering Jews to accept bills on the Sabbath and on Jewish holidays, he declared publicly that he would take no notice of this regulation.

S. M. von Rothschild, Vienna

The capital of the Habsburg monarchy and the city in which the Austrian Emperor resided was characterized by churches and noble palaces, court societies and salons. The Congress of Vienna in 1815, at which peace on the Continent was concluded, transformed Vienna into the hub of the forces of the Restoration, and the atmosphere in the city was shaped by secret police surveillance and a police state. By contrast, the bourgeoisie, influenced by liberal ideas, fostered a highly varied cultural life in the city.

Klemenz Lother
Prince zu Metternich
1773–1859, after
a painting
by Th. Lawrence

»Of benefit and useful for the Imperial Government«

As of 1819, the extensive business transactions with the Austrian Government necessitated the presence of a member of the Rothschild family in Vienna. Salomon Mayer took on this task, but probably did not intend to stay in Vienna in the long term.

Count von Metternich was the most powerful representative of the Austrian House of Habsburg. Named after him, his »Metternich System« successfully combated all national and liberal currents in the country. Metternich had originally been very reserved towards attempts by the House of Rothschild to approach him. The Austrian government preferred to work with large established Viennese banks and was endeavouring via the Austrian National Bank, founded in 1816, to cut the government deficit. It was only when Salomon, together with the Parish Bank, which was widely respected in Austria, had floated an Austrian government bond worth 55 million guilders, that Metternich recognized the importance and potential of the family.

The Rothschilds were in contact with Metternich via Friedrich von Gentz. The latter, a statesman and political commentator, was the adviser and staff member closest to Metternich. In his writings, above all for the Österreichischer Beobachter, he provided massive support for the Chancellor. As of 1817 he had been in close contact with the Rothschilds, whom, like many of his contemporaries, he both admired and despised. In December, 1818, Gentz wrote to his friend Adam Müller:

»... The Rothschilds in fact [constitute] a unique species with their own specific characteristics. They are common, uneducated Jews, show decency on the outside, are pure naturalists in their work, without any inkling of the higher interconnection of things, but gifted with an admirable instinct which always enables them to choose the right thing, and from two right things, to choose the best. Their immense wealth (they are top of the pack in Europe) is thoroughly the product of their instinct, which the masses tend to term luck.«

Salomon paid Gentz a salary for his work as a go-between and his regular reports. In fact, the salary was higher than that which Gentz received from the Imperial Court. »Europe's quill«, as Gentz was called, in return put to paper a treatise in defence of equal rights for the Frankfurt Jews and was the author of the first public description of the Rothschilds, which appeared in 1827 in the Brockhaus' »Allgemeine deutsche Realenzyklopädie«.

When anti-Semitic rioting troubled the Frankfurt Jews, Baron von Handel, the Austrian emissary in Frankfurt, wrote to Metternich: »… The large and rich House of Rothschild should not be completely adverse to leaving here and if this happens, it will probably choose one of its fixed places in Paris or London. – The question arises here,

whether it would not be commensurate with interests here to convey to them how well received they would be in the Imperial States and thus encourage this House to move to Vienna?« This did not in fact happen, because the Rothschild Bank did not seriously contemplate leaving Frankfurt. However, the Austrian government ensured that the Rothschilds knew that a Rothschild branch in Vienna was fully in line with the interests of the Austrian state.

»A privileged exception in the midst of my fellow believers«

The legal preconditions for Jews to settle in Vienna were worse than in most other places. A condition for someone to be granted long-term residence was that they were first »tolerated« by the Emperor. At the time, eight Jewish families were »tolerated» in Vienna in this manner, all of whom had been ennobled, and there were about 1,500 Jews living there with the status »foreign Jews«, i.e. with temporary residence permits. Salomon refused to petition for »tolerance« and also did not apply for a residence permit. However, he had to go along with the restrictions imposed on »foreign Jews«. Thus, he was not permitted to buy either real estate or a house. Instead, Salomon rented rooms in Hotel »Zum Römischen Kaiser«, a »superlative inn« which was located on the corner of Renngasse and Freyung, and thus lay on the edge of the city centre and in the immediate vicinity of the Imperial Court and the Government Chancellery.

Initially Salomon rented only rooms, then a whole floor and eventually the whole building. After having been made an honourary citizen of the City of Vienna in 1843 he was in a position to buy property. He thereupon bought the inn and the building next to it and had both properties

Hotel »Zum
Römischen Kaiser«,
No. 138 Freyung,
after the renovation
work of 1844

extensively renovated. Salomon was, incidentally, the first Jewish honourary citizen of Vienna.

Salomon was fortunate in having Leopold von Wertheimstein as an adviser, a member of one of the few tolerated Jewish families. A further member of his staff, Moritz Goldschmidt of Frankfurt, was granted »tolerance« in 1833. Without the assistance of these exceptional staff members Salomon would hardly have been able to reach such a position of prominence in the Austrian financial world. Both acted as his representatives when he was away on one of his countless business trips and in fact they travelled in his name to all the main centres of Austrian financial policy. Moreover, they took on social engagements on the Rothschilds' behalf and nurtured contacts to the Jews in Vienna. Salomon remained an outsider in Vienna, »a privileged exception in the midst of my fellow believers« as he stated in a letter to the representatives of the Vienna City Parliament on being made an honourary citizen.

Von Wertheimstein and Goldschmidt both played key roles in the expansion of Salomon's business activities. They supported, for example, the »Nordbahn« (Northern Railway line) project, von Wertheimstein being one of the directors of the company of the same name from the very outside (see below, pp 130 sqq.).

»Justice and Liberty«

Although support for the reactionary »Metternich System« crumbled swiftly after 1830, Salomon continued to orient his activities toward Metternich and the Austrian Emperor. However, the doors of the Court remained closed to him; it was not until 1884 that his grandson was granted entrance to Court as a gift for his family by way of thanks for his investments to foster the Hungarian economy. Salomon did not seek links with bourgeois society, which attempted intellectually and culturally to find a path of its own, opposed the censorship of the police state and advocated the emancipation of the Jews. In 1848 it was precisely the bourgeoisie that rose up and called for the abolition of the order based on feudal estates, called for civil rights, freedom of the press and a new constitution. There were naturally many Jews among the ranks of the revolutionaries, who hoped that a bourgeois revolution would lead to the emancipation of the Jews. »It is at long last time,« they demanded, »that Jews in Europe are granted justice and liberty instead of a few rights and freedoms.«

Metternich, as the personification of state power, was the first target of the revolutionaries. They succeeded in forcing him to be dismissed and he had to quit Vienna. Soon thereafter, the Emperor and his family also fled the city. Salomon von Rothschild also felt it advisable to flee, as he had become a representative of the »Metternich system« to too strong a degree. Salomon went to Paris, where he already owned palatial property in the town, never to return to Vienna.

Ups and Downs of the Stock Exchange. Caricature, Vienna, 1848

Anselm Takes Over at the Bank

The revolutions in Europe in 1848 led to a stock exchange crash. The House of Rothschild also found itself in difficulties: the prices of their government securities fell and numerous banks, including ones with whom they were affiliated, collapsed. Owing to liabilities not being paid, there was a severe cash squeeze. The Rothschilds sustained substantial losses above all in Vienna. They managed to survive the crisis thanks to the London branch of the family, which was not affected by the troubles and supplied sufficient quantities of gold coins to ensure the liquidity of the other branches.

Salomon's son, Anselm, who had entered the Frankfurt bank after completing his education, succeeded in reestablishing the Vienna Bank after the Revolution. Yet it was never again to have the size or significance that it had had in the first half of the 19th century.

In 1855 Anselm put up the lion's share of the capital stock on the foundation of the Österreischische Credit-Anstalt für Industrie und Gewerbe; this bank, one of the new generation of joint stock banks, was intended to ward off the competition of France's Crédit Mobilier bank and its affiliates (see below, pp. 134sqq.).

In 1861 Anselm was made an Austrian peer. Nevertheless, like Salomon and his family before them, Anselm and his family were never to feel fully at home in Vienna. He trained his sons to take on the business, while his wife Charlotte moved with her daughters back to her home country, England. It was Anselm's sons Nathaniel and Salomon Albert who first succeeded in becoming integrated into life in Vienna.

C. M. de Rothschild e figli, Naples

With its 360,000 inhabitants, Naples was the third largest city in Europe in the early 1820s. The city featured the sumptuous palaces and gardens of the nobility which looked out over the Gulf and the attractive town houses of the prosperous middle classes. Day and night, the streets were filled with the bustle of trade and fun, life and laughter.

This outward appearance was somewhat misleading, however. Approximately one third of the inhabitants lived in abject poverty and in the smallest of confines, eking out an existence as craftsmen, fishermen, day labourers or beggars.

»Viva la libertà – Viva la constituzione«

The foundation of a branch of the Frankfurt Rothschild Bank in Naples occurred in connection with the Austrian intervention to block the successful uprising in the city in 1820.

During the Wars of Revolution, Naples, then centre of the Italian Enlightenment, had become a Republic. The Congress of Vienna in 1815 decided to reinstate the Bourbons in Naples and to found a Kingdom of the Two Sicilies under Ferdinand I. The latter instituted absolute rule and used force to put down any liberal groups and demands. An uprising by the secret Carboneria organization, whose members came from the propertied and educated middle classes, forced the king to recognize a liberal constitution based on the sovereignity of the people and a division of powers.

The King took his oath on the constitution and yet immediately turned to Austria for help. Metternich was already alarmed, for he saw his European system under threat

»Blauschild (Blue
Shield) as Exemplary
Knight«. Caricature
of Carl Mayer von
Rothschild, 1825

was the only trustworthy and competent partner for such a difficult transaction. The bond was intended to finance the military campaign, pay for restoration of the absolute monarchy and cover the costs of the Austrian troops in Naples. The European powers put up the security for the bond, with the Kingdom of the Two Sicilies putting its state territories up as collateral. The Rothschilds declared that they were prepared to provide the prefinancing.

Salomon called in his brother Carl from Frankfurt for assistance. The latter then followed the troops to Italy and financed the army's supplies. The campaign was soon over, the troops remained in Naples for six years, protecting the reinstated absolutist Bourbon King's regime.

Carl's business trip led to a bank branch being established. Together with his brothers he issued three further bonds and organized covering the high maintenance costs of the army of occupation. The House of Bourbon thus became fully dependent on the Rothschilds.

While Austria did not have to pay for the military campaign, the population of Naples had to fund repayment of the bond and the interest in the form of the higher taxes it was forced to pay. The Rothschilds made substantial profits from the transfer of large sums of money, the high commission they charged and by placing the bonds in Frankfurt, London and Paris.

The Naples bank C. M. de Rothschild e figli, that remained a subsidiary of the Frankfurt M. A. von Rothschild & Söhne bank, was never of great significance. The financial business conducted neither essentially went beyond the borders of the Kingdom of both Sicilies, nor did it serve as a launchpad for expansion into blossoming areas of industry. The Paris Rothschild bank was much more active in Italy, floating bonds, for example, on behalf of the Vatican.

from the revolutionary movements in Spain, Portugal and Italy and had the Holy Alliance give him absolute power to intervene with military means if necessary. As he regarded Italy as part of the Austrian sphere of influence and also had a secret agreement with Ferdinand I, directly after the revolt had broken out he had the Holy Alliance give him full powers to intervene with military means. However, Austria did not have the money to finance the campaign in the field against Naples. To finance the war, the only avenue open to Austria was to raise cash by floating a bond.

Financing the War and Founding a Bank

Metternich negotiated exclusively with Salomon von Rothschild, who he believed

Between Naples and Frankfurt

Prior to setting up the branch in Naples, Carl Meyer, the second youngest of the brothers, was accustomed to being on the road on business. He thus served as a courier between Frankfurt and the Court of the Elector of Hesse in exile. Later he travelled on similar missions between Paris, Frankfurt and Vienna and represented the Rothschilds at the Congress of Aix-la-Chapelle.

In 1818, Carl married Adelheid Hertz, daughter of a rich and esteemed Hamburg merchant. His brothers initially objected to the match because her family was liberal in

Album of visiting cards belonging to Adelheid de Rothschild, 1843

Adelheid von Rothschild, née Hertz, 1800–53. Anonymous portrait

its religious opinions. However, Adelheid swiftly adjusted to Carl's orthodox lifestyle.

At first Carl and Adelheid had difficulties being accepted. Even the conservative nobility and upper class regarded them merely as carrying out Austrian commands. It was not until the Rothschilds petitioned Austria for a reduction in the occupation costs that local society opened its doors to them. Moreover, matters were aggravated by the fact that Jews were not legally admitted to Naples and only four or five families lived there. They were tolerated, albeit without there being a legal basis for their residing in the city.

Carl probably lived in a hotel during his first few years in Naples. In 1841 he purchased a villa, the interior and outside of which was truly sumptuous, with large gardens in a prime location on the Via Chiaia. For a few years Carl and Adelheid ran the largest and most renowned house in town. The regular visitors included nobles, ministers, diplomats, painters and writers.

In front of the Palazzo Rothschild in the Via Chiaia, c. 1855. Adolph and his wife Julie de Rothschild and possibly other members of the family are to be seen in the picture.

In the 19th century Naples was a preferred holiday destination, and receptions and dinners were frequently given in honour of visitors. Despite numerous printed travelogues of the day, we have little information about the life of the Rothschilds in Naples. In 1827 Moses and Judith Montefiore, who were related to the Rothschilds through marriage in England, visited Naples, travelling there by yacht, which then moored in the harbour. Their diary entry gives the following report: »Wednesday, January 16th. - Mrs. Montefiore dined at Baron Charles' ... It was a large dinner party, and the guests included the Austrian Ambassador with his wife, the Duke and Duchess D'Ascoli, the Duke and Duchess Theodore, Sir Henry and Lady Lushington, and others ... Thursday, January 17th. ... In the evening Mrs. Montefiore accompanied Baroness Charlotte to the ball at the Sardinian Embassy ... there were about five hundred of the nobility present...«

Carl and Adelheid spent as much time in Frankfurt as they did in Naples, and it was in the former city that they were buried.

Bust of Adolph
de Rothschild,
1823–1900

1863: The Bank is Closed Down

Mayer Carl and Wilhelm Carl, both Carl's sons, took over the helm of the Frankfurt bank in 1855. The middle son, Adolph, joined Bank C. M. Rothschild e figli, Naples, continuing the business of banker to the Court without much zest. He occasionally received complaints from London and Paris that he was taking too little interest in railway construction and the industrial development of Italy, which the House of Bourbon had been strongly supporting as of about 1830.

After the unification of Italy and the end of the Kingdom of the two Sicilies, Adolph moved to Paris and closed the Naples branch. He was the first member of the Rothschild family to give up banking altogether and sold all his shares in the Rothschild banks to his relatives.

He nevertheless maintained links with Naples. When, on the basis of the new Italian constitution, it was at long last possible to establish a Jewish Community there, Adolph and his sisters and brothers financed all the necessary institutions: synagogues, salaries for the rabbis, a hospital, a children's home, a poor house and, at a later date, even a Jewish school.

What Pigeons Have to Do with Stock Market Profits

The five brothers made their greatest profits after 1815 by speculating in bonds, by exploiting differences in quotations on the various exchanges and by conducting money transactions swiftly. If you were the first to be informed of planned bond launches, quotations, government crises and the dangers of war, you stood to make a huge profit, to be able to conclude contracts on a safe basis and to avoid incurring large losses.

Fast and clear information also brought with it power, influence and a reputation. The Rothschilds became important sources of information for various governments and certain orders were not put until their couriers had arrived with new information.

The Rothschilds linked up all the means possible to create an extensive news and information system. By 1820 no political power or business enterprise was able to compete with their logistics, let alone their deployment of funds and contacts.

Gathering Comprehensive Information

The Rothschild brothers' communication system consisted of two elements: gathering comprehensive information and forwarding it swiftly and reliably.

Like all major trading houses, as of approx. 1800 the Rothschilds had agents working for them at the major transport hubs, the main trade and political centres as well as stock exchanges. These agents were merchants, bankers, relatives or political journalists. It was their job to keep the five brothers constantly informed on financial, economic and political events. As the scope of their financial activities expanded and their power as financiers and merchants

increased, the Rothschilds had to also expand this network of agents and correspondents – it was soon the largest in Europe.

From correspondence which has survived we can ascertain that by 1840 the Rothschilds had correspondents working exclusively for them in Amsterdam, Baltimore, Brussels, Constantinople, Florence, Milan, New York, Odessa, Rome, St. Petersburg, San Francisco, Trieste and Turin.

Stock Exchange Telegraphing, J. J. Grandville, 1841.
This drawing shows the information instruments used for stock exchange speculation.

Transmitting Information Quickly and Safely

The Rothschilds forwarded information by an effective but costly linking of all available means of transport. Thus, Nathan had his own couriers operating between London and Dover. Agreements with ships' captains allowed letters, bills or other documents to cross the sea to the Continent without delay. There, James' agents were waiting to receive them and send them on with couriers. Frequently, the established, quite extensive regular postal service was used between Paris, Frankfurt and Vienna. Post to Italy, by contrast, was despatched using their own couriers. The Rothschilds used couriers to convey urgent news, irrespective of the distance. The high costs involved were soon recouped via price gains. Short urgent news was sent via carrier pigeon. The Frankfurt branch of the family had an estate in Hemsbach in South Hesse where carrier pigeons were trained and a similar facility in Kent.

The advantages of swift information via carrier pigeons can be seen from a letter

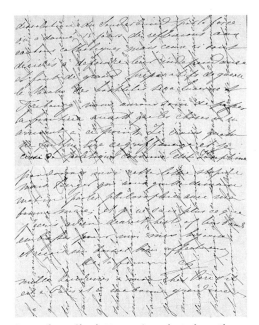

Letter from Charlotte to her husband Nathaniel de Rothschild, August, 1847.

In order to keep the mail as light as possible, letters were sometimes written both lengthways and sideways

Despatching a carrier pigeon bearing news

to the London Times of October 7, 1836: »There is a very earnest desire at the Stock Exchange and indeed all over the city, to get rid of the system of 'pigeon' expresses from Paris which give a most unfair advantage for those who have exclusive access to the information conveyed by them … The only thing that has suggested itself in the shape of a remedy for the evil has been the collection of hawks, falcons, and other birds of prey near to the spot, on the coast of Kent, where the pigeons are understood to deliver their charge … «

Daily Letters

In the days before the telephone, telegraph and fax, letters were the only way of communicating over a distance. The Rothschild brothers had undertaken to inform one another in daily letters about financial transactions, stock market prices and political events. This information was backed up by personal comments and concrete instructions on the action to be taken. The numerous personal letters formed the basis of all the financial transactions the five brothers engaged in.

The fact that only a very few letters arrived at their destination unopened if sent by the regular mail was a danger to their operations. The governments of the day had hordes of civil servants whose job it was to intercept letters, open them artfully and copy out their contents. However, various items of disinformation were planted on governments in this way, among others by the Rothschilds.

The Advantages of Being a Consul

When, as of the end of 1817, Nathan and James de Rothschild endeavoured to be appointed Austrian consul in London and Paris respectively, they had their eyes not just on the social prestige this position brought with it, but also the practical advantages. Firstly, the consuls had access to political and economic information. Secondly, the couriers of such emissaries needed no passports or passes; the post they carried with them was particularly protected and could also be entrusted to other diplomats for forwarding.

The Austrian government dragged its feet over appointing Jews as its state representatives. In 1820 Nathan was finally appointed consul, and James was given the same position a year later. In 1836 Salomon's son Anselm became Austrian Consul General in Frankfurt. In that city, one Rothschild family member became Consul of the State of Bavaria and another General Consul of the Kingdom of the Two Sicilies.

Always on the Road

The efficiency of the Rothschilds' information system was helped by the fact that they and later their sons were constantly travelling. It should be remembered that travel in the early 19th century was by no means enjoyable. Initially they travelled between Frankfurt, Paris and London, but soon their journeys were taking them further afield: to Berlin, Constantinople, Madrid, St. Peters-

The brothers wrote in German, but also used Hebrew letters, a practice they were familiar with from their days in the Judengasse

Letter from Nathan to his brothers, January 2, 1816

Uniform of a Consul
General of the
Kingdom of the Two
Sicilies, uniform
of Baron Wilhelm
Carl von Rothschild

burg and Vienna. The Rothschilds also travelled to numerous congresses held by the Holy Alliance, congresses that lasted months and were not only political conventions but also social events. There, they established new contacts and created the conditions for major deals. Always very well informed and able to combine information from various different places, their counsel was ever more frequently sought and heeded.

»Tomorrow evening about 7 o'clock I purpose sending you a Post Office express with despatches for Mr. Leveux of Calais, and the purport of the present is to request the favour of you to prepare a boat to be in readiness to convey them to Calais without delay.«
Nathan to his agent in Dover, 1808

»Am 14. früh erhielten wir durch einen Courier des Hauses Rothschild die erste Nachricht von der Erhebung des Herzogs von Orleans auf den französischen Thron.«
Friedrich von Gentz, 1830 in his diary

»The interval between this and Wednesday must probably ... bring the confirmation from Constantinople, of the report received yesterday by the House of Rothschild, that the Porte had consented to all the demands of Russia at Ackermann.«
Letter from the British Foreign Minister to the King

»Je profite d'une occasion que m'offre M. Rothschild, pour vous donner avis que ...«
Comte Villèle to the French emissary to the Congress of Verona, 1822

»Le courier de Rothschild fait monter nos fonds, comme vous le verrez par le bulletin de la Bourse, que je vous envoie«
Op cit, November 18, 1822

»Um Dich mit dem Beispiel anderer wegen des Postgeldes zu trösten, kann ich Dir sagen, daß Rothschild hier seine Ausgaben an Postgeld jährlich im Durchschnitt auf 5000 Pfund rechnet«
Wilhelm von Humboldt from London to his wife, 1818

»Sir ... said he had seen at Naples a Courier newspaper of that day week, produced by Rothschild and brought by one of his couriers.«
Sir Charles Greville, Naples 1830

Arrival and departure
of the Thurn und Taxis
post coach in Frankfurt
on Main at the Rotes
Haus on the Zeil.
Around 1840, water-
colour by J. B. Bauer

Coach. England, early
19th century. The
door bears the Roth-
schild coat-of-arms

The House of Rothschild: A European Family

On the occasion of his 70th birthday Salomon von Rothschild was given a congratulatory gift mounted in a leather cover with gold-plated silver ornamentation by an Austrian wholesale merchant Gastl. The Rothschild coat of arms is positioned in three-dimensions at the centre of the ornamented side of the cover - for some inexplicable reason, however, the hand only holds three arrows. It is surrounded by six depictions of the family's business successes: In the middle at the top, sits Mercury, the god of trade, prosperity and the arts. The two uppermost pictures show ships carrying cargo, goods in tied-up packages, bales and crates, clearly a reference to the cloth trade between England and Frankfurt. Coins and paper roll out of a jug that has been knocked over; fluttering paper alludes to state bonds. Barrels symbolize the transport of coins.

Some other symbols have also been integrated into the pictures: the bee's hive for the Rothschild's diligence, the globe for their comprehensive business, the easel for their interest in the arts.

The two lower pictures with the locomotives belching out steam refer to the Rothschilds' achievements in railway construction.

In the middle below stands a Mercury-like herm equipped with an anchor and Mercury's stave as signs of prosperity and solidity. The figure is surrounded by crates, barrels and bales of cloth.

In the first decades of the 19th century the Rothschilds overtook all the other banks. They built up a monopoly on loans to the major European powers and established a second pillar for their business, namely railway construction, at an early date before the business in state bonds declined. Their wealth had reached an unprecedented size.

From its first base in Frankfurt, the family enterprise had not only founded banks in the most important European cities, but also ensured that these were embedded in the fabric of the emerging modern nation states. Importantly, the unity of the House of Rothschilds was never cast into question but always accepted as the precondition for the company's success. The following generation of family members also felt duty-bound above all to uphold the family company and the social position this Jewish family had gained for itself. The linkage of aristocratic and bourgeois ideals proclaimed in the motto of »Concordia, Integritas, Industria« was realized by means of innovative business practices and exceptional flexibility, but also decidedly within the conservatively tinged political framework of the first half of the 19th century. In this context, the Rothschilds climbed into the uppermost ranks of business and society.

Despite the differing talents and interests of the various family members, the family did not owe its ascent to the special talents of one individual, but rather to the uninterrupted exchange of ideas and news between all the Rothschilds, to the joint action they took and their family discipline.

Commemorative gift given to Salomon von Rothschild on the occasion of his 70th birthday by Gastl, a wholesaler

The Price of Success

Self-Perception, Self-Presentation and Criticisms

Marriage of Alphonse and Leonora de Rothschild at Gunnersbury Park, 1857

The rapid rise of the Rothschild family was already a source of amazement to their contemporaries. Not surprisingly, public reactions ranged from admiration to hostility.

The family responded to their own success and the public's reaction to it by devising a very precise strategy regarding their role in society, and by projecting a specifically designed perception of themselves. The strategy was based on intrafamily marriages, carefully chosen educational paths, and the cultivation of a Jewish identity.

The public face of the Rothschilds was shaped by their extravagant lifestyle and by their charitable works. They also began at an early stage to make use of the press as a means of defending themselves against the repeated attacks and defamatory articles which appeared there as they became increasingly successful.

How to Become a »Rothschild« The Self-Perception of the Family

Based on its »Grundvertrag« and its ennoblement, the family developed a unique perception of itself in which pride at having risen to prominence by one's own efforts was combined with an awareness of the family's Jewish origins.

The family ethos manifested itself in the motto of the family crest: »Concordia – Integritas – Industria«. Here, two traditional concepts taken from the world of the nobility, namely »concordia« and »integritas«, were linked with a virtue associated with the modern bourgeois world of work, namely that of »industria«. This self-perception, unique in bringing together tradition, modernity and Jewish heritage, separated the Rothschilds not only from the non-Jewish aristocratic families, but also from the Jewish *haute bourgeoisie*. It has left its mark on the family to this day, and helped to create the mythology surrounding the name Rothschild.

Intrafamily Marriages

The imperative of solidarity meant that striving for strong family ties was tantamount to a programme. Once the five sons had set up businesses in European capitals and several branches of the family had been created, the maintenance of family ties was guaranteed by the intermarriage of the children. Certainly from the mid-1820s onwards, if not earlier, such marriages were actually arranged by the five brothers. By insisting on marriage within the family, the Rothschilds were following a custom which even in the 19th century was still common among the European aristocracy. Family solidarity was regarded as the precondition for maintaining economic and social dominance.

The first to engage in the practice of marrying a relative was James de Rothschild, who married his Viennese niece Betty in 1824. In the generations of the five brothers' children and grandchildren, this virtually became a rule, thus producing complicated kinship relations. This phenomenon was noticed by outsiders too, who expressed their amazement – like Heinrich Heine: »There is reigning great harmony among these Rothschilds. Curiously, they always intermarry and there is such a criss-cross of relationships that a historiographer would have a devil of a job trying to unravel the knot.«

The advantages of intermarriage were obvious: dowries stayed within the family, and the money was jointly available as a shared pool of capital. Commercial continuity could be guaranteed by systematically raising the sons to take over the family business. They spent their years of apprenticeship in Rothschild banks.

By the 1830s at the latest, the Rothschilds' self-image was already fully developed. This is demonstrated by a letter from Baron James de Rothschild dated July 16, 1839, which he wrote to his nephew Nathaniel on the occasion of the marriage of Nathan's daughter Hannah to a Christian English aristocrat. Not at all in agreement with the marriage because he felt that marrying a Christian was in itself a violation of the Rothschilds' self-perception as a Jewish family, he explained: »The point is not that I am a fanatical admirer of Judaism, even if I do wish to retain my faith, … but that in our family we have always endeavoured to uphold the cohesion and sense of belonging together. And it has been more or less agreed from the outset, from their earliest childhood, that our children should never wish to marry outside the family. This way our wealth always stays in

the family … and Mayer will marry Anselm's daughter, just as Lionel's daughter will marry one of our sons, to do honour to the name of Rothschild.«

Family Rituals

Aware of their own uniqueness, the Rothschilds developed their own special rituals in connection with family occasions. Weddings and funerals afforded opportunities for the family to appear in public and demonstrate family unity. As long as the matriarch, Gutle, was still alive, the weddings were celebrated at the place where the family's rise to prominence began, in Frankfurt. In ceremonial fashion, the engaged couple would be officially introduced to Gutle – despite the fact that they were members of the family and well known to her. A sense of the rigid, almost businesslike nature of one such marriage in this early period of family history is conveyed by this rendering of Anselm and Charlotte's wedding in 1826, which has

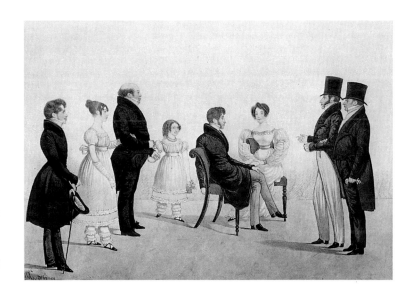

Marriage of Anselm and Charlotte von Rothschild in Frankfurt in 1826, drawing, pencil and watercolour

the air of a legal document in pictorial form. The bride and groom are seated in the middle; on the right stands the bride's father, Nathan Rothschild, who is also the groom's uncle, with his two youngest daughters Hannah and Louise and his eldest son Lionel. On the left stand the father of the groom, Salomon von Rothschild, and his brother Carl.

An important part of the marriage were the financial transactions involved. They were part of the marriage contracts, which specified who had the right to use which possessions, right down to personal objects such as expensive clothing – laces and Kashmir-shawls, for example – as well as jewellery. Accordingly, the personal presents took on a particular significance. Most wedding presents consisted of jewellery. Prior to the wedding the gifts were usually small items such as bracelets, necklaces or brooches, whose value was mainly as a memento. Yet at the wedding itself, the couple would be presented with very expensive jewels; the Rothschild pearls and diamonds became famous in their own right. The wedding ceremony was recorded in albums printed specially for the occasion, most of them elaborately decorated. Medals were also minted to commemorate the wedding, as used to be the custom of sovereign princes. The honeymoon – even in the latter part of the 19th century – was always spent visiting relatives, and was thus a duty.

By the 1830s at the latest, Rothschild weddings were being reported extensively in the press. From these reports we are able to conclude that the press was explicitly admitted to such occasions and that the family used them as an opportunity for public display. As their social standing grew, the Rothschilds' weddings became more and more opulent. The London marriage of Alphonse, son of Baron James de Rothschild, to his cousin Leonora on March 4, 1857, was a major European social event. Numerous guests from aristocratic and diplomatic circles were invited to attend the Jewish marriage ceremony, which took place at the Rothschild country estate of Gunnersbury Park. Detailed descriptions of the reception and the ball appeared in the press, including commentaries on the costumes worn by the guests. The bride's jewels received special mention. According to the marriage contract, these remained the private, inalienable property of the bride and, like her Kashmir-shawls, could not be made part of the Bank's assets. The wedding portrait shows Leonora with a bracelet, with very personal-looking jewellery on her left wrist and magnificent jewels out of emeralds in an Oriental style, as well as a valuable Kashmir-shawl.

Leonora de Rothschild as a bride. 1857, oil on canvas

Marriage ceremony of Leopold de Rothschild and Marie Perugia beneath the wedding canopy in the Portland Street Synagogue, London, 1881. Lithograph from »The Graphic«, January 19, 1881

On January 19, 1881 Leopold de Rothschild, son of Baron Lionel, married Marie Perugia in the Portland Street Synagogue in London. The wedding was attended not only by politicians and diplomats, but also by the Prince of Wales, making his first ever visit to a synagogue.

The response of the press was enormous, and concentrated on the Jewish marriage ceremony, which was described in detail: Following the ordinary weekday service and the recitation of the prayer for the Royal Family, the bridal procession entered the synagogue. The choir led the singing of the psalms … and the bride and groom were led to their place under the Chuppa, the marriage canopy, which was set up in front of the Ark. The bride wore a gown of white satin and the usual orange blossoms in her hair, yet not a single piece of jewellery. The groom wore a silk tallith (prayer shawl), a gift from the bride. Its four corners were richly embroidered in gold, and it bore his monogram surrounded by the bridal wreath with lover's knots. During the course of the ceremony, following the opening prayer, the Rabbi. A.L. Green addressed the bride and groom, recited the betrothal blessings and handed each of them the kiddush cup. As the groom placed the ring on the bride's finger, he spoke the following words: ›Behold, thou art wedded to me with this ring according to the law of Moses and Israel.‹ Afterwards, the ketubba, the marriage contract, was read out and, following an ancient custom, the groom broke a wine glass. The ceremony ended with the recitation of the seven marriage blessings and the singing of the 150th Psalm.« After the ceremony, the gifts were put on public display at the house of Alfred de Rothschild, one of the groom's brothers. Visitors virtually besieged the house, and the press published the list of presents. The commentator, fascinated by the fabulous jewels, especially the pearls and the bride's diamond tiara, concluded his report with the exclamation: »What a wonderful people these Jews are.«

The list of wedding presents is an excellent document of cultural history regarding the family's status and public esteem. The list of people who gave presents was headed by Edward, Prince of Wales, whose gift was a silver ewer and basin. He is followed by the British aristocracy, foreign diplomats and the bourgeoisie, listed in alphabetical order, as well as employees of the Bank. The presents were mainly objects made of silver, from bibelots to tableware, including a large number of letter-openers, cigarette cases and riding crops. The members of the Rothschild family themselves chiefly gave very valuable jewellery.

Solidarity as a Jewish Family

The weddings, with all their pomp, and the grand-scale funerals were conducted according to Jewish custom. That meant that the family events which were put on show for the public always emphasized the Jewish identity of the Rothschild family. The retention of this identity was determined not at all by economic exigencies, but was – as James de Rothschild puts it in his letter of 1839 – a personal and a family matter. In his life and the lives of his brothers, especially that of his eldest brother Amschel in Frankfurt, adherence to the Jewish faith played a more significant role than one might conclude from reading the letter. In his library in the Bank, James not only had a Mahzor, a Jewish prayer book for the whole year, but also the »Guide to the Perplexed« by Maimonides, one of the most famous works of mediaeval Jewish philosophy, which suggests that James was well educated in Jewish culture. And either he or his brother Salomon probably owned the delicate Esther scroll, which was so small that it could be taken on one's travels. Charlotte de Rothschild received wedding presents

not only of beautifully bound prayer books but probably also the small prayer mirror for the blessings of Sukkoth, the étui of which bears her colours.

The Education of a Rothschild –
An Arduous Apprenticeship

Work at the Bank determined the education of a Rothschild. The first lessons were given by private tutors or at exclusive schools. From about the age of 16 on, the boys also had to do an apprenticeship at the Bank. They were sent to the various Rothschild branches, where they were taught the business under the supervision of their uncles and cousins. After studying, the sons joined the Bank and became – at least during the first half of the 19th century – »slaves to business«, as Anthony de Rothschild put it.

Their educational programme was based on the bourgeois ethos of education and work, and followed the necessity, already recognized by Meyer Amschel, of combining secular education with Jewish religious knowledge. Both the boys and the girls of the Rothschild family received an education that was unusually comprehensive, even by 19th-century standards. Its twofold purpose was for the children to acquire linguistic, literary and scientific knowledge to as high a level as was possible at that time, and also to instruct them in the traditional social skills, such as dancing, riding and conversation. Outstanding academics were called in to teach the children. The portrayal of the two brothers Mayer Carl and Wilhelm Carl on horseback is a perfect illustration of this educational goal:

The brothers are wearing immaculate school uniforms – as they would have done had they attended public schools, although

The brothers Mayer Carl and Wilhelm Carl von Rothschild on horseback. Watercolour by Raffaele d'Auria, 1833

in fact they were exclusively taught at home by private tutors – and their posture on horseback is elegant and self-assured, as befitting future gentlemen.

The children's moral education was the responsibility of the Rothschild women, who theorized on the subject in publications or their diaries. The children were strongly encouraged to reflect upon their own education, with the result that the daughters of Anthony de Rothschild became so interested in the subject that they wrote about it and even asked to have a school set up as a birthday present where they could teach the children of the village that formed part of their country estate. Carl von Rothschild devised detailed lesson plans for his sons Mayer Carl, Adolph and Wilhelm Carl, making sure that the contents were appropriate to their respective age. The plan compiled for Wilhelm Carl in 1843, when he was 15 years

old, included a total of 20 subjects, including five languages, the main one being Hebrew, and five science subjects.

Henri Blanvalet, a renowned French physiologist, was charged with coordinating the work of the various private tutors who taught Carl von Rothschild's sons. He had to commit himself to writing assiduously detailed reports on the level of knowledge attained by his pupils. All the children had to write weekly reports. Parallel to their lessons, the sons were given a grounding in office work, in the course of which they were expected to take responsibility for performing minor tasks, such as copying letters. The daily routine was organized down to the last detail, leaving little room for free time. Just how precisely their father in far-off Naples organized the education of his sons in Frankfurt is shown by the highly detailed instructions he wrote to Blanvalet. His son Wilhelm Carl had to move into a small house of his own – evidently on his father's estate – and was not allowed to receive visitors without Blanvalet's consent, and then only to a limited extent. The teachers were only permitted to enter the house during lesson time. They were strictly forbidden to smoke. Wilhelm Carl was only allowed to go out in the company of his tutor, and he required his tutor's approval to visit people. However, he had to pay regular visits to his relatives, in particular his Uncle Amschel, with whom he had to attend synagogue on Sabbath. He had to submit written reports on everything – his academic progress, his daily expenses, his correspondence and also his conduct.

»What grace and goodness is to be seen in the institution by virtue of which we draw pleasure from fulfilling our duties!«
(Louise de Rothschild, 1859)

The education of the Rothschild girls was characterized by learning »to be useful«. To this end, the Rothschild women, such as Louise de Rothschild, wrote texts on moral education. Their ideas combined an extremely conservative vision of woman's role with an awareness of the importance of education for women and a confidence that were positively avant-garde for their day. »Homage to the woman morally and intellectually strong – to the woman of sound judgement, powerful thought and independent action.« »According to the old Hebrew idea, the Perfect Woman must possess energy, strength of purpose and active zeal. Her home must be the abode of order, purity and cheerfulness.« A knowledge of science and the humanities was considered necessary not only for boys but also for girls, as is borne out impressively by

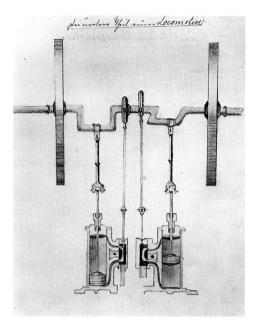

Drawing of a locomotive's connecting rod by the 16 year-old Emma Louise de Rothschild, 1861

the technical drawing of a locomotive connecting rod produced by Emma Louise von Rothschild, who was only 16 at the time. It could by no means be taken for granted in the 19th century that girls were taught scientific subjects. Moreover, the girls and women in the Rothschild family were supposed to acquire the knowledge of business matters required to run a bank, as Carl warned his daughter Charlotte when she married into the London branch of the family. This was not at all to say that the girls had to neglect traditional subjects, such as drawing, painting and music. They received professional artistic training, and some of them became accomplished artists and musicians.

Portraits –
A Rothschild Custom

The way the family saw itself found visual expression in the numerous portraits of family members, the earliest of which date from the 1820s. During the course of the century, different types of portraits evolved, each used for specific kinds of events, such as weddings, or particular places, such as the bank, the salon or the private study. The typological model on which this development was based was that of the aristocratic portrait, although it was adapted to fit the needs of the Rothschild family in projecting a public image of themselves. Of key importance was the series of portraits of the five brothers, produced by the Frankfurt painter Moritz Daniel Oppenheim in 1836, shortly after Nathan's death.

The five portraits show the brothers sitting in demonstratively formal posture and attire, each wearing a medal. This type of representation takes its cue from portraits of civil servants and diplomats common during the 19th century, and thus emphasizes the aim of the five brothers to belong to the leading political and social class in Europe at the time. Apparently, this series was not only copied for each of the branches, but also served as a model for the print that was used to advertise the Bank, and were thus a visual expression of a »Rothschild corporate identity«.

In addition to these head-and-shoulders and knee-length portraits, large-sized individual portraits were also produced of the heads of each of the Houses of Rothschild, which were hung in the bank and the formal reception rooms of the residences.

Series of portraits of the five brothers, painted by Moritz Oppenheim in 1836, from old photographs, as the originals are supposedly lost. The portraits show Amschel and Salomon, as well as Nathan, Carl and Jakob (James)

The Grand Salon in
Château Lafite.
Watercolour by
A. Serebriakoff.
Representative
portraits of the five
brothers hang
on the walls

An impressive example is the portrait of James de Rothschild painted by Hippolyte Flandrin in 1861. It shows the leading Parisian banker at the pinnacle of his success in a demonstratively relaxed pose, wearing smart, elegantly fashionable clothes.

One of the masterpieces of 19th century European portrait painting is the portrait of Betty de Rothschild painted by Jean Auguste Dominique Ingres. It portrays her as an exotic beauty – a discreet reference to her Jewish origins. Her clothing and jewellery identify her as one of the wealthiest and most elegant ladies of Parisian high society. Her likeness, of which the family possesses numerous copies to this day, formed the model for a style of portraying Rothschild women which was emulated in numerous later works.

Carl von Rothschild specified in his will: »… the family portraits in the house are for Mayer Carl (the eldest son). Duplicates go to my dear son, Baron Adolph Carl von Rothschild, triplicates to my dear son Baron Wilhelm Carl.«

Each of the children was also permitted to have copies made from the originals. This demonstrates the special importance of the portraits as a means of strengthening family bonds. The small size of many of these representations, in particular the more personal portraits of the children and the family, indicates that they were intended to be hung in the family's private quarters. Most private of all, often conceived and collected as objets d'art, were the miniature medallions.

The family had its own portrait artists, the most prominent of whom was Moritz

Portrait of Baroness
Betty de Rothschild,
wife of Baron
James de Rothschild,
Paris.
Oil on canvas, Paris,
1848, Jean Dominique
Ingres (1780–1867)

Daniel Oppenheim of Frankfurt, whose style was also imitated in England. In Paris it was Ary Scheffer who was commissioned to paint the Rothschilds; in Vienna the likenesses were produced by miniaturists of the Austrian nobility, such as Moritz Daffinger and Karl Kriehuber. In terms of style, the Rothschild portraits' deliberate evocation of traditional portraiture placed them in a category of their own within the context of 19th-century representative art. As works of art, the outstanding specimens in this category are the large individual portraits of Betty and James. These are complemented by a masterpiece of modern portraiture, Lucian Freud's likeness of Jakob Lord Rothschild.

At the Pinnacle of European Society

Perfectly Managed Fairy-Tale Castles

In the second half of the 19th century, the family had large pseudo-historical castles built in France and England, surrounded by fairy-tale grounds. In 1850/51, Joseph Paxton, who designed the original Crystal Palace in London, built Mentmore Castle, Buckinghamshire, for Baron Mayer de Rothschild.

Three years later he was summoned to Paris by James de Rothschild, who had him build an imposing hunting lodge, Ferrières Castle, to the south-west of Paris, surrounded by a large park.

The interiors of Ferrières were designed by the painter Eugène Lami. One of his most beautiful creations is the Blue Salon, which is dominated by the Rothschilds' colours, blue and gold.

Between 1874 and 1883 Ferdinand de Rothschild commissioned the French architect Hippolyte Destailleur to build Waddesdon Manor in Aylesbury. In their mixture of styles, ranging from the Italian Renaissance to French Baroque and Rococo, all these castles reflected the architecture of the princely residences of Europe.

The interior setting of the suites and reception rooms, which in Ferrières and Mentmore were arranged around a huge central hall, followed a traditional layout of a castle. By contrast, a progressive design of the side- and service rooms met the most advanced standards of conveniences available at that time. Thus Waddesdon Manor was equipped with a »state-of-the-art« kitchen. In Ferrières, a unique solution to the »kitchen problem« was found. In his memoirs, Baron Guy de Rothschild

Mentmore Castle, Buckinghamshire, built by J. Paxton for Baron Mayer de Rothschild in 1851

recalled: »Who could imagine the kitchens of Ferrières? It is in the nature of such places that they do not always exude the pleasantest of odours, odours against which one cannot easily protect oneself. The simple solution to this problem was to isolate the kitchen. Not sufficient to locate it at the other end of the castle, for then the wind could still have blown the undesirable fragrances across. No! It was quite simply built a long way away from the castle. More precisely, it was built underground! It was a veritable underground command post, consisting of several rooms. It was connected to the castle by a passageway, along which the food was conveyed by a little train running on rails. The dishes were kept warm on little hotplates. There was nothing frightening about this vision from another age – on the contrary, this place was one of our favourite playgrounds. We sometimes helped to push the little train with its heavy trucks by climbing between two baskets of tableware.«

The upkeep of these country estates required a large number of staff, who were accommodated in their own outhouses. At least 30 or 40 persons were needed to maintain Ferrières Castle, and another 50 to tend the grounds. Nathaniel de Rothschild had so many English gardeners looking after his famous gardens on the Hohe Warte near Vienna that it was possible to set up Vienna's first football club for their benefit.

The culmination of life on these luxurious country estates was marked by the visits of crowned heads. In 1862, the French Emperor Napoleon III came to Ferrières, ostensibly for a hunt, although the real reason was a reconciliation with his political opponent, James de Rothschild.

The »Salon Bleu« at Ferrières Castle, decorated in the Rothschild colours of blue and gold.
Watercolour by A. Serebriakoff

In 1890 Queen Victoria visited Waddesdon Manor. Other guests at Waddesdon included the two prime ministers, Gladstone and Disraeli. The Prince of Wales – later to become Edward VII – was a personal friend of Ferdinand de Rothschild and his cousins.

By shining in their roles as hosts to international society, Ferdinand and Alfred de Rothschild made a significant contribution to building the family's worldwide network of business associates.

The palatial town houses were smaller but no less luxurious. In Paris and Vienna they all stood in the same district, and in London even in the same street. Londoners referred to Piccadilly as »Rothschild Row«. Their luxurious appointments are described in numerous memoirs. The Austrian Ambassador, Count Apponyi, for example, gave an account of Baron James de Rothschild's Parisian residence on rue Laffitte. He was amazed at the perfect imitations of paintings on a gold background decorating the walls, the sculpted marble fireplaces and the priceless grandfather clocks, studded with precious stones. The height of opulence in his view were the chairs, decorated with ormolu and bearing two figures on the backrests holding up the coloured enamel crest of the Rothschild family.

The Rothschilds as the Hosts of International Society

The Rothschilds' town houses, country estates and castles formed the perfect setting for the lavish hospitality for which they became renowned. The task of organizing the representative, social side of the

Queen Victoria at Waddesdon Manor, May 5, 1890. The event was commemorated by planting a tree.

Rothschilds' lives was left mainly to the women, who thus made a significant contribution to the family's prestige and at the same time lent effective support to the business interests of their husbands and brothers. For a salon also provided an opportunity to obtain important informations quickly and confidentially.

Carl wrote in a letter of March 1839 to his daughter Charlotte: »Business or just being busy – tell your husband he should assiduously visit diplomats in order to hear the news...They should try to find out what is happening in London, and can go visiting every Sunday in London.«

During the 19th century, especially in Paris, the salon developed into a forum for exchange of intellectual ideas, and played an important role in the formation of political and cultural opinion. For decades, the salon of Baroness Betty de Rothschild was

The Grey Drawing Room at Halton Hall, a country estate built for Alfred de Rothschild in 1884

considered one of the most illustrious in the French capital. Leading politicians and diplomats rubbed shoulders with important writers such as Heine and Balzac, or leading musicians like Rossini, Liszt and Chopin.

The House's Trump Card: Its Cuisine

If the Rothschilds' salon in Paris attracted so many guests, it was in no small part due to the marvellous concoctions by Antonin Carême, the master chef. He was responsible for a high table serving at least 50 every day, as well as ensuring that the service was immaculate. He dreamed up menus famous for their refinement and decoration. His speciality was creating table decorations out of confectionery and gigantic, architecturally arranged buffets.

Carême (1783-1833) was one of the leading professional cooks of his day, who made the sumptuous dinners of the salons and the major restaurants the absolute

pivotal attraction of bourgeois society, establishing the 19th century as the golden age of classical French cuisine. His cookery books still form the basis of French cooking today.

For the Rothschild family he created what has since become a classic dessert, Soufflé Rothschild, made from glacé fruit with a dash of »Danziger Goldwasser« (a brandy).

The report by Lady Morgan, a society lady writing around 1830 on an invitation to dine with James de Rothschild, is testimony to the reputation enjoyed by Carême at that time and the significance that was attached to invitations to the Rothschilds' table. Lady Morgan describes the table as expensively but tastefully laid with gold, silver and porcelain. The dishes met the standards of modern haute cuisine: »… neither were there old-fashioned, strong-tasting sauces, nor over-concentrated jus. Rather, the delicate gravies were made with almost chemical precision, … each vegetable still had its fresh colour, … the mayonnaise was whipped ice-cold … Carême deserves a laurel wreath for perfecting an art form by which modern civilisation is measured.«

Lady Morgan, evidently seated next to Baron James de Rothschild as a guest of honour, received a special accolade from Carême: her name was written in icing on an arrangement of columns, also made of sugar, which formed the table decoration.

Music in the Salon = Salon Music?

Aside from conversation before, during and after dinner, the salon was also the scene of another form of entertainment: the musical recital. In the 19th century, music was one of bourgeois culture's most important ways of expression. It was cultivated not only in

Silver platter by Karl Thomas and Johann Martin Schmidt, Frankfurt, 1842. It belonged to the set of tableware made for the wedding of Mayer Carl and Louise von Rothschild

The kitchen in the basement of Gustave de Rothschild's palatial town house at 23 Avenue Marigny, Paris. Watercolour by A. Serebriakoff

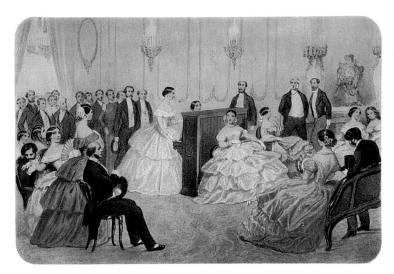

Concert held in a salon of the Parisian bourgeoisie, c. 1845. Watercolour by Eugène Lami

public concert halls and opera houses, but to an equal extent in private salons.

The pianoforte was the favoured instrument of the day, and the travelling piano virtuoso became a type of musician in his own right. A number of the Rothschild women developed a particularly keen interest in music: in London there was Hannah, Nathan's wife; in Paris, Betty de Rothschild and her daughter Charlotte; and in Frankfurt, Charlotte, Anselm's wife, and their daughter Hannah Mathilde. They regularly played host to nearly all the famous musicians and composers of the day. Rossini was a personal friend of Betty and Charlotte in Paris, and dedicated a number of his oeuvres to them. He also wrote the music for the reception given for Napoleon III at Ferrières, the »Chorus of Democratic Hunters«. Chopin taught Charlotte and Hannah Mathilde, and dedicated some of his piano pieces to Charlotte. On many occasions, Betty de Rothschild's Paris salon heard Liszt play the piano and Paganini and Joachim perform on the violin.

As one of the leading musical salons in Paris, the Rothschilds' did not offer the superficial musical entertainment only for which the salons were so frequently criticized, but instead also formed a backdrop for new developments in music and composing. Thus it was the brilliant virtuosity of Paganini's violin which inspired Liszt to create new forms of melodic expression.

The Rage of the Day – Horticulture

In her »Paris Letters«, Emile Girardin describes the new fashion in the salons: magnificent bouquets of flowers, filling the rooms with a fragrant mass of blooms. The Rothschilds' guests were regularly treated to the sight of exquisite, tastefully arranged floral pageants. These decorations were extremely expensive, especially in the winter months, which coincided with the social season, as the flowers had to be ordered from greenhouses. Needless to say, the

Rothschild properties included extensive flower gardens and greenhouses, in which not only exotic flora grew, but also useful plants, so that fresh flowers, fruit and vegetables were available all year round.

Horticulture and greenhouse-keeping were highly-regarded social pursuits in the 19th century, and many a Rothschild was a passionate »gardener«. Nathaniel von Rothschild's gardens at Hohe Warte near Vienna were characterized by a combination of the useful and the leisure, of parkland, flowerbeds and vegetable patches as well as greenhouses. His greenhouses were famous for their superbly modern equipment and their precious flowers that were difficult to grow and keep, such as orchids and cactuses. The selection of rare flowers reflected the latest in botanical research worldwide and thus alluded to their owner's broad education and knowledge of the world. These gardens, which the people of Vienna were permitted to use as a place of recreation, also enhanced the family's reputation as public benefactors.

Extravagance as a Lifestyle

In 1884 Alfred de Rothschild was presented by the magazine Vanity Fair as the epitome of the Rothschilds' »savoir vivre«. The statement »he is known by everybody« shows the degree to which the family had become socially accepted. The extravagance of his lifestyle set the tone for the society of the day, as is reflected in numerous anecdotes. Both he and his cousin Ferdinand are credited with having invented the »Rothschild tea ceremony«, a non-plus-ultra in attentive service first thing in the morning: »When the curtains were drawn, a powdered footman entered the room, followed by an underling with a tea trolley, and would query politely: ›Tea, coffee or a fresh peach, Sir?‹ – ›Tea, please.‹ – ›China, Indian or Ceylon, Sir?‹ – ›China, if you please.‹ – ›With lemon, milk or cream, Sir?‹ – ›Milk, please.‹ – ›Jersey, Hereford or Shorthorn, Sir?‹«

An integral part of life as a Rothschild was and still is the passion for the Turf. Mayer and Leopold de Rothschild's stables were famous in England for breeding horses like St. Amant, winner of the 1913 Derby.

1871 went down in the history of English horse-racing as the »Year of the Baron«, as Mayer's horses won the four major classics of the season.

Thanks to the favourite British pastime of betting on the horses, the Rothschilds achieved an extraordinary popularity as horse-breeders. The name »Rothschild« was just as well known on racecourses as it was in international banking. Both their extravagant lifestyle and their involvement in horse-racing were seen as an expression of the »Rothschild myth«, according to which the Rothschilds were a family that could not be measured by any normal standards.

The Rothschilds' »Public« Face

As of the end of the 18th century broad strata of the population started availing themselves of educational possibilities as well as participating in political discussions and economic activities. Simultaneously, a rapid expansion was seen in the technological means of exchanging information. The press mushroomed and became the symbol of the public sphere in the modern sense.

For the Rothschilds, who as of about 1820 had established themselves at the head of the European financial world, this development both afforded new opportunities and posed new risks. On the one hand, a large part of their business relied on absolute discretion and took place far away from the public eye in business offices, audience chambers and salons. On the other, the family was keenly aware of the importance of the press for its business, as we can learn from their correspondence as of roughly 1817. Thus, in 1839 James de Rothschild wrote to his nephew that he attended to »attack« the French government »in all the press« if they did not support a railway project, as it was the press which as a rule tended to have the best effect. When, three years later, anti-Jewish and tendentious articles appeared in the European press covering a purported ritual murder in Damascus, James ensured that an article was widely circulated in which the innocence of the Jews persecuted in Damascus was made plain for all to see, thus stressing how scandalous their persecution was.

How the Rothschilds Presented Themselves to the Public

If you are successful then you want and have to legitimate your success, to explain the reasons for it. Almost inevitably, the Rothschilds' public presentation of themselves focused on interpreting their rapid ascent to become Europe's richest and most influential bank and trading house. After all, the times in which this success story occurred, namely the turbulent political age prior to, during and after Napoleon, gave enough fodder for speculation in themselves. Two legends purport to indicate what the Rothschilds' attitude and business ethics were like at that time.

The one, far from friendly towards the Rothschilds, claims that they made their wealth by exploiting the Battle of Waterloo. Nathan Rothschild deliberately, so the legend would have it, spread false reports on how the battle was going, intimating that Napoleon had won, and thus manipulated prices on the London Stock Exchange in his favour.

The other, friendly legend focuses on how the Elector of Hesse's assets were saved from the French. Elector William I had fled into exile with the lion's share of his wealth and entrusted management of part of his securities to the House of Rothschild. Documents concerning him were therefore deposited in the house on Judengasse, where they were kept safe despite a raid by the French police. By exaggerating and dramatizing this state of events, the legend arose in Frankfurt that the Elector had had all his assets kept safely by the Rothschilds and was able to collect them unharmed on returning to power.

Fifty years later the Vienna branch of the Rothschild family commissioned Moritz Daniel Oppenheim to record the legend for posterity in pictorial form.

The first painting shows Meyer Amschel Rothschild in his house in the Judengasse receiving the treasure from the Elector, the second depicts the same lo-

Meyer Amschel's
five sons return
the treasure to the
Elector.
Moritz Daniel
Oppenheim, 1861

cation with the five sons returning the treasure, as Meyer Amschel had meanwhile died. In these pictures, the prince and his Jewish bankers are portrayed as if close social links existed between them, which was certainly never the case at the time. The House of Rothschild, so the message these pictures convey, guarantee the safety of assets entrusted to them during difficult times and over the course of generations. The claim is, in other words, that their wealth does not stem from their mis-appropriation of the funds, as some might have liked to believe. At this level, they are placed on a par with the prince, his trust being met by equally deep loyalty.

On the other hand, the differences be-tween the clothes and the interiors in the two paintings points to modernization and the family's ascent up the social ladder in the second generation. Oppenheim's pic-tures were intended for public display and

were presented at an exhibition, first in Frankfurt, then in Vienna:

The painter could be sure that his historicizing interpretation was of a well-known legend, for as early as 1827 the »Allgemeine deutsche Realencyklopädie« (General German Encyclopedia) printed by Brockhaus had contained an article on the Rothschild family. A footnote there de-scribes the »rescue of the Elector's assets« in a form that could be misunderstood. It was added by a Frankfurt editor, who relied on a text by Friedrich von Gentz (that had not yet been published). The latter, who had, among other things, established contact between the Rothschilds and Count Metternich, had been commissioned by the Rothschilds to write their family history. The encyclopedia entry of more than four columns was an extract from his piece. It describes the Rothschilds' exceptional position as being the result of a sense of family, skillful exploitation of circumstances, great sincerity and, above all, the highly reliable way in which they treated assets entrusted to them. Although the writer initially alludes to Meyer Amschel having studied, mention is made neither of the family's Jewishness, nor is the great efforts by Meyer Amschel and his sons on behalf of equal rights for Jews.

The picture the author paints in this article, and Brockhaus was a leading opinion maker at the time, is one of a purposeful bourgeois family completely in line with the values of the day and which therefore deservedly ascended to the ranks of the aristocracy and high society but had nevertheless stuck true to its original values.

The article was adopted for »Encyclopédie des Gens du Monde« and thus ensured that this image of the family also became widespread in the French-speaking world.

Twenty five years later Moritz Daniel Oppenheim was engaged to create a pictorial image of the family's »corporate philosophy« for public presentation. His design was then used for a lithograph, prints of which were used to ornament the walls of the branches of the Rothschild Bank. In the centre he placed portraits of Meyer Amschel's five sons. Arranged around them are views of the five cities in which these men respectively resided as heads of the local bank. The cities are in turn each allocated specific symbols: London is complemented by a still-life of barrels and bales, Naples by

palm trees. A view of Frankfurt is positioned at the top of the picture, corresponding to the family coat of arms and motto, which is placed at the bottom. The motto »integritas, concordia, industria« is repeated across the full width of the picture, accompanied by explanatory motifs. Genesis 14.21 is used to illustrate the family's integrity. There, Abraham refuses to allow the King of Sodom to make him rich. The family unity is symbolized by a parable by Plutarch in which a family father shows his sons that one arrow can easily be broken whereas a bundle of them cannot. And industry is symbolized by Genesis 26.12, in which Isaac sows and plants in order to harvest a hundredfold with the blessing of the Lord.

The motto, which in the Rothschilds' coat-of-arms conveys above all the values of bourgeois entrepreneurs, is particularly emphasized in this depiction. By contrast, the aristocratic elements in the crest, which refer back to a baron and warrior class, clearly recede into the background here. The family, so the message of the picture, not only rules over lands and people, but has succeeded in establishing itself in the most important financial and trading centres in Europe primarily owing to its bourgeois values.

Images of the Rothschilds in Literature

Needless to say, the public images of the Rothschilds were not restricted to the picture they had painted of themselves. Nineteenth-century literature repeatedly deals with the Rothschild phenomenon, although the angle taken differs strongly from writer to writer. When the Rothschilds started holding larger salons, writers were among the guests. It was above all Heinrich Heine, who profited from the Rothschilds as his patrons while in exile in Paris; he

The five sons of Meyer Amschel. Lithograph after a design by Moritz Oppenheim, 1852

incorporated the experiences thus gained in various of his works. In England it was in particular the statesman and novelist Benjamin Disraeli, who, for example in his novel »Sybil«, created a literary monument to the family. Honoré de Balzac, who also moved in the Rothschild circle in Paris, used members of the family as models for his figures in various of his socially critical novels, such as »La maison Nucingen«.

But even writers who did not have such contact with the family referred to them. The liberal politician and writer Ludwig Börne, who himself had been born in the Judengasse in Frankfurt, was highly critical of James de Rothschild. In Joseph von Eichendorff's »Libertas und ihre Freier« there is a figure who is the archetypal enemy of freedom, and who can be recognized in part as Amschel Mayer Rothschild. In the pamphlet »Les Juifs rois de l'époque« by Alphonse Toussenel, which is considered to have laid the foundations of French anti-Semitism, the Rothschilds play the key role in bringing ruin upon society in the Jewish-capitalist social order the author dreams up and attacks.

Just how rigid the literary image of the Rothschilds had become by the turn of the century and how recourse could be had to it without knowing anything about the persons themselves can be seen from Emile Zola's »L'argent«. Saccard, the protagonist, is up against a figure called »Gundermann«, alias James de Rothschild. Both men embody different variants of money. Saccard, a gambler, forms a joint stock bank not only in order to conquer the economies of the Orient but above all to break the stranglehold of Gundermann and the other major Jewish bankers have on the stock exchange. Gundermann, who is immeasurably rich, counteracts Saccard's passionate ploy by relying on the cold logic of the money business and, finally, wins out after a dramatic battle on the stock exchange. Zola makes clear use of anti-Semitic clichés which he repeatedly had his protagonist utter. He portrays the close family life of the Rothschilds satirically as uncivilized chaos, in the midst of which he places Gundermann as the emotionless king of money who pulls all the strings at the stock exchange. And in Zola's book, at the other end of the exchange, where stocks that have lost all value and promissory notes that have not been redeemed are traded, it is again Jewish figures who do the business: dirty, slimy and insistently seeking financial gain.

Admittedly, Madame Caroline, one of the favourable figures in »L'argent«, opposes her anti-Semitic friend Saccard by saying that for her Jews are humans like all other humans. However sharp Zola's criticism of Rothschild the Jew, it was not least that simple principle that all humans

N. M. Rothschild, Esq., Caricature by W. M. Thackeray

are alike that led him a few years later to take his vehement stance on behalf of the rehabilitation of Captain Dreyfus and become a fierce opponent of anti-Semitism.

The Rothschilds in Caricatures

Images of the Rothschilds reached a broad public in the form of contemporary caricatures. The medium first started to be widespread with the invention of lithography at the end of the 18th century, because it enabled drawings to be reproduced in large numbers relatively cheaply. As a rule, political caricatures present criticism in personified form, making use of exaggeration and distortion of the individual's physiognomy. About 1820 the first caricatures of Nathan Rothschild arose in England. He was immediately recognizable for his contemporaries with his short, roundish figure. The Rothschilds were the center of the cartoonists' attention specifically in their role on the stock exchange and in financing government projects. The core of stock market business, rising and falling prices, was repeatedly given pictorial form, e.g. by drawing a seesaw, as manipulation of a balance, as paper inflated by a bellows. The success of the Rothschild business stemmed, in the view of the cartoonists, above all from dubious if not criminal activities. The presentations are frequently shaped by anti-Jewish feelings, for example in William Makepeace Thackeray's »N. M. Rothschild, Esq.«, which combines the picture of Nathan at the pillar in the Royal Exchange with a poem that bestows the role of a king upon him:

»HERE'S the pillar of 'Change! Nathan Rothschild himself / With whose fame every bourse in the universe rings; / The first Baron Juif; by the grace of his pelf. / ... Not ›the king of the Jews,‹ but ›the Jew of the kings.‹ / The great incarnation of cents and consols, / The eights, halves, and quarters, scrip, options, and shares; / Who plays with new kings as young Misses with dolls; / The monarch undoubted of bulls and of bears!«

From about 1848 onwards, in France and Germany an explicit visual code of anti-Semitic and nationalistic images increasingly emerged. It culminated in the Anti-Dreyfus campaign and the German anti-Semitic movement at the turn of the century. Cartoonists started consistently creating a »typical« outward appearance for Jews. In so doing the individuals were given traits and signs of an inborn (moral) baseness to the point of being rendered

The General Lender,
1848 or 1869

Die Generalpumpe.

animal-like and therefore no longer human.

In the minds of people who thought this way, the Rothschild became the negative symbolic figures of a new social order and its Jewish representatives, in which the universal validity of money ties was conceived of as a threat to their own identity, which they construed in terms of nation and race. Thus, a myth had finally become linked with the name »Rothschild« – the myth of the power of money to rule society and turn the world order on its head. »The General Lender«, a caricature from the German-speaking world, strikingly shows this: the House of Rothschild is depicted as the incarnation of a financial system that covers and dominates the whole globe and on which Oriental and European princes are dependent. The English government is placed directly to the left, the French government to the right of the stomach; the figures on the far left are (probably) Mehmet Ali and Ibrahim Pasha, and on the far right General Espartero with the Spanish Queen Isabelle.

The cartoonists' imagination constantly focused on their opinion that Jews as a collective group should leave Europe, be it voluntarily or by the use of force. An anti-Semitic cartoon from the turn of the century is called »The Jews Leave Germany« and propagates all Jews being driven out of Europe to Egypt. The mass of people in the picture is predominantly made up of criminals, cheats and other dubious figures. The Rothschilds, on the right, are the only people on a horse-drawn cart in the midst of people walking laden down with baggage. They thus represent a Jewish upper class which inconsiderately looks only to its own advantage.

As early as 1848 a caricature had taken up this motif. The subtitle reads: »The Children of Israel enter the Promised Land in order to found a Republic«. Rothschild rides on a mule, while the other Jews have to travel by foot to the Orient. Even earlier, in 1829, a newspaper article wrote favourably of the possibility of Jews setting up a colony in Jerusalem and Palestine, under the active and able leadership of the Rothschilds. The article appeared in the United States, however, where the Rothschilds were, as a rule, admired as the epitome of successful financial business, as is to be seen from a large number of Rothschild anecdotes that circulated in the US press at the time.

Jewish Voices

The Rothschilds enjoyed a varying reception among the Jewish public. A few highlights will serve to show how, on the one hand, people linked high expectations with the family's immense wealth and traditional philanthropy, something that, on the other, easily turned into criticism.

With regard to its wealth, many gentile families were far better off, wrote Amschel Mayer Rothschild in 1818 to his brothers Nathan and Salomon, and went on to say that the family was admired precisely because it was a Jewish family. Amschel was evidently certain that in the future being a Rothschild and being a Jew would be like hand and glove.

In 1834 Moritz Abraham Stern, a mathematician who at a later date was to be the Jew to be a professor at a German university, addressed a letter to Amschel Mayer von Rothschild. In it he maintained that Amschel »in the opinion of all Jews in Germany can do most to achieve their liberation.«

Those were great expectations, but there were also very small expectations. At about the same time, Heinemann Rosenthal, who was then only an eight year-old Jewish pupil agreed with his friends in the then Province of Saxony »that we should secretly leave home and first make the pilgrimage to Frankfurt on Main and beg the money we needed for our onward journey to Palestine from Rothschild ... «

The »Allgemeine Zeitung des Judenthums«, which was published in Leipzig, had greater expectations, writing in 1837: »All attention is directed more than ever at the House of Rothschild. ... For the House of Rothschild has now unerringly placed itself at the head of a movement which will completely reshape the European monetary system: the destruction of trade in paper, the injection of capital into industry and real estate. What will now be said, given that this major transformation is being accomplished by Jews, and Europe is thus benefiting from a group, from whom one would expect it least...«

The newspaper was of the opinion that the trade in money and securities was an unproductive cycle that was definitely damaging to overall economic development. And it was precisely this area, hitherto the domain of the Jewish bankers, that the Rothschilds were about to give up, which would have not only a decidedly favourable impact on the economy but also on the »image« of Jews as a whole.

Yet by 1839 the newspaper had thoroughly revised its opinion, expressly voicing its disappointment at the fact that its hopes had not been fulfilled: »Well we know to our dismay that the repulsive attitude towards the Jews in Germany, which had almost disappeared completely at the time of the Wars of Liberation, increased with the increase in the House of Rothschild, and that the latter's great wealth and their partners have adversely affected the Jewish cause, so that as the former grew so the latter sank all the further. Well we know to our dismay that the example of the House of Rothschild has seduced many a diligent man of our faith away from the blessed path of industry and onto the hollow boards of trading in paper ... We must sharply separate the Jewish cause from the whole House of Rothschild and their consorts. Who can come forward to say that these people have done anything substantial for Judaism, for its external or inner emancipation, for its civil or spiritual elevation?«

In the eyes of the columnist, the Rothschilds let all Jewry down with their insistence that they continue to do business in their traditional terrain and the fact that they did indeed only hesitantly start engaging in financing industrial and transport projects. Not only had they with their business practices provoked the Renaissance of anti-Jewish feeling in the country, but, so he goes on, they had also spawned a negative image for themselves among Jews. The »Jewish cause« and the House of Rothschild, so his bitter summary, had in future to be kept completely separate.

The Jewish jokes about the Rothschilds that circulated at the time were a far cry from such critical and one-sided deliberations on the role the Rothschilds played in the complex process of integration into the society of the day. Here, a far simpler yardstick was applied, as the following joke exemplifies: A cadger, spellbound on seeing Rothschild's magnificent gravestone: »What a great lifestyle these guys have«.

Wealth Obliges

The Charitable Foundations of the Rothschild Family

An important area in which the Rothschild family presented itself in public was that of charity. Countless charitable institutions in many parts of Europe and Palestine served as a constant reminder of the Rothschild name they bore. Obituaries to family members repeatedly emphasized their commitment to charitable works. The family was at pains to extend their image as a financial power to include their role as benefactors. By the end of the 19th century at the latest, the name Rothschild had become equally synonymous with wealth and with charity.

The Religious Tradition

The charitable work of the Rothschild family stands in the tradition of the Zedaka. Zedaka, the Hebrew word for charity, implies working for social justice by means of offering material support for the needy.

In Frankfurt, the Rothschilds' efforts were mainly directed towards promoting the numerous social welfare institutions attached to the Jewish community, and it was here that they set up their first foundations. In 1829 a donation from the family led to the establishment of the hospital run by the Men and Women's Health Insurance, housed in a building which was destroyed in the Second World War. The text of the commemorative plaque read:

»Barons Amschel, Salomon, Nathan, Carl and Jacob von Rothschild built this house in accordance with the wishes of their late father; for the care of the sick, the good of the community, the embellishment of their home town; a memorial to filial respect and fraternal harmony.«

The »Baron Amschel Mayer von Rothschild Foundation to Provide for Impecunious Young Israelite Women«, which was

1299

Freiherrlich
Amschel Mayer von Rothschild'sche
Stiftung zur Ausstattung
unbemittelter Israelit. Jungfrauen
in Frankfurt a. M.

Aus dieser Stiftung sind gegen Ende dieses Jahres Sechstausend Gulden als Heurathsgut einer unbemittelten und unbescholtenen Jungfrau, Bürgerstochter aus der hiesigen Israelitischen Gemeinde, zu verwenden.

Die Bewerberinnen dürfen nicht jünger als 17 und nicht älter als 36 Jahre seyn; unter mehreren nach den näheren Bestimmungen des Stiftungsbriefes gleichberechtigten Angemeldeten entscheidet eine Verloosung, welche am Sterbetage des seeligen Herrn **Mayer Amschel von Rothschild** (Vaters des Stifters), am 14. des Monats Tischri, in diesem Jahre am 18. September, stattfindet.

Der Ablauf der Anmeldungsfrist wird hierdurch **auf den 15. August 1861** bestimmt und Anmeldungsformulare sind bei der unterzeichneten Stelle (Fahrgasse 146) zu erhalten.

Frankfurt a. M., den 14. Juni 1861.

Die Verwaltungs-Commission.

set up in compliance with Amschel Mayer's will of 1849, also conformed to the purpose and orientation of traditional Jewish foundation work.

In the early 19th century, Christian institutions and foundations also began to receive donations from Jews. Thus, for example, Meyer Amschel's will of 1812 already calls for a bequest to »the three praiseworthy Christian charitable foundations« of Frankfurt.

Working for the Jewish Community

Whereas the Rothschilds in Frankfurt still acted jointly on behalf of the Jewish community, when Salomon moved to Vienna, Nathan to London, Carl to Naples and James to Paris, they each took over individual responsibility for the Jewish communities in those cities, and made outstanding contributions to their development. From 1850 onwards, the Rothschilds were particularly prominent in sponsoring the erection of large, representative synagogues. Thus the Christian public sphere was being called to witness a Jewry which used the nature of its buildings as a confident manifestation of its newly acquired legal status and its integration into mainstream society. The synagogue of Versailles (1886) and the one built in 1874 in Rue de la Victoire, in Paris, were both funded by the Rothschilds. The architect, Alfred Philibert Aldrophe, was a Jew, which at that time was still far from usual. He also designed the Rothschild Orphanage and the private houses for Gustave de Rothschild in Paris.

The building of hospitals, equipped to the most modern medical standards, remained a foremost concern of all the family members, as did the founding of schools which offered not only secular but also religious education.

The English branch of the family showed great interest in the Jews' Free School, which was founded in 1822 in London. The school was set up in response to the poverty among large sections of the Jewish population and the educational disadvantages experienced by the children of these families. The poorest children received lunch every day and a new set of

A youth group on the occasion of the Purim festival at the Jews' Free School, 1910

clothes each year at the Rothschilds' expense. In 1847 Sir Anthony de Rothschild was made president of the School's Board and played a prominent role in its expansion. Around 1900 the school had over 3,000 pupils and was thus probably the largest in the world.

Brought Up to Serve Worthy Causes

Religious instruction was a major part of the Rothschild children's upbringing. Great importance was attached to encouraging the girls in particular to engage in charitable works. The mothers played a key role here in imparting these values.

On the Sabbath, Louise von Rothschild, who came from England and lived in Frankfurt, would lecture her children on religious and ethical subjects. A collection of these talks published in England in 1857 and translated into French and Russian. The German edition, published by Leopold Stein, was reprinted time and again. Alongside chapters headed »Truthfulness«, »Honour thy father and thy mother«, »Peace in the home« and »Thoughts for the New Year«, there is also a lecture which deals with the subject of »Charity«.

Louise's notion of charitable work corresponds to Jewish tradition. God-given wealth brings with it a responsibility to care for the poor and the sick.

The speech ends with a prayer: »Oh Lord, Thou hast made me so much happier, Thou hast vouchsafed to me so many more blessings than to thousands of Thy creatures, that I know not how I can ever thank Thee sufficiently. I can only pray to Thee to make me charitable and compassionate towards those who suffer and are in want, and to prevent me from being selfish and from thinking only of my own gratification. Place in my heart, O Lord! the wish and incli-

nation to feed the hungry, to clothe the naked, and to console the sorrowful, as long as I have the power and the means to do so, that I may thereby be less underserving of all Thy bounteous goodness to me, and less unworthy of Thy favour and merciful protection, O my God! Amen.

The Rothschilds' wills placed their children under an obligation to set up foundations in accordance with their parents' wishes and to assume personal responsibility for running them. One member of the family was always to be on the governing body of the foundation, or a member of the administration. The foundations thus became institutions whose development was influenced by several generations of Rothschilds. It was not until the advent of National Socialism that this tradition was brought to a violent end. Today, only Britain still has foundations which can look back on an unbroken tradition of Rothschild membership of the board of governors.

Charitable Works – A Duty of the Women

In 19th-century society, charitable works were a typically female field of activity. At the beginning of that century, responsibility for social welfare matters, which had previously been managed exclusively by men, passed into the hands of women. The Rothschild women were no exception. Charity was the only area in which they were able to act freely on their own responsibility. The women and daughters of the family, who had received just as comprehensive an education as the male members of the family, behaved as society expected them to behave – and some of them came to be looked up to by their generation as models of social commitment. The fact that, despite their education and wealth, none of them broke out of the confines laid down for them by society to go their own way is an indication of just

Israelitisches Kurhaus, Bad Soden a. T.

Israelite Sanatorium,
Bad Soden in the
Taunus hills. Postcard,
c. 1902

foundations had now been transferred to the women.

Yet it was not merely a sense of duty, but also a personal interest and a genuine desire to help that motivated the Rothschild women to become involved in charitable work to a far greater extent than might have been expected. Even in the vicinity of their summer residences they supported existing foundations or built new, generous institutions. In each place the Rothschilds would almost always set up several social foundations – for instance a school, a hospital and an orphanage – and lend their support to countless others. Thus, Hannah Mathilde founded the Israelite Children's Home and the Israelite Home for Women in Bad Nauheim, as well as the Sanatorium for Poor Israelites in Bad Soden, both towns being near to her summer residence in Königstein.

how narrowly society and the family defined their role. It is possible, however, that in the second half of the 19th century, a few of the women – like Hannah Louise – decided to remain single in order to escape the constrictingly stereotyped role of a married woman.

From the mid-19th century onwards, it was increasingly the Rothschild women who took the initiative in setting up new charitable foundations. Although the institutions were still generally named after the husband or the late father – following the death of her father, Hannah Louise set up two major foundations in his memory, the »Baron Carl von Rothschild Public Library« and the »Baron Mayer Carl von Rothschild Foundation Carolinum« – responsibility for the establishment and supervision of the

It was her financial support that rendered it possible to erect a clinic for respiratory disorders in Ruppertshain. And she even welcomed the rather eccentric-sounding proposal to buy a plot of land near the Israelite Sanatorium in order to grow potatoes for the soup kitchen.

The women not only gave their money but also took an active role on behalf of, and in, their institutions, as is shown by the example of Hannah Mathilde, who designed the architecture of the Israelite Children's Home in Bad Nauheim herself. This also showed, however, just how limited were the opportunities for women – even for one such as Hannah Mathilde von Rothschild – to apply knowledge and skills which did not fit in with contemporary notions of a woman's place.

After the death of her husband, Laura Thérèse continued to manage the hospital he had set up at Berek – sur – mer, their summer residence. She also founded a boys' and a girls' school in the town.

Welfare

Once they had begun, in the latter half of the 19th century, to acquire country estates, the English Rothschilds also turned their attention to helping the inhabitants of the villages attached to them. It was above all the women who, moved to pity by the poverty and disease they encountered, decided that something must be done to help. They had houses, medical facilities, schools and orphanages built. For each village a separate social welfare system was devised and implemented. These measures were conceived by the Rothschilds not only as a means of improving the living conditions of »their« villagers, but also as a way of averting social unrest.

The same paternalistic attitude – although here the fear of protests was probably uppermost in their minds – was also expressed in the efforts of the Rothschilds to cater for the social welfare of the workers employed in their industrial enterprises. In 1848 the workforce at the Witkowitz ironworks totalled 2,775 – representing a sevenfold increase within the space of 20 years. What was once a little village had grown into a town. The Rothschilds created all the facilities which the workers and their families required, from living quarters and shops to hospitals and schools. Essential though they might seem, the provision of such facilities could by no means be taken for granted in those days, and was regarded both by the Rothschilds and by society as a whole as an act of charity.

New Times – New Tasks

In the latter part of the 19th century, new social problems began to emerge in the wake of industrialization. In response, the Rothschilds extended their charitable activities to take on new tasks. The French Rothschilds, for example, donated 10 million francs towards the building of affordable housing for workers.

At the same time, with the situation for Jews in Eastern Europe deteriorating, there was a large influx of Russian and Polish Jews into Britain. This resulted in a wave of anti-Semitic incidents which were also directed against the London's Anglo-Jewish community. Nathaniel Mayer Lord Rothschild saw Anglification of the immigrants as the best way of solving this problem.

Many of the immigrants found a home of sorts in London's East End. Nathaniel realized that the housing shortage in that area was a key barrier to the integration of the Eastern European Jews into British society. He called for the setting up of the »Four Per

Cent Industrial Dwellings Company Limited«, a housing development company which, as the name suggested, would be able to keep the rents down by offering a dividend of only four percent. Within the space of 11 years, the firm had built four estates providing homes to 4,000 people. Initially, no attention was paid to the external appearance of the houses, as this would only have added to the cost.

From the time of its foundation up to the present day, a Rothschild has always held a seat on the board of directors of the company.

Relief for Persecuted Jews

The provision of relief for Jews who had suffered persecution or who had fallen upon hard times had always been a major concern for all the members of the Rothschild family. They always did their best to help victims of anti-Jewish feeling – whether faced with a charge of ritual murder in Xanten, anti-Semitic unrest in Corfu or pogroms in Russia – and to ease their difficulties. To this end the Rothschilds made use of their extensive connections to influential politicians and governments.

Carl Mayer von Rothschild and James, his brother, made a loan to the Vatican conditional on an assurance to improve the lot of Jews living in Rome's Jewish ghetto.

The Rothschilds also lent their support, both financial and personal, to the international relief organizations which evolved around the turn of the century, such as the Alliance Israélite Universelle.

During the National Socialist era, members of the family made substantial contributions to welfawe foundations, such as the Lord Baldwin Fund in Britain. Lionel de Rothschild was involved in the founding of the Central British Fund for German Jewry. In France, Edmond de Rothschild appealed for support for the victims of National Socialism.

During this period, the Rothschilds' efforts again went far beyond the mere provision of funds. James Armand de Rothschild and his wife Dorothy organized and financed the emigration of orphans to Palestine, and in 1939 arranged for Jewish children to be evacuated from Frankfurt and brought to their estate in England, where their education was taken care of. James Armand and Dorothy also received a hundred evacuee children who had fled

Evacuated children in Waddesdon Manor, Aylesbury

London to escape the threat of air raids and allowed them to stay at Waddesdon Manor.

The French branch of the family also supported efforts to save persecuted children, offering their own property as shelter.

Support for the Needy

In addition to establishing large foundations and supporting charitable institutions, the Rothschilds were always responsive to the pleas of individuals in need.

The legendary wealth of the Rothschilds and their reputation as great benefactors led countless people to turn to individual members of the family for help in their hour of need. Whether it was a carter who had lost his only horse and was now asking for money to buy a new one, or a widow begging for help in supporting her children, every request was taken seriously and received a reply. The family employed secretaries whose sole responsibility was to deal with letters from people like this, sent in from all over the world. In his memoirs, *Erinnerungen 1870–1920*, Jacob Rosenheim gives an impression of the work performed by these employees, who were jokingly referred to as »beggars' secretaries« by the other members of staff.

»Every evening, often as late as eight or nine o'clock, my father would go to the Baron [Wilhelm Carl von Rothschild] at his business premises on Fahrgasse, and sometimes also to the Grüneburg, in order to present him personally with a list, carefully drawn up by mother, of the petitions – 20 to 30 of them, on average – received from all over the Jewish world, personal appeals for help, letters from the most esteemed rabbis in every country, the yeshivot and welfare institutions in the East and the West. In each individual case the Baron personally decided on what seemed to him to be an appropriate amount. Incidentally, he also read with a certain amount of satisfaction every single letter of thanks received. Before it was presented to the Baron, information on each request had to be sought from one of the rabbis in the Baron's confidence who were located throughout the world. Each item of information was registered and copied verbatim into a book ... The vast amount of paperwork involved in carrying out this Zedoko work became even greater in the weeks leading up to religious feasts.«

The Rothschilds' activities as benefactors were to a large degree carried out by the women of the family, who were urged to engage in this kind of work by the dictates of the period. It was here – and only here – that they were able to make use of their knowledge and their talents. Yet the energy which the women invested in the foundations also shows that they enjoyed performing their task and did so with great dedication.

In the early days, the social policy of the family, which was derived from the ideas of the Jewish Zedaka, was conducted in a thoroughly traditional paternalistic manner. As modern society evolved, however, their charitable work gradually took on the character of preventive social measures, increasingly motivated by the desire to protect their own interests. It is legitimate to talk of »social policy« to the extent that the institutions set up by the family contained important elements of a forward-looking, systematic conception of social welfare provision such as later came to be practised within the framework of state-implemented social policy. The Rothschild family's work as benefactors went far beyond traditional forms of relief provision, not only in terms of its magnitude but also in terms of the approach on which it was based.

The Advent of the Age of Industry

»Baron Rothschild'sches Eisenwerk Witkowitz« (ironworks at Witkowitz).
Section from a colour lithograph by Ernst Wilhelm Knippel, c. 1850

For many years the main activity of banks was floating government securities. However, as of the 1830s an area of business emerged on the Continent which was to become the dominant economic sector and one that had heavy credit requirements: industry.

Banks only gradually started tapping this sector, as it was still not clear what risks were involved in financing industry. The Rothschilds, too, took their time before entering this future-oriented business. Yet, even though precisely they had the reputation of being conservative bankers, they were pioneering in that field which marked the beginning of industrialization on the Continent, namely railway construction.

The Steam Railway Comes to Austria

The railway was developed in England, but it was not Nathan but his brother Salomon in Vienna was the first Rothschild to recognize the profits that could be made. Salomon was fortunate to become acquainted with Franz Xaver Riepl (1787–1857), who held the Chair of Mineral Sciences and Merchandising at the Vienna Polytechnic and was active as a consultant to the Witkowitz Ironworks company in Moravia.

Riepl conceived a complete 2,200 kilometre-long railway network – a gigantic project at the time and completely without parallel. Salomon immediately recognized the potential that the railway offered and was willing to support the enterprise, albeit only the northern section of it, with a total of 450 kilometres of track. The planned line connected Moravia with the capital, Vienna. To ensure its profitability it was, however, necessary to extend the railway east into Galicia and to incorporate numerous towns that were trading centres into the plan. Riepl had initially thought of using a horse-drawn, rather than steam-powered train. Salomon sent him to England, where he was able to inform himself on the latest developments in the railway sector. The impressions he made there convinced him: Riepl planned the railway using a steam locomotive.

Salomon's support did not in itself suffice, for the expropriation of land necessary for the railway project's realization required the concession of the Emperor. In 1830 Salomon submitted a petition for permission to build the railway, but Emperor Franz rejected it because, to quote the heir apparent, »not even the coach to Kagran is always full«.

Salomon put the plan on ice and involved himself instead in the only Austrian railway at the time, the line from Gmunden to Budweis, which was, however, horse-drawn. It had been built in 1825 and primarily served to transport salt.

In 1835 Emperor Ferdinand ascended the Austrian throne. Salomon immediately resubmitted his application, and this was finally approved. He was granted the Royal privilege to build a railway from Vienna to Bochnia in Galicia, including branch lines, and to set up a joint stock company. By insisting that a joint stock company be established the government officials made certain that a project of such great public import was not solely in the hands of one private person. On the other hand, this type of organization suited the banker's interests, because the money invested in the railway was thus committed over the long-term, which was not usually the case with government bonds or trade loans.

Salomon then got together with Viennese financiers and drew up an outline for the corporation. This foresaw raising the construction costs of 12 million guilders via 12,000 shares at 1,000 guilders each. The administration had insisted that the shares

Ankunft der Dampfwagenzüge auf der Kaiser Ferdinands Nordbahn im Bahnhofe zu Brünn bei der Eröffnungsfahrt am 7ten July 1839.

Welcoming the inaugural trains at Brno Station on the occasion of the formal opening. Lithograph, 1839

be denominated in this manner, as the officials were skeptical whether the project would be successful. The high par value was intended to prevent larger sections of the population becoming involved in what might turn out to be a bankruptcy. However, only a third of the shares were even up for public subscription, as the founders of the railway had reserved the first 8,000 for themselves.

In 1837, seven years after the first petition for the concession, work began. Up to 14,000 workers were involved in building the first track section, which was formally opened in 1838. The overall line, with over 400 kilometres of track, was not completed until 1856.

The building project encountered various difficulties. Most of the workers had no experience in laying track, and Austrian foundries were unable to produce tracks of adequate quality. Both had to be procured from England, as did the locomotives. The importation of the first locomotive was a complex affair: disassembled into various pieces it was shipped to Trieste and then tortuously transported by horse-drawn cart to Vienna.

The first section between Deutsch-Wagram and Florisdorf was ready in the autumn of 1837 after eight and a half months' work. In November, the first trial runs were made with selected guests. The average speed of 33 kph was something contemporaries felt was very fast indeed.

In order to point up the fact that the government had approved the project, Salomon succeeded in arranging for the railway to bear the Emperor's name. Metternich's state continued to view the new means of transport with suspicion: in order to purchase a ticker, each passenger had first to procure a certificate that the police had nothing against him or her travelling.

The dawning of the age of the railway in Austria prompted fascination and skepticism among the public. Prior to the building of the »Nordbahn« (Northern Railway) track, Johann Strauss had composed a waltz on the theme. For one section of the public the railways were a technical achievement that constituted a patriotic deed; others, such as the poet Nikolaus Lenau, regarded them with dismay. The railway company correspondingly devoted great effort to obtaining public recognition. Naming the line after the Emperor was such a step.

Austria was not the only country where the Rothschilds financed railway building. The Frankfurt Rothschild bank had a stake in some German lines, e.g. the Taunus Railway, the Bavarian Eastern Railway, the Rhine-Nahe Railway, etc. However, it usually left it to other banks to initiate such projects. Only James in France was equally pioneering in the railway sector.

Salomon Becomes an Industrialist – The Witkowitz Ironworks

After Salomon had become familiar with the ins and outs of the »Nordbahn« project he started to think about track production. He immediately showed an interest in the Witkowitz Ironworks company, which was in the middle of the Ostravian coal and iron fields. Franz Xaver Riepl had introduced a modern oxidizing process there, puddling. Oxidizing, the process for transforming iron ore into workable iron, had hitherto been effected using costly charcoal. Puddling could be done with cheaper mineral coal. And only with the puddling technique could suitable railway tracks be produced.

In 1831, Cardinal Archduke Rudolf, the owner of the ironworks, died. But Salomon's application to lease the works was turned down. The Archbishopric of Olmuetz intervened, which owned other ironworks. They feared the other works would be rendered uncompetitive by the banker, with the enormous capital resources at his disposal. It therefore elected to purchase the works itself.

When Salomon's application to build the Northern Railways had been approved, he made use of a ruse to get at the ironworks. He deliberately started a rumour that the Northern Railway Company intended to build a puddling works of its own. Fear of an all-powerful competitor persuaded the Archbishopric to lease the works to Salomon. It was leased to a company set up by the Viennese wholesaler Geymüller, the four partners of which, including Salomon, all belonged to the founding committee of the Northern Railway Lines. A few years later Geymüller bought the works, but soon went bankrupt. Salomon was not able to acquire the works until 1843.

»Baron Rothschild'-sches Eisenwerk Witkowitz«. Colour lithograph by Ernst Wilhelm Knippel, c. 1850

Witkowitz was one of the most modern ironworks in Austria and the first to use mineral stone. It was here that, in 1836, the first Austrian coke-fired blast furnace was erected. It was needed to manufacture pig iron that was suitable for puddling. Witkowitz also had a rolling mill which was mainly used to produce rails. The foundry remained exclusively in Rothschild hands for 30 years before other partners, the Gutmann Brothers, were taken on, who possessed large coal fields in the Ostravian area.

Competitive pressure and growing demand from the railways for puddle iron made it necessary to extend the plant. The workforce, which totalled 42 in 1828, had risen to 2,775 by 1848. Towards the end of the century, the plant began producing additional material for the arms industry. In 1908 it employed nearly 20,000 people. As the workforce grew, the ironworks built numerous dwellings and social facilities.

Witkowitz, once only a village, grew into an industrial city.

Salomon's involvement in railway construction led to his interest in mining and industry. This led consequently to other participations, such as in the Viennese Locomotiv Fabriks AG.

The same was true of the Paris branch. The development of the various Rothschild branches thus moved in differing directions: the Frankfurt branch, which had been wary of an involvement in the railways, also showed no interest in industrial projects.

The Rise of Two Competitors: The Pereires

The credit needs of industry grew quicker than private bankers were able or wanted to handle. In France, it was the disciples of the philosopher Saint-Simon who first considered the idea of a different type of banking organization more suited to the new corporate world: a joint stock bank. By issuing shares they could draw money from broader segments of society, raise capital as required and place the most capable bankers at the head of the company. Capable entrepreneurs could realize plans with the assistance of such a bank that went far beyond his own capital resources, or, by making savings deposits with the bank, participate in that manner in the economic boom. The new type of bank was therefore superior to the private banks, which usually only did business up to a ceiling set by their own capitalization and were constrained by the fact that on occasion no talented younger member of the family was forthcoming to take over the helm.

The plan for such a vast joint stock bank was devised by two brothers who had, at the beginning of their career, worked for James de Rothschild, only to later become his fiercest rivals: the Pereire brothers.

Émile and Isaak Pereire were Sephardic Jews from Bordeaux who had moved to Paris, where they worked in the financial sector. Via a relative, they were admitted into the group of Saint-Simonists, most of the members of which came from banking circles. There, they received the motivation to develop two projects, which were first to closely connect them with the Rothschilds and then to make them bitter opponents.

Henri de Saint-Simon (1760–1825) had called the completion of the French Revolution, by which he meant that the ongoing power of the aristocracy and large landowners needed to be broken and an »industrial society« created in which bankers played a central role. He therefore argued for the economy to be placed under centralized control and for a single bank to be responsible for satisfying society's borrowing requirements.

The Pereire brothers wished to apply the principle of centralization to the railways and erect a nationwide rail network. Yet it was difficult to find sponsors, so they initially designed two short lines, from Paris to St. Germain and to Versailles. Both lines went to favourite Parisian leisure destinations. The hope was that this would sway public opinion in favour of the railways.

The search for financial backers was not easy in France, either. Eventually, James de Rothschild and a few other bankers agreed to finance the first two lines. James took over as administrative head of the project. Émile Pereire became director of the railways. But the competition was not about to be caught out. Immediately after the Versailles track had been built on the right bank of the Seine, a competing company acquired the concession to build a train to the same destination along the left bank.

James de Rothschild was involved in the construction of other French railway lines, which together created a large network. The most important was the Northern Railway Company, which ran to the Channel ports and Belgium. Accustomed to the cooperation between the Pereire brothers and James de Rothschild Émile Pereire had long since become James's »shadow« in the opinion of the press. Yet the ambitious brothers were aiming at higher things: They planned to form a joint stock bank as a counterbalance to the power of the Rothschilds.

The Battle of the Giants

The private bankers had hitherto neglected the nascent industrial sector. They were accustomed to dealing only with a small select clientele whom they usually also knew personally. Against this background, the odds were stacked against industrial companies, which took the form of stock companies being given loans. Bankers were not least suspicious of the industrialists' ongoing credit requirements.

In the wake of the economic crisis of 1848, which had also severely shaken the banking world, the Pereires' idea of founding a joint stock bank fell on fertile ground. 1852 saw the establishment of »Crédit Mobilier«, under their directorship. Its main purpose was financing industrial and railway companies. James was formally offered a stake in the bank, but such a minor one that he had no choice but to refuse.

Crédit Mobilier kicked off activities with a bang. Shares of a par value of 500 francs were immediately sold at double that price. By 1856 shares had almost reached the 2,000 francs mark, which was hardly surprising, as the dividend payment in 1855 had been over 40 percent.

Crédit Mobilier soon started founding railways and banks all over Europe, markedly intruding into erstwhile Rothschild territory. To do so, the new bank joined forces with other banks; the Rothschilds' response was to do the same. As a consequence, both banking groups set up numerous companies in direct competition with one another.

The first direct confrontation between the two groups took place in Germany. When Crédit Mobilier helped to set up the Darmstädter Bank für Handel und Industrie (Darmstadt Bank for Trade and Industry), right on Frankfurt's doorstep, the Frankfurt

bankers responded by setting up a bank of their own. Frankfurter Bank was thus founded in 1854 under the management of the Rothschilds. It was not, however, a credit and deposit bank, but instead served to support the private banks. Thus, it was authorized to issue banknotes, in the hope that this would relieve the shortage of currency in Frankfurt.

Crédit Mobilier also initially scored successes in Austria. The finance group it headed managed to acquire the concession to build the second largest Austrian railway line, the Südbahn or Southern Railways. However, the Rothschilds pre-empted the move to found a joint stock bank in that country. The Rothschilds adopted their competitor's strategy and established the Österreichische Credit-Anstalt für Handel

Share of the »Creditanstalt für Handel und Gewerbe«

und Gewerbe (Austrian Credit Institution for Industry and Commerce). The Pereires and the Rothschilds also both applied in Berlin for concessions to set up strongly capitalized joint stock banks. The two competing applications were filed within only days of each other at the relevant office, but the Prussian government rejected both. It feared that the government's influence on the economy would be impaired by the inauguration of a large joint stock bank.

The struggle continued in many European countries, from Spain to Russia. However, in the final analysis the Pereires' strategy proved to be wrong. Crédit Mobilier had retained for itself too many of the shares in industrial companies it had set up, had distributed excessively large dividends, and created overly meagre reserves to cope with difficult times. When economic activity panned out, the bank and the industrial companies it had established were caught up in a crisis. Crédit Mobilier's shares fell to 145 francs in November, 1867. The Pereire brothers were dismissed and the bank, although it continued to exist, thenceforth no longer posed a threat to the Rothschilds. The banks the latter had founded were more successful. The »Österreichische Creditanstalt« soon surpassed the Viennese branch of the House of Rothschild and became Austria's leading bank. The Frankfurter Bank still exists today, having merged with another bank.

Unequal Partners – Rothschild and Oppenheim

At a time when banks had no subsidiary offices, cooperation with other banking houses played an especially important role. Each of the Rothschild branches had its own network of correspondent banks: the banks held accounts with one another, offered one another preferential terms when floating bonds and exchanged trainees. One of the banks with which the Rothschilds collaborated throughout the 19th century was the Jewish banking firm »Sal. Oppenheim jr. & Cie« of Cologne. The form cooperation took changed in the course of time.

The Oppenheims had been in contact with the London House of Rothschild at an early date. During the first few decades of the 19th century, the two banks issued reciprocal letters of credit for people travelling abroad. Rothschild customers visiting the Rhineland received cash from Oppenheim, while Oppenheim customers in England were supplied by Rothschild. There were also family ties between the two families. In 1834 Abraham Oppenheim married Charlotte Beyfus, a granddaughter of Meyer Amschel. During the 1830s the London House of Rothschild had started sending its clients travelling in the Rhineland region to Schaaffhausen, Oppenheim's competition, and Abraham Oppenheim took the occasion of his wedding to ask Nathan to reinstate the links between the two banks.

The banks in Frankfurt had taken a stranglehold on government bond business and the Oppenheims as a consequence sought a new area of activity to accompany money exchange, current account loans and trade in bills. In the first half of the 19th century, the Rhine-Ruhr region gradually became industrialized, and the Oppenheims – like other Cologne-based banks –

capitalized on their geographical proximity to the developing areas by participating in the financing of industrial firms and transport enterprises. The Frankfurt House of Rothschild – and with it numerous other Frankfurt banks – in contrast retained a more conservative policy. It did not become directly involved in this line of business. Instead it confined itself to providing liquidity to the Cologne banks when they ran short.

Cooperation between the Oppenheims and Rothschilds intensified at the end of the 1830s, when banks first entered into the insurance business. Up until the 1840s, foreign firms controlled the insurance market in the Rhineland. However, a law of 1838 took away these firms' licences. The Paris House of Rothschild held shares in some of the French insurance firms which were now squeezed out. In order to avoid losing the firms' existing business, the Rothschilds teamed up with the Oppenheims and other Cologne bankers and founded a new insurance firm, Köln-

ische Feuer-Versicherungsgesellschaft, later known as »Colonia«. The insurance firms »Concordia«, Germania and »Kölner Rückversicherungs-Gesellschaft« were other joint operations set up at this time.

Links to the Rothschilds offered new business contacts and access to the necessary capital, making a partnership with them especially attractive. The cooperation took two forms. Firstly, the Rothschild banks themselves took on shares in the insurances. Secondly, they undertook to place shares with their illustrious customer base. Numerous French names among the list of initial shareholders demonstrate how active the Paris branch of the Rothschilds was. The Rothschilds contributed their name, which stood for security, their money and their connections, while the Oppenheims were active in the locality, conducting the founding negotiations and sitting on the board of directors. There were also numerous forms of secret cooperation. Via their seat on the Supervisory Board, the

Oppenheims improved the commission rate which the Rothschilds received for placing shares, and, in return, the Rothschilds cut them into the profits made on the sales.

The Cologne bank also involved the Rothschilds in its railway and mining operations. Business relations between the two families were not, however, always rosy. The Oppenheims were related to the Fould family, bankers in Paris. Fould was one of the co-founders of Crédit Mobilier and had also ensured that the Oppenheims had a stake in the project. The »German« Crédit Mobilier, namely the »Bank für Handel und Industrie« in Darmstadt, was also set up with the Oppenheims' help. This certainly did not make for an easy relationship, but it also did not bring cooperation between the two banks to a close. In 1870 the Frankfurt Rothschild bank and the Oppenheims, the banking firm of Bleichröder and Berlin »Discontogesellschaft« together founded the Preussische Centralboden bank. The initiative had again been made by the Oppenheims. It was they who had got the Rothschilds and other friendly banks involved.

For the Oppenheims, the success of the Rothschilds epitomized what they too were striving for. When they were elevated to the nobility in 1868, they incorporated their rivals' motto »Integritas, Concordia, Industria«

The Transfer of 5 Billion Francs

The growth of nationalism led to a loosening of ties between the various branches of the Rothschild family. They now became increasingly oriented towards the interests of their respective government. A visible sign of the separate ways the branches went was their behaviour during the Franco-Prussian War of 1870/71.

Following its victorious wars against Austria and Denmark, Prussia had consolidated its status as a major power. This led to tense relations between Prussia and France. On the question of the succession of the Spanish throne, in July 1870 the governments were on the verge of war. Prussia was in favour of a German prince, which France viewed as an affront. The Rothschilds wished to prevent a war; after all, they had banks in both countries and since the outcome of any war was unclear, it potentially threatened prices in government bonds. Emperor Napoleon II hoped England would act as a go-between and persuade Prussia to drop support of the German prince. To do so, he did not engage the services of a diplomat, but of Alphonse de Rothschild, whom he asked to get into contact with Gladstone, English Prime Minister of the day, via his cousin Lionel. Lionel received a telegram in code from Alphonse and immediately contacted Gladstone, who stated that England did not intend to become embroiled in the conflict. The English Rothschilds thereupon attempted via Gladstone's predecessor Disraeli to persuade England to block the threat of war. However, their efforts were in vain and war broke out between the two superpowers.

German and French nationalism blossomed with the outbreak of the Franco-Prussian War. The political agenda was shaped by patriotic deeds and gestures. Alphonse de Rothschild immediately surrendered his title as Prussian General

Consul. »Political events,« he wrote to Federal Chancellor Bismarck, »place me in the unfortunate position, of having obediently to inform your Excellence that I must resign as General Consul of the Northern German Confederation.«

Bismarck was admittedly not a friend, but certainly an old acquaintance of the Rothschilds. During his days as Prussian Emissary to the German Diet in Frankfurt the Rothschilds had managed his money for him and he had been their guest on several occasions. When Bismarck left that city in 1859 he had asked Mayer Carl von Rothschild whom he should contact in Berlin as a reliable banker. Mayer Carl proposed Gerson Bleichröder, the Rothschilds' long-standing correspondent in Berlin. Bismarck approved and Bleichröder became manager of his funds and soon the most important private banker in Prussia.

Above all, Bleichröder supplied the Paris Rothschild bank with political and economic information. And the link was maintained during the war. Bleichröder also participated along with the Frankfurt Rothschild bank and other banks in issuing a German War Bond.

German troops advanced swiftly on Paris. On September 19, 1870, Paris was surrounded and besieged. For some weeks, Ferrières Castle was the headquarters of the advancing German army. Alphonse de Rothschild had previously fled to the French capital. On entering the glorious rooms of the castle, the Prussian king is said to have remarked: »We can't match this; you have to be a Rothschild to make something like this.«

In Paris, it was difficult for the Rothschilds to obtain information from outside. Getting information out of the city was easier. Alexandre Guyard de Saint-Chéron was a political informant who kept the Lon-

don House of Rothschild abreast of the mood and events in Paris during the siege. Every day he sent them reports and political commentaries. A sign of the times, his letters were carried across the lines by balloon, a method that involved certain difficulties, as it was not possible to control the direction in which the balloons flew. Some of them fell into the hands of the Germans.

After a siege lasting more than four months, Paris capitulated. The Germans demanded that the city put up 200 million francs towards costs of the German war effort – a taste of what was to come when France as a whole capitulated. This happened a few months later, and the Germans specified that the French had to pay war reparations amounting to 5 billion francs. Alphonse de Rothschild was the financial expert representing the new French Republic at the peace negotiations. Gerson Bleichröder acted in the same capacity for the Germans.

Alphonse de Rothschild organized the transfer of the reparations, effected via a group of banks headed by the Rothschild bank. The five billion francs were taken to Germany in the form of cash, bills of exchange and foreign banknotes. The Rothschilds asked the banking houses with which they were associated to contribute to the extensive transfer. In order to pay for the war reparations, two bonds were issued, one worth three billion, the other two billion francs. On the first bond, the banks guaranteed to absorb securities amounting to 1 billion francs. The London House of Rothschild organized the sale of the bond in England and also guaranteed that a share of the bonds would be taken up by English banks.

The Purchase of the Suez Canal

Even if joint stock banks were increasingly squeezing private banks out of the marketplace, the Rothschilds initially managed to assert their leading position. Handling payment of the French reparations had after all shown just what means the Paris bank had at its disposal. And just a few years later the London Rothschild bank demonstrated that it was in a position to mobilize considerable capital resources very swiftly.

The Suez Canal was built in the 1860s by an international consortium. Britain had shown no interest in taking part in the venture. In order to ensure the success of the project, Egypt's ruler bought a large shareholding. The Canal was opened in 1869 and the steadily increasing volume of traffic now convinced the British go-vernment of the Canal's importance. London signalled its greater interest in a stake, especially as the Canal considerably shortened the time needed for the trip to India, which was still an English colony.

In 1874 Prime Minister Disraeli gave Lionel de Rothschild the task of finding out whether the Suez Canal Company would sell its shares. The company declined. Soon, a new opportunity arose, however. By 1875 the Egyptian ruler's financial difficulties had become so serious that he was forced to sell his shares. A French group of banks also showed an interest in buying. It was then a matter of which side could be first to raise

»HMS Malabar« in the Suez Canal. The Malabar transported the Khedive's shares – over 176,000 of them – to England in 1875.

the asking price of £4 million. Disraeli, who had still not received parliamentary approval for the expenditure, turned to the Rothschilds. A few days later they supplied him with the money without waiting for parliamentary ratification. This clinched the deal for the British government. In December 1875, more than 176,000 Suez Canal shares changed hands. The Rothschilds received 2.5% commission (= £100,000). To this they added 5% interest.

In a letter, Disraeli reported to Queen Victoria in euphoric terms on the acquisition of the Suez Canal shares: »You have it, Madam«, even though the Canal did not belong to England entirely, for the country was now solely largest shareholder. Disraeli emphasized that only the Rothschilds were capable of raising the required sum at such short notice. The parliamentary opposition took a different view, and criticized the high rate of interest which the Rothschilds were charging.

As long as the Egyptian viceroy ruled his country, the Rothschilds let other banks deal in Egyptian bonds. The feudal ruler was an unreliable debtor. When selling his shares to England, he had already pledged the interest on his Suez Canal stock for years to come. It was not until Britain took control of the country that they too issued a bond, payment of which was guaranteed by the European powers.

Black Gold

One consequence of industrialization was an increasing need for raw materials. The Paris branch of the Rothschilds was less involved in trade and extraction of raw materials as such, and concentrated on a select few products. They committed themselves solely to markets where few suppliers existed and where their capital resources as a result gave them an edge. This included the petroleum market, the great future of which only gradually became apparent. At around 1870 the French Rothschilds already had a stake in the importation of American crude oil to France. There were few uses at that time for mineral oil, which was mainly used for petroleum lamps and as machine grease. In this context, the Rothschilds had oil refineries built in Fiume in Austria and in Spain.

The need for cheap oil supplies for their refineries soon sparked the Rothschilds' interest in the oil fields around Baku in Russia. The world petroleum market was dominated by American oil. Russian oil was yet to make any impact: a government monopoly on oil extraction was preventing the development of a private oil industry there. It was only when the monopoly was lifted in 1872 that an oil industry began to grow. However, the poor transportation facilities prevented Russian oil from conquering more remote markets. The leading company in Baku, which belonged to the Swedish Nobel Brothers, therefore focussed on supplying the domestic Russian market. Around 1880 work started on building a railway from Baku to Batum on the Black Sea coast, with the intention of opening the European market up to Russian oil. When the rail link to the Baku oilfields appeared to be in danger of failing due to a shortage of funds, the Paris Rothschild bank recognized its chance. It guaranteed the

Oil plant near
Balakhani near Baku,
c. 1900

financing of the railway in exchange
for rights to oil plants. Soon thereafter it
founded one joint stock company for oil
extraction and another for transporting the
oil. Within a short time the Rothschilds had
become the second most powerful oil group
in Russia, headed only by the Swedish
Nobels.

In the early 1880s, 200 refineries were
operating in Baku (Azerbaijan). Batum,
some 850 kilometres west from Baku, was
where the oil companies concentrated their
storage tanks and operating equipment.
The first pipeline went into operation in
1906.

Within only a few years, Russia was
able to increase its oil output to such an extent that between 1898 and 1901 it was actually the world's leading producer. The
continuous rise in production forced firms
to seek new markets.

When the Rothschilds and other Russian oil producers started to target markets
in Central Europe they came into conflict
with Standard Oil. Under John Rockefeller,
the latter company had more or less established a monopoly on US oil extraction
and thus almost the whole world market
prior to the Russian fields being tapped. In
order to survive in the battle of the giant
corporations, the Rothschilds looked
around for allies. They had long since had
cooperation agreements with the Nobels
and other Russian producers, but these soon
transpired to be inadequate. Oil had increasingly come to be used as engine fuel
and this had prompted drilling for oil in
Indonesia, a Dutch colony. This led to the
company Royal Dutch being set up, which
soon merged with the transport firm Shell.
The Paris House of Rothschild decided to
join this new group, which became ever
more powerful. Price competition between
the them and Standard Oil was often fierce.
Frequently, one of the two lowered prices in

a region that was being fought for to a figure lower than that at which the competition could sell while at the same time hiking prices in another region via a company that belonged to their group. Standard Oil started selling petroleum lamps in Asia at cost price in order to generate demand for oil there.

The coalitions between companies within a group were highly unstable at the turn of the century. The Rothschilds at one point considered siding with Standard Oil while simultaneously negotiating with Royal Dutch. In 1912 the Rothschilds swapped their holding in the Russian joint stock company, worth a total 27.5 million roubles, for shares in Shell/Royal Dutch. Yet the Rothschilds had to accept that the oil companies were highly aggressive. Moreover, oil activities required a far greater organizational capacity than that afforded by an office on the top floor of the Paris bank. The Rothschilds had to recognize that the oil companies were simply superior – by abandoning independent Rothschild oil companies.

Receiving Tsar Nicholas II at the Rothschild Oil Company in Batum, c. 1900

Worldwide Expansion

During the second half of the 19th century the Rothschilds' business ventures were characterized by two trends: they expanded operations to embrace the whole globe while at the same time forfeiting their leading role in banking.

The expansion in Rothschild operations resulted from the burst in industrialization, which led above all to the countries with large raw material deposits being integrated into the world economy. The Rothschilds issued bonds for such countries or became involved in the trade in and extraction of raw materials. Yet, hand in hand with the wider spread of the Rothschilds' capital resources across various economic sectors went a decrease in the importance of the Rothschild bank. Groups emerged in the different industrial segments specialized in particular products and the Rothschilds were not in a position to dedicate all their resources to one such segment to compete with such groups. In banking, the expanding large banks gradually squeezed the private banks out of the market.

Bonds

The Rothschilds' main area of business remained the bonds business. The main clientele was composed no longer of European governments, who meanwhile approached rather bank consortia when availing themselves of credit; the member banks of such consortia were prepared to accept a lower profit margin in exchange for a better risk spread.

Non-European countries, by contrast, continued to be important for the Rothschilds. The English Rothschild bank, for example, had both Chile and Brazil as steady customers.

In 1824, the London bank issued first bond on behalf of the fledgling Brazilian state, and many more were to follow.

Brazil remained a client of the Rothschilds throughout the 19th century. In 1855 the House of Rothschild was appointed as Brazil's official state banker in London. It issued all Brazilian bonds and carried out all of the government's foreign payment transactions.

In 1886 the English Rothschilds issued their first bond for Chile. They hoped that, like Brazil, the Chilean government would soon declare them to be its exclusive bank. However, in 1889, when Chile needed more money for railway construction, the government turned instead to two German banks. The Chilean credit was fixed in such a way that the government was able to exploit the competition between the banks. In the years that followed, Chile continued to steer an independent course, changing banks at will. All the same, the Rothschilds remained Chile's most favoured bank until well into the 20th century. In the period 1886-1912 alone, the Rothschilds issued 14 bonds worth a total of £30 million. Yet the large banks soon butted on in this area, too, thus in the course of time reducing the significance of the private banks. The geographical expansion of the Rothschild banks was, however, not just confined to banking, but also extended to the raw materials extraction.

Raw Materials

The Rothschilds had already done trade in raw materials, such as tobacco, cotton, mercury and precious metals in the first half of the 19th century. Mercury was of particular interest to the Rothschilds from that point onwards when it controlled the complete output of the mine in Almadèn in Spain. In the first half of the 19th century, Almadèn was one of only two European sources of mercury. The government used its mercury production as a pledge on loans granted by the Rothschilds. This left them in control of the mines' entire production in the 1830s and '40s. It was a profitable business for them, while state income from the mines was very low. Given that the Rothschilds also controlled the entire output of the second European mercury mine in Idria, they totally dominated the mercury market during the 1830s and '40s. With the Spanish government in permanent need of credit, production remained in the hands of the Rothschilds, with only a few short interruptions, until 1921.

For the Rothschilds, mercury was an interesting raw material precisely because it was needed to refine precious metals, and the company was also active in trade and processing of gold and silver. As early as 1792, Meyer Amschel offered to sell silver to the Electoral Mint in Hesse. Nathan was involved in the minting of Portuguese coins for Wellington's army. Throughout the 19th century, all five Houses of Rothschild were involved in the precious metals trade. When gold was struck in California in 1849, they immediately sent an agent to San Francisco. By virtue of its gold and diamond fields, South Africa became one of the domains in which the London branch operated. The Rothschilds occupied such an important position in this market that from 1919 until the present day the world price of gold has been fixed on the New Court premises of the Rothschild Bank in London.

The Rothschild stake in the traditional gold and silver trade was complemented toward the end of the 19th century by a commitment to diamond mining. When diamonds were discovered near the South African town of Kimberley in 1870, a huge wave of adventurers descended on the area.

Diamond mine near
Kimberley, 1890

They were only able to acquire small plots of land in the diamond fields and lived in hope that their one-man operation would be the one to strike it rich. In the course of time, however, it became necessary to mine underground, which required large sites and large volumes of capital. Soon the rights to the mines were owned by only two firms.

However, with prices fluctuating widely, any kind of competition in the diamond market was a danger. Therefore, under the leadership of Cecil Rhodes, one of the two firms tried to buy the other one out. The necessary capital was put up by the English House of Rothschild. In 1889, for the sum of £1.4 million, the French firm was incorporated into a new company, De Beers Consolidated, which now held a monopoly of diamond mining in Kimberley. The Rothschilds were this company's largest shareholders.

Further raw materials, such as nickel and mineral oil, were later also included in the Rothschilds' range of holdings. The Rothschilds' strategy focused on those raw materials for which there were few suppliers and whose markets were therefore easy to control. In 1880 large nickel deposits were discovered in the French colony of New Caledonia. The Rothschilds joined »Société Le Nickel«, a company formed to extract the raw material, and soon they were in charge. For a time, supplies from New Caledonia were able to meet the total world demand for nickel. Around 1902 the firm already employed a workforce of 1,800. When it was discovered that steel became more durable when enriched with nickel, this metal took on great significance for the armaments industry. A frantic search began for new sources of nickel. New mines were discovered, new companies founded. By striking agreements with other groups, Société Le Nickel was able to secure a segment of the world nickel market for itself.

The Rio Tinto mines, which until 1873 belonged to the Spanish government, were Europe's largest producers of copper. Even so, the mines operated at a loss. The main reason for this was the lack of adequate

1

transport facilities, the improvement of which would have entailed huge investments. In 1873 the mines were taken over as a joint stock company by a group of foreign financiers. At the time, the Rothschilds were only indirectly involved in the copper trade: they supplied large firms with credit to purchase copper. Out of this they developed an interest in extracting the raw material itself. However, in the initial stages, their purchases of Rio Tinto shares remained hidden from the public eye. They did not sit on the company's board of directors either, but undoubtedly sent their people to its meetings. According to a remark by Guy de Rothschild, the family made it a rule not to adopt a high profile in companies that they did not actually control. In 1905 the London and Paris Houses held over 30 percent of the Rio Tinto shares between them.

Industrial enterprises also provided the Rothschilds with an opportunity to do banking business: in 1895 the English Rothschild bank took on the task of issuing a bond on the company's behalf.

The growing demand from the manufacturing industry led to intensified exploitation of mineral resources. In many regions, the hunt was on for raw material deposits and the number of suppliers soon increased. Thus the Rothschilds soon lost their strong influence over the market. By the end of the 19th century, the name Rothschild was still regarded by the public as a synonym for wealth. But the family's power had waned: industrialization had brought forth larger concentrations of capital, and those new names that came to be equated with modern wealth were the names of industrialists.

Rio Tinto mine
in Spain, c. 1905

The End of a Bank Steeped in Tradition: Frankfurt 1901

For a long time, the Frankfurt bank had been declining in importance relative to the other Rothschild banks. Around 1900 it was the branch with by far the lowest business volume. In 1901 the head of the bank, Wilhelm Carl von Rothschild, died without leaving any male successors. Salomon Albert von Rothschild of Vienna announced that he was willing to keep the bank running on a temporary basis until such time as a younger member of the family was able to take over the firm. Yet eventually the family decided otherwise: in June 1901 the bank that was so rich in tradition was finally closed down. Disconto-Gesellschaft, a joint stock bank based in Berlin with which the Frankfurt branch had already been collaborating for some time, took on the staff and the business of the private bank. Indeed, as early as 1885, this collaboration had earned the Frankfurters the criticism from their French cousins that they were no more than a satellite of the Berlin bank.

The closure of the Frankfurt House of Rothschild marked the end of an era. The heyday of the private banks was over.

The Rothschilds
in the Twentieth Century

Palace in Prinz-Eugen-Straße, Vienna, residence of Louis de Rothschild, May, 1943.
Round salon with a portrait of Adolf Hitler

The end of the Frankfurt bank and the termination of the partnership agreements between the Rothschilds in Austria, England and France marked a major turning point in the family's history. From now on the Rothschild banks in the various countries went their own ways, the unity of the family ceased to be of importance for the companies. Not a few family members quit the traditional paths ordained for them and devoted themselves to tasks outside banking. Only two issues affected the family as a whole in the 20th century: anti-Semitic defamation and persecution during the Nazi period and a commitment to Palestine and later to Israel. The activities to support east European settlers in Palestine was originally the work of only one family members: Edmond de Rothschild, who, as of 1882, together with his wife made promoting the early Jewish settlements his life's work. He is a typical example for the trend seen in the fourth-generation family members, many of whom turned their backs on banking and devoted themselves to tasks beyond the traditional career in banking. It was not until later that supporting the Jewish settlements in Palestine and building the State of Israel became a project that a large part of the family dedicated itself to.

Propaganda, Persecution and Relief Work

The Rothschilds during the Nazi Era

In the 20th century, although they no longer played the prominent public role that their financial dominance had allowed them to play in the first half of the 19th century, the Rothschilds retained a certain celebrity and a presence in the public eye as private bankers, collectors and philanthropists. Yet it was the Nazis who first exploited this public awareness of the Rothschilds to make them a favourite target of anti-Semitic propaganda. The Nazis were able to draw on the defamatory portrayals and caricatures of the 19th century, as well as on numerous popular publications about the history of the Rothschilds which had appeared since the beginning of the 20th century. The fate of the Rothschilds during the Nazi era shows with exemplary clarity how the methods of anti-Semitic propaganda work and what its murderous consequences can be.

The Rothschilds as Portrayed in Nazi Propaganda

The Rothschilds drew the attention of Nazi propaganda because, as a European family of bankers, they seemed to epitomise the anti-Semitic cliché of the »power of international Jewish finance«. Nazi writers deliberately revived widespread legends and myths about the family, which gave their defamatory portrayals an air of plausibility and historical accuracy. Aside from countless newspaper articles, this is shown with particular clarity in Erich Waschnek's film »Die Rothschilds« (The Rothschilds), which dates from 1940. This was the first in a series of anti-Semitic and anti-British films which – so Goebbels' Ministry of Propaganda hoped – would help to reinforce the German war effort. It was followed by two more anti-Semitic films, »Jud Süss« (Jew Süss) and »Der ewige Jude« (The eternal Jew), which served as the propagandistic prelude to the deportation and murder of the Jews.

»Die Rothschilds« reproduced two of the best-known legends surrounding the family's rise to prominence. The film opens in Meyer Amschel's office in Jews Lane. Elector Wilhelm of Hesse, fleeing Napoleon's advancing armies, has entrusted Meyer Amschel with his fortune. This money, characterised as »blood money« because the Elector earned it by selling Hessian soldiers, is taken by Rothschild's sons, James and Nathan, who use it in shady and unscrupulous dealings to increase the family fortune. This is shown above all in the depiction of how Wellington's army in Spain was financed. The money entrusted to the Rothschilds passes through so many – Jewish – hands that only a fraction of it actually reaches the troops at the front. The message of these suggestive images is clear: while English or German soldiers spill their blood on the battlefield, the Rothschilds, their Jewish helpers and the British officials and generals who collaborate with them, are syphoning off for themselves the money that was supposed to go to the troops.

The film's central figure is Nathan, who is using the elector's money to do successful business but who, despite his growing wealth and his efforts to be accepted by society, is spurned by the British bankers. Nathan lands his greatest coup over the Battle of Waterloo, as he is the first person on the London stock exchange to learn the outcome. By spreading false rumours of Napoleon's victory, he reaps huge speculative profits and is at the same time able to ruin his rivals, the British bankers.

The film presents this famous legend, and all the other episodes that surround it, as historical fact. This was underscored by the book whose appearance was timed to co-incide with that of the film and bore the programmatic subtitle: »A True Account«. In order not to undermine the claim of the film to historical accuracy, the Ministry of Propaganda had issued

Meyer Amschel Rothschild and Elector William I. Still from »Die Rothschilds«, 1940

Nathan Rothschild.
Still from
»Die Rothschilds«,
1940

instructions to writers of reviews and previews not to refer to it as an anti-Semitic film.

Yet its anti-Semitic intention is not only evidenced by the – ostensibly true – representation of the Rothschilds' fraudulent business practices but above all in the portrayal of the characters. Meyer Amschel is shown as the cliché of a traditional ghetto-dwelling Jew: wearing a kaftan and side curls, obsequious, devious and wily. Nathan and James, by contrast, appear as modern businessmen in frock coats and top hats, yet their behaviour, their gestures and facial expressions reveal - and this is the message of the film – that they too, no less than their father, are haggling and cheating Jews.

However, the unscrupulous accumulation of wealth is not the only goal of Nathan and his brothers, according to the film, which implies that their true aims are more ambitious than that. In the closing scene, Nathan stands in front of a map of Europe and explains his plans for the future to his

James Rothschild.
Still from »Die
Rothschilds«, 1940

most important business associate, a British treasury official named Herries. He aims to set up branches in the capitals of Europe, which he joins up on the map with lines that form a Star of David, its lowest point touching Jerusalem. What the Rothschilds are really striving for - so we are meant to conclude – is Jewish world domination. Their ally is the British Empire, and in particular its unscrupulous leaders who, like Herries and Wellington, collaborate with the Rothschilds in return for personal gain. This shows up the anti-British sentiment behind the film, which it shares with numerous UFA productions of this period.

The film is more subtle in the way it portrays a further aim of Nathan. He tries to win the favour of the wife of his main rival, the banker Turner. Yet at their very first encounter, even before she knows he is a Jew, Turner's wife – the stereotypical blond-haired Aryan woman – snubs him out of an instinctive sense of racial propriety. And she also rebuffs his later approaches, which are made to look utterly ridiculous in the film, with pride and contempt, thus thwarting his goal of »defiling Aryan blood«.

The figure of Nathan thus stands in the film as a paradigm for all the anti-Semitic stereotypes regarding the aims of Jewish existence: deceit, world domination and »defiling the blood« of »pure« races. Yet the film was not the success its makers had hoped for, and indeed was withdrawn from the distributors' lists not long after the premiere for fear of endangering the reception of »Jud Süss«, which was in fact seen by over 5 million cinema-goers.

Erich Waschnek's Rothschild film had two precursors. The first, a German silent movie made in 1922, was based on the play »Die fünf Frankfurter« (The five Frankfurters) by Carl Rössler. No surviving copies exist today. The second, »The House of Rothschild«, a 1934 Hollywood production, based its plot on precisely the same legends and period as the Nazi film. Here too, Nathan and his activities are at the centre of interest. However, the rise of the

Nathan Rothschild talking with the wife of Baring, his competitor. Still from »Die Rothschilds«, 1940

Rothschilds is presented in a favourable light as the realisation of the American dream. This film, which in its depiction of the Frankfurt ghetto makes allusions to the contemporary Nazi pogroms, was not shown in Germany. Erich Waschnek's version was thus in a certain sense a response to the American production, inverting its democratic message in affirmation of the American tradition. The Nazi film »Der ewige Jude« (The eternal Jew) even takes some of the scenes from the Hollywood production and uses them, in a distorted reproduction, as quasi-documentary material to demonstrate »Jewish business practices«.

When the Rothschild film was re-released in 1941 under a new title, »Aktien auf Waterloo« (Shares in Waterloo), it appeared with a significant new epilogue: »Since the making of this film, the last descendants of the House of Rothschild have fled Europe as refugees. The struggle against their partners in crime, the British plutocracy, continues.«

This was a gloating summary of the »achievements« of anti-Semitic propaganda and policy as they had affected the Rothschilds in the territories now controlled by the Nazis.

Vienna 1938: Detention and Aryanization

Immediately after the occupation of Austria by the German army and Hitler's enthusiastic reception in Vienna, Louis de Rothschild was arrested. Realising the danger in time, his brothers Alphonse and Eugène had been able to flee for safety. Louis de Rothschild spent over a year in Gestapo custody as a bargaining lever which the Nazis hoped would force the Rothschilds to surrender their assets and in particular to sell the Witkowitz steelworks.

Hermann Göring was the first to appreciate how important the Rothschild steelworks in Witkowitz could be for German war production. After protracted negotiations with Dresdner Bank, acting

Cheering masses greet Hitler in Vienna on March 12, 1938

Louis de Rothschild and the socialist politician Leopold Kuntschak in Gestapo custody, 1938-9

under orders from Göring and Himmler, the family eventually had no choice but to agree to the sale. Only then was Louis released. The family's extensive assets in Austria were »aryanized«. Yet before he was allowed to emigrate, Louis de Rothschild also had to pay over 5 million marks in so-called »Tax on Persons Fleeing the Reich« after his total assets were estimated at 21 million marks.

The family's houses in Vienna were particularly highly coveted objects for Aryanisation. The SS Security Service set up headquarters in the requisitioned residence of Alphonse de Rothschild. The Palace in Prinz-Eugen-Strasse, home of Louis de Rothschild, was requisitioned in 1938 and turned into the »Central Office of Jewish Emigration« run by Adolf Eichmann, which was responsible for organising the expulsion of the Jews from Austria. The famous art collections of the three Rothschild brothers were also »aryanized« in 1938/39 and handed over to Austrian museums. Many of the most important paintings were selected for the »Neue Kunstmuseum« in Linz, founded by Hitler himself for the purpose of exhibiting the crowning achievements of German art. As he was never able to bring his gigantic plans to

Palace in Prinz Eugen
Strasse, residence of
Louis de Rothschild,
May, 1943.
Staircase with a
swastika

Paris 1940: Persecution and Escape

As had happened earlier in Vienna, the German invasion of France in the summer of 1940 was followed by the seizure of the Rothschild's houses and collections. The German press ran propaganda articles depicting the ostensibly extravagant and decadent lifestyle of the French Rothschilds and their wealth. Portrayals such as these were meant to justify the German actions, not only against the Rothschilds but against all Jews.

The members of the family attempted to escape the Nazis, and fled to Britain or the United States. Élie and Alain de Rothschild, who were soldiers in the French army, were taken prisoner and held in German prisoner-of-war camps without being recognised as Jews. Guy, Philippe, James and Claude de Rothschild were later to join de Gaulle's forces. Some of their dependents – Philippe de Rothschild's wife, Elizabeth de Chambure, for example – were deported and sent to concentration and extermination camps, where they were murdered.

The family's confiscated art collections – at least, those works that could not be hidden – were shipped to Germany and put in storage in Neuschwanstein and other depots. A special fate awaited the Rothschilds' libraries. Like all the major book collections owned by Jews, they were seized by the task force sent out by Reichsleiter Rosenberg and taken back to Frankfurt to form part of the Institute for the Study of the Jewish Question, which was founded in 1941. From Paris alone, 1,400 crates of books were shipped to the Institute, which was part of the National Socialist »Hohe Schule« (the cadre school for the Nazi elite) and was devoted to researching Jewish history and culture from an anti-Semitic standpoint. Jewish prisoners were forced to translate Hebrew and Yiddish texts.

fruition, the works ended up in storage in various places, one of which was Neuschwanstein Castle.

Most of the Rothschild town houses in Vienna were destroyed in the war, so that hardly any of these impressive buildings have survived to the present day.

After 1945, by no means all of their seized property was returned to the family. When the works of art were returned, Alphonse's widow, Clarice de Rothschild, donated a number of very valuable pieces to the Austrian nation. This explains why, for example, the famous Rothschild prayer book, dating from the 16th century, is still in the possession of the Österreichische Nationalbibliothek.

Furniture from the Parisian houses of the Rothschilds, in storage at Neuschwanstein, photographed in 1945

Library at the »Institut zur Erforschung der Judenfrage« in Frankfurt on Main. Photograph by Paul Wolff, 1941

London 1938: Relief Work and Rescue Operations

As early as 1933 the Rothschilds in Britain and France became involved in the work of aiding refugees, and played a prominent role in the founding of committees to help Jews who were suffering persecution in Germany. They made public appeals and organised charity events on behalf of the German Jews.

In particular, the family supported the evacuation of children, some 10,000 of whom were thus enabled to emigrate from Germany and Austria and settle in Britain up until 1940. One of the ways in which the family helped was to provide buildings in Britain and France in which the children could be housed. One example was the rescue of children from the orphanage run

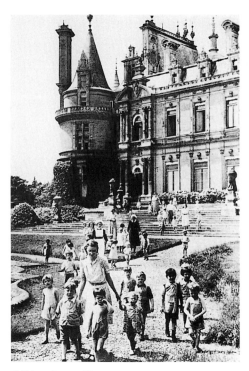

Children housed in
Waddesdon Manor.
Photograph, 1941

Semitic propaganda; in Austria and France as well as Germany, the Goldschmidt-Rothschild family suffered personally under the Nazis' apparatus of oppression which they - following the family tradition of defending persecuted Jews – did their best to oppose from their bases in Britain and, until 1940, in France.

by the Flersheim-Sichel Foundation in Frankfurt. Thanks to the support of the Rothschilds, the 30 children who lived there were able to leave Germany in 1939, together with the staff, and travel to Britain. Here they lived in an outhouse of Waddesdon Manor. Evacuee children from London were also brought here to escape the German air raids.

The fate suffered by the Rothschilds is a particularly chilling example of how anti-Semitic portrayals are followed by murderous deeds. The image of the worldwide Jewish conspiracy, embodied by this family whose activities spanned Europe, was deliberately evoked in order to justify persecution and mass murder. However, the Rothschilds were not merely the victims of anti-

Why There Are Countless Streets Named Rothschild in Israel

Edmond de Rothschild and Palestine

In Haifa, Jerusalem and Tel Aviv, in Rishon Le-Zion and in numerous other places in Israel, streets and buildings are named after Edmond and Adelheid de Rothschild and their son James Armand. Banknotes and coins bore portraits of them, and bottles of wine woo customers with the name »Rothschild«. What is less well-known is that countless locations in Israel themselves bear the names of this family. For example Zikhron Yaakov, named after Jacob/James; Maskereth Batya named after Betty; and Kefar Meir Shefaya named after Meyer Amschel himself.

This honour dates back to Edmond de Rothschild's commitment to the cause of Palestine. From his 37th year onwards, he devoted himself predominantly to establishing Jewish settlements in Palestine. And he dedicated the larger part of his wealth to this undertaking.

It is unclear what actually sparked Edmond's interest in Palestine. There was admittedly a Rothschild family tradition of regularly donating money to Jews living in Hebron, Safed and Tiberias, and Edmond's father James had paid for a hospital to be built in Jerusalem's Old City in 1855. However, no direct link obtains between this tradition and support for Jewish immigrants from eastern Europe who wished to live not from donations but from the fruits of their own labour.

When the west European Jewish communities heard the terrible reports of the persecution of Jews in Russia and how many were forced to leave that country, they organized extensive assistance to help their uprooted brethren reach the United States. Appeals for help by Russian Jews who wanted for national Jewish reasons to immigrate to Palestine fell for the main on deaf ears.

Edmond was almost the only person who promised them help. His personal situation left him much scope for a new activity. At that time he had devoted the lion's share of his time to his art collection. Banking did not really interest him. He was admittedly a partner in the bank and discharged certain duties in railway management, but he more or less left the business side of things to his brothers. In 1877 he had married his cousin Adelheid. Born in Frankfurt, she was the eldest daughter of Wilhelm Carl and Hannah Mathilde von Rothschild.

Edmond de Rothschild, 1845–1934, c. 1890

Rishon Le-Zion, 1885.
After a drawing by a
settler

»It is my desire to facilitate the development of the settlements that currently exist.«
Edmond de Rothschild, 1882

Edmond's commitment to the Palestine cause commenced in the summer of 1882. At that time, the Chief Rabbi of the Jewish community in Paris recommended to two delegates that they turn to Edmond. The one, Rabbi Mohilever from Russia, sought support for his plan to settle Russian Jews who had been trained in agriculture in Palestine. The other, Josef Feinberg from Palestine, sought on behalf of the settlers to raise money for the Rishon Le-Zion (»The First in Zion«) settlement, which would not have survived without outside assistance. Together, these men brought about a complete change in Edmond's life.

Edmond de Rothschild's commitment started with concrete promises of help for the settlers in Rishon Le-Zion. The twenty founding families arrived in Turkish Palestine in 1882 to find awful conditions awaiting them. They had paid out much money for sandy soil that was covered in alfalfa grass and therefore could not be tilled without agricultural equipment. Water was the main problem. When the Rishon Le-Zion settlers sent Josef Feinberg, one of their number, to Europe, they desperately needed money to drill for water. Edmond granted them 25,000 francs to this end. He also sent technical equipment and experts. When, in February, 1883, the settlers at long last struck water, 60 metres down, Edmond was already full of ideas and plans for the construction of this and additional settlements.

»Father of the Yishuv« –
Father of Jewish Colonization

From the very outset, Edmond was aiming at more than merely providing philanthropic support. He sensed that in view of the ongoing persecution, Jews would continue to be forced to leave eastern Europe and he therefore wished to create the basis for them to be able to live in Palestine. To do so, the goal was to transform the existing settlements into centres in the vicinity of which immigrants could then settle. Edmond was prepared to promote all settlements which were not able to secure their own existence.

Almost all the settlements founded around 1881-3 in Palestine by Jewish immigrants from Eastern Europe applied to Edmond for help.

These included the Samarin settlement at the foot of Mt. Carmel, roughly 30 kilometres south of Haifa. Romanian Jews had founded a settlement there, which Edmond later named Zikhron Yaakov after his father.

When the settlers first contacted the Baron, approximately 400 of them lived in Samarin in great poverty. Many had contracted malaria, yellow fever or cholera. Moreover, they were in debt to Romanian financiers who had lent them the money for the trip to Palestine and to purchase land.

Approximately one year after founding the settlement, they turned to the »well-known benefactor« in Paris for help. Their situation was so desperate that they were willing to be completely dependent on Edmond:

»We place ourselves in Your Hands; the land of Samarin shall belong to You. We

Zikhron Yaakov.
Around 1890.
In the foreground the factory for producing wine barrels. In the background is the Bat Shlomo settlement.

give ourselves over to You and undertake with this letter to reorganize the colony as You should so wish. We shall blindly obey the administrator whom You shall choose to send to lead us. We promise not only to follow the advice he shall give us, but also to completely obey his instructions. We wish to work as real settlers.«

The settlers had taken advice beforehand in order to find the tone that best appealed to Edmond. Edmond accepted their request for support, paid off their debts for them and took on the further financing of the settlement. In the years that followed he did indeed give many orders and instructions via his administrators. However, at a later date the settlers were not as willing to obey as at the time of their greatest distress. Edmond wanted to assist Jews emigrating from Russia at all costs, but he was convinced that in the difficult initial period it was better to have settlers with experience in agriculture than idealists and enthusiasts

from the cities. When Rabbi Mohilever found eleven farming families in Russia who wanted to emigrate to Palestine, Edmond redeemed the promise he had given. He had land bought near Rishon Le-Zion, houses built and provided a basic financial framework.

Compared with other settlements, this site, called Ekron, developed better than did the others in economic terms, until, that is, Edmond forced the settlers to use some of the land for wine-growing. During Edmond's visit to Palestine in 1887 Ekron was renamed Maskereth Batya (in memory of Betty) in honour of his mother.

The settlements were always established in line with one and the same pattern: The houses in the settlement were built along one road; behind it lay gardens used by the individual inhabitants. Alongside the settlers' houses were small houses for Jewish labourers and larger houses for the administrators. The settlers' houses as a rule consisted of two rooms and a stable in the courtyard. They were built of local lime-

Synagogue in Rishon Le-Zion

Workers in a silk
factory in Rosch Pina,
c. 1890

stone, whereas the red roof tiles were imported from southern France.

Edmond also provided the religious
and social institutions. He had synagogues,
schools, medical stations and, at a later
date, community halls, built in all of the
settlements. Edmond was strongly in
favour of children receiving religious instruction and of Hebrew being used as the
»lingua franca«. The school in Rishon
Le-Zion was the first school in Palestine in
which classes were all held in Hebrew.

As we know from countless handwritten letters sent by him, Edmond concerned
himself with all the different sides to the
settlements. He set no great store by the
abilities of the settlers themselves. He sent
gardeners, engineers and administrators
from France, furnishing them with far-rea-
ching powers. These officials were instructed to inform Edmond in great detail about
the settlements and the settlers. Edmond
devised numerous ideas for farming in the
settlements and then instructed the settlers
to put them into practice. Alongside the
fields of grain, fruit orchards, almond

orchards, orange groves and vines were
planted. Edmond introduced silk production to the settlement of Rosch Pina, the
first in Galilee: French mulberry trees were
planted and a factory built to spin and
weave the raw silk. The plan was to employ
children from orthodox Jewish families in
nearby Safed, whose families had hitherto
lived solely off donations. This educational
objective was not reached, nor was the
industrial enterprise successful.

Edmond believed that setting up industrial companies alongside the agricultural sector was highly important for the
overall development of the utterly neglected country. All the other projects, such
as the production of perfumes and glass,
also had to be abandoned. Nevertheless, he
repeatedly launched new projects, albeit
without much support from the settlers,
who wished to live as farmers.

The most complex and undoubtedly
the most controversial of Edmond's projects was his introduction of viticulture.
Encouraged by the Rothschild vineyards in

southern France, he sent cuttings from the best vines in Bordelais, but the soil and climate were unsuitable for them. Only after many years were vines cultivated that survived. Processing was no less difficult. All the plants, such as wine presses and distillation equipment, had to be imported from France, as were the materials for producing pipes and barrels.

Between 1884 and 1899 Edmond invested roughly 12 million francs in viticulture, without there being any sign that the enterprise would be profitable. In Palestine itself there was no market for table wines, which counted as luxuries at the time; and the quality was not sufficient to ensure sales on the Central European market. A limited amount of kosher wine, in other words wine produced in keeping with ritual prescriptions, was sold in Russia and Poland. But a large part of good harvests could not be sold at all and Edmond simply bought it up. We do not know just how large the enormous losses made were, as until 1900 no books were kept.

Against all economic common sense, Edmond stuck with viticulture. Numerous settlers in Zikhron Yaakov, Rishon Le-Zion and Ekron attempted in vain to get him to change his mind. They had to make part of their land available for wine-growing and had to work tending the vines and in wine production. They thus lost any independence they once had. Over the years, the introduction of the vines as a monoculture changed the social structure of the settlements. Thus, around 1900 roughly 100 of the colonizers in Zikhron Yaakov were supervisors for the Arab and Jewish workers, carters and artisans. Approximately 90 administrators organized planting, harvesting, purchasing and the cellars. During the harvests additional day labourers were employed. All were economically utterly dependent on Edmond's subsidies.

The development imposed on the colonies by Edmond and his French administrators inevitably led to conflict and revolt. Many settlers felt they were controlled, patronized, robbed of any economic independence and their personal dignity violated. Settlers rose up against the highhanded administrators; in Ekron they refused to till the fields in the Sabbatical year; some refused to give up their land; others tried to found interest groups to

1

combat the Baron's overwhelming power. They were not successful. The power of money in distant Paris decided the day and Edmond ruled with an ever more iron fist. Some of the settlers were forced to leave the area. They included Josef Feinberg following an uprising among settlers in Rishon Le-Zion.

Even during his first trips to Palestine in 1887, 1893 and 1899 and his visits to the settlements, Edmond did not come into contact with the settlers or familiarize himself with their interests.

»It is not a private, but rather an historical and national undertaking.«
Edmond in a speech in 1894

In 1900 the era of Edmond's personal and patriarchal management of the settlements and the high-handed treatment of the settlers by his French administrators came to end. Edmond had recognized that things could not go on that way. It had been his aim to help Jewish immigrants from Eastern Europe who were in distress and to create a sound economic basis for the development of the various settlements. With his numerous ideas and projects and the substantial funds he had committed to them, he had worked against precisely achieving this goal. Edmond transferred administration of the settlements to the Jewish Colonization Association (JCA). The latter was an international organization predominantly promoting the emigration of Jews to South America. The management in Palestine was placed in the hands of a Palestine Commission, founded on signature of the contract, of which Edmond was chairman. Work in Palestine itself was entrusted to people who had a long-standing knowledge of conditions there and better cooperation with the settlers evolved. By taking this organizational step, Edmond severed the ties

between the project and his person, for, as he had said at a much earlier date, »it is not a private, but rather an historical and national undertaking.«

After but a few years things had changed for the better. Viticulture was cut back and agriculture and cattle-grazing prioritized and the successful citrus fruit plantations expanded. The settlers founded their own purchasing and sales co-operatives and formed interest groups.

In 1903, at the end of the first wave of immigration (Aliya Alef), 28 Jewish settlements existed in Palestine, of which 19 were partially or completely financed by Baron Edmond de Rothschild. Furthermore, he had purchased large tracts of land for future settlements.

»I am here to give the Rothschilds and great Jews an historical mission.«

Theodor Herzl wrote this in his dairy on June 7, 1895, at a time when he was drafting a 90-page plus »Speech to the Rothschilds«. It is the first systematic presentation of his views and plans, a draft version of his book on the »Jewish State«. In view of the constant increase in anti-Semitism, Theodor Herzl wished to bring about the return of the Jews to Palestine from the Diaspora. He was convinced that the affluent Jews in Western Europe would support him and place their capital resources at his disposal for the project. The Rothschilds did not react and, like most of the West European Jews, ignored Herzl. Edmond finally received Herzl a good year later, after all. He was the only member of the family willing to listen to Herzl's opinions. At the meeting he stated unequivocally that he did not agree with Herzl's movement, which called itself Zionism. The differences of opinion were clear. Herzl wanted to fan a Jewish political movement and prompt Jews to return to Palestine. Edmond wanted to make it possible for Jews persecuted in Eastern Europe to settle in Palestine. Many Zionist leaders sharply criticized Edmond's work in Palestine as a form of charity that forced people to remain dependent on him.

»Without me, the Zionists could not have accomplished anything; without the Zionists, my project would have died.«
Edmond de Rothschild, quoted by Weizmann

Twenty years later the political situation led to cooperation between the Rothschilds and the Zionists. After Turkey had entered the war on the side of Germany in 1914, the two Zionist leaders Chaim Weizmann and Nahum Sokolow tried to whip up support in Great Britain for a Jewish homeland in Palestine. This was by no means easy. The Zionists were dependent in this context on the aid of non-Zionists, such as the Rothschilds, with their high public profile and their contacts to English politicians.

Alongside Edmond and his son James Armand, Lord Walter Rothschild, his sister-in-law Rozsika, his brother Charles and his mother avidly supported the Zionist cause after the outbreak of World War I. They were convinced that Britain was the only power capable of protecting the Jewish population in Palestine.

The joint efforts culminated in the declaration made by Lord Balfour, the British Foreign Minister, that the government would support setting up a national homeland for Jews in Palestine. This declaration was passed on to Lord Walter Rothschild on November 2, 1917 in the simple form of a letter, because it was addressed to world Jewry and not exclusively to the Zionists: »Dear Lord Rothschild, I have much pleasure in conveying to you, on behalf of his Majesty's Government, the following declaration of sympathy with Jewish Zionist aspirations which has been submitted to, and approved by, the Cabinet. ›His Majesty's government view with favour the establishment in Palestine of a national home for the Jewish people, and will use their best endeavours to facilitate the achievement of this object, it being clearly understood that nothing shall be

Edmond and his wife Adelheid during their last visit to Palestine in 1925

done which may prejudice the civil and religious rights of the existing non-Jewish communities in Palestine, or the rights and political status enjoyed by Jews in any other country.‹

I should be grateful if you would bring this declaration to the knowledge of the Zionist Federation.«

For all the differences between the Zionists' goals and the development of the »Baron's colonies«, practical cooperation soon emerged between the two parties in Palestine. These joint efforts were intensified after 1918 in large-scale electrification and land development projects. For this reason, Edmond again changed the organizational form of his Palestine administration. He founded the Palestine Jewish Colonization Association / Edmond de Rothschild Foundation (PICA), which was headed by his son James Armand.

As the largest Jewish landowner in Palestine, the PICA made land and money available for the immigrants, who were again arriving in large numbers above all from Russia. In addition, they also concentrated on initiating and supporting projects that served the overall development of the country and the creation of arable land: projects involving draining swamps, building canals and irrigation channels, power stations, streets and harbours.

Without the land that Edmond made available from 1918 onwards through the PICA, and without the technicians and engineers, whom he had employed and paid, without the reports that he commissioned and the machinery he had bought, Palestine would not during the politically difficult years of the British Mandate have developed into a »national homeland« that could serve as the basis for the foundation of the State of Israel.

Edmond died in 1934, his wife Adelheid in 1935. Both had expressed the wish that they be buried in Palestine. Only after the foundation of the State of Israel was it possible to fulfil this wish. In 1954 the two coffins were transported from Paris to Israel and placed to rest on Ramat Hanadiv, named in their honour the Hill of the Benefactor, near Zikhron Yaakov.

»I want to make some modest contributions towards the advancement of science, art and culture in Israel.«
James Armand de Rothschild, 1957

Edmond's son James Armand was highly dedicated to the work of the PICA and continued his father's work after the latter's death in 1934. He welcomed and supported the State of Israel as founded in 1948 and contributed £6 million towards the building of the Knesset, the new Parliament building in Jerusalem.

Shortly before his death in 1957, James Armand de Rothschild announced in a letter sent to David Ben Gurion, the President of Israel, that he wished in future to finance in particular those institutions of popular education and the arts as well as scientific institutions which the young state did not yet have the means to maintain. After his death, his wife Dorothy de Rothschild set up the »Yad Hanadiv« Foundation (»Memorial of the Benefactor«) to pursue this goal.

The foundation continues to be active in many areas in Israel today. It funds institutions such as the »Instructional Television Centre« with a wide range of learning programs for kindergartens, schools and new immigrants, as well as Israel's Open University, a chain of public libraries and the Music Centre in Jerusalem. Moreover, Yad Hanadiv promotes and funds archaeological excavations and reconstruction work. Thus the reconstruction of the fort at

Massada and the harbour at Caesarea were supported by the foundation, as was after 1967 the restoration of Sephardic synagogues in Jerusalem's Old City.

At the end of 1992, the new Supreme Court building proposed and financed by Yad Hanadiv and Dorothy de Rothschild was officially opened in the presence of most of the members of the Rothschild family.

Beyond the Domain of the Bank

It is unusual for the principles of a company with numerous branches to be upheld for over a century and for the members of the founding family to be both willing and able to continue to manage the banking business. However, even Meyer Amschel's grandchildren no longer all dedicated themselves exclusively to the family business; some turned to other interests, such as collecting art, building country mansions and palatial town residences, or horse-racing. Frequently these interests were clearly not just regarded as mere hobbies,

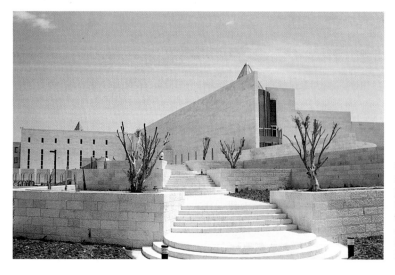

Supreme Court of the State of Israel in Jerusalem. Proposed and financed by »Yad Hanadiv«. Inaugurated in November, 1992

but pursued with a scholarly devotion bent on perfection.

Initially, the focus was on art, in which the Rothschilds had traditionally been interested. But as of the fourth and fifth generations, various members of the family also involved themselves in other areas, leading to their giving up active banking altogether.

Walter de Rothschild became a zoologist and at the tender age of 24 he already had an outstanding reputation in the field in England. Walter's career shows just how difficult it was for a Rothschild to shrug off the family tradition and expectations, despite his recognized superb achievements. Walter studied natural history in Cambridge. Nevertheless, as expected of him by his father, in 1889 he joined the Rothschild Bank in London and remained there until 1908, even if he probably was not responsible for any important business there. He exploited the opportunities the bank offered to expand his unique zoological collection, to correspond with his agents and to organize worldwide expeditions. As he was a Member of Parliament he had a good reason to leave the bank during office hours, although as a rule he did not do so in order to attend sittings of Parliament but to visit the Natural History Museum in Kensington.

As early as 1892 he created a museum for his extraordinary collection in his mansion at Tring Park, a museum that was open to the public. Together with the custodians, he conducted scientific research on the collection and published on the topic. Some of the animals thus discovered or researched received the name of Rothschild, for example the »Giraffa camelopardalis rothschildii«, a type of giraffe with five horns.

Walter shared his interest with his younger brother Nathaniel Charles, who, out of a sense of responsibility to the family

Henri de Rothschild, 1872–1946

and the bank, spent most of his life at New Court, as the English branch of the family simply had no other male progeny at the time. Charles was particularly interested in preserving nature and protecting animal species and was well ahead of his day with the nature reserves he set up. He conducted extensive research into fleas and made an important contribution to our knowledge of the transmission of diseases. His daughter Miriam continued his work. She compiled a seven-volume illustrated catalogue of his comprehensive flea collection and made a name for herself in the research world with numerous scientific papers.

However, it was even more difficult for women to leave all tradition behind them and no longer spend their lives only running a large house, educating the children, engaging in philanthropic works and concerning themselves with art and music. It was precisely in the latter areas that female members of the family were able to create great scope and an independent area for themselves, and they received great recognition for their efforts. Wherever they were given the opportunity, they competently continued the men's work: the activities of Alice de Rothschild at Waddesdon Manor being a perfect example. Yet work in the bank to this day remains off-bounds for the women, even though some of the female Rothschilds have been exceptionally talented in financial and banking work and would have dearly liked to play an overt part in them and not just operate behind the scenes. These women included Nathaniel's wife Emma who was born in Frankfurt and Rozsika (née von Wertheimstein), the wife of Charles, who died young in 1924. Even the fact that by the turn of the century the number of male Rothschild progeny had declined and, as mentioned, some developed no interest in banking, did not lead to a change of the principles laid down in 1810-2, according to which daughters-in-law and daughters were not permitted to become partners in the bank.

Henri de Rothschild quit the bank altogether; he studied medicine and published numerous articles on pediatrics. He also worked on numerous inventions and managed highly differing companies, such as a car factory and a soap factory. However, the capital he committed to these projects exceeded the returns. He later devoted himself completely to writing and the theatre. Out of consideration for the family he published his books under a pseudonym. In 1929 he founded the Pigalle Theatre and thereafter wrote numerous successful plays. His son Philippe initially followed in his footsteps, but then opted to head the Château Mouton vineyards: the wines, together with those from the nearby Château Lafite vines, which have achieved a new, unique popularity since being associated with the family name.

Whenever a bottle of fine claret is sold for the maximum prize at international wine auctions it is, most likely, a bottle from

The brothers Walter and Charles de Rothschild in Tring Park

View of Walter de Rothschild's Natural Science Museum in Tring Park

the two famous Bordeaux-vineyards owned by the Rothschild family.

The Bordeaux wines first became world famous after the wine classification introduced at the 1855 Paris Exposition. The two uppermost categories, »premier cru« and »second cru« were soon used as synonyms for a refined, luxurious lifestyle. It therefore comes as no surprise that acquiring a prestigious vineyard became a desirable goal among members of Parisian society as of the mid-19th century. Nathaniel de Rothschild had already bought the Mouton vineyard in 1853, two years before the World Exposition classified it as a top vineyard in the second highest Bordeaux category. In 1868, the year of his death, probably at the insistence of his sons, Baron James de Rothschild acquired a vineyard in the top category, namely Château Lafite near Paulliac. Thus, not only did the Rothschild family own two of the most prestigious and best vineyards in the country, but a rivalry was set in motion between the two to see who could produce the best wines. The rivalry has lasted over a century and the wines' are meanwhile of a legendary quality, so that the name »Rothschild« has become synonymous with the best and most expensive wines in the world. The vineyards continue to be owned by the family and the rivalry continues: to the good of the wines' exceptional quality – witnessed by the fact that Mouton has since been reclassified as a top category Bordeaux.

The Rothschilds continue to be active as bankers to this day. The London N M Rothschild & Sons Limited continues to exist. The Paris Rothschild Bank was nationalized in the Eighties, yet soon

The Wine Cellar
(called Chai) at
Château Lafite-Roth-
schild, watercolour by
A. Serebriakoff

thereafter refounded. In recent years, a
Rothschild Bank has opened in Zurich, set
up there by the London bank. The Rothschild Group has representative offices
throughout Europe, and as of the last few
years they include an office in the city in
which the Rothschilds' started out on
their incredible climb to success, namely
Frankfurt.

The Rothschilds in Frankfurt

View of Frankfurt from the west, J. J. Tanner, 1840

Rothschilds in Frankfurt?

Little in Frankfurt today points to the family which, in the 19th century, owned the most important bank in Frankfurt, indeed in the whole world.

The Rothschild Park, the Rothschild Avenue and the Jewish Museum in the Rothschild Palace are the first traces you notice when you start looking around. A closer study of the family history soon turns up other traces. Streets such as Luisenstrasse or Mathildenstrasse were named after family members. Then there are further parks and other buildings, which they had built, and numerous foundations for the Christian and Jewish citizens of the city. The tracks lead you to the Grueneburg Park or the »Carolinum« Dental Clinic, where memorial plaques stand in memory of family members. Each of these persons shaped in his or her own, unmistakable way the image of the Rothschilds in the minds of Frankfurt's inhabitants.

The following section will therefore focus less on the financial transactions of the Frankfurt M. A. Rothschild & Söhne bank and more on the three heads of the bank who succeeded its founder, and the impact they and their wives had on Frankfurt.

»In terms of money, Rothschild is still the most distinguished« (Otto von Bismarck)

Amschel Mayer von Rothschild (1773–1855)

Leaving the Ghetto Behind

It was Amschel Mayer, the eldest son of Meyer Amschel Rothschild, who decisively influenced the family's climb into the upper echelons of society at the beginning of the 19th century.

Amschel was born in the Judengasse in Frankfurt and worked in his father's trading company. On behalf of his father, Meyer Amschel was frequently travelling up and down Germany, buying and selling coins or effecting money exchange or loans business. He spent many years of his life travelling in uncomfortable post coaches or in foreign cities. In 1796 he married Eva Hanau, who came from one of the Juden-

Amschel Meyer
von Rothschild

The Rothschild Bank
in the Fahrgasse

gasse's most affluent families. As of the 1790s, Amschel Mayer participated in the soaring financial fortunes of the family as his father's partner.

Although after 1800 the Rothschild trading house was one of the most important private banks in Frankfurt, the family's social life was initially confined to the Judengasse. Even the Fire of the Judengasse in 1796 and Frankfurt's occupation by the French in 1806 did little to change this state of affairs. The ghetto remained, if in expanded form, under Napoleonic rule.

The burned-down northern section of the Judengasse and streets nearby were intended as the Jewish quarters. However, the Jews had no interest in continuing to live in a closed-off quarter, especially as many had concluded long-term rental contracts outside the Judengasse following the fire. No

Jew therefore bid in the auction of building sites in its northern section. Only after pressure was exercised by Prince Primate Karl Theodor von Dalberg in early 1809 were all 23 sites between the synagogue and Bornheimer Gate finally sold.

Amschel Mayer and his brothers acquired one of the best locations at the northern entrance on the corner of Judengasse and Fahrgasse. Here, they had representative commercial premises built taking up the space of five former houses. While the City Council ouce had forbidden eye-catching buildings in the Judengasse, the Rothschilds had their new bank building given a discreetly restrained outer appearance, but its style was still very up-to-

Baroness Eva von
Rothschild

Mayer's wish to gain entry into the established bourgeois circles in Frankfurt was his purchase at this time of a mansion with large gardens on the avenue to Bockenheim. It was above all Reformed and Catholic families, who had originally only been tolerated in Frankfurt because of their money, and had then been given civil rights in 1806 by von Dalberg who lived here.

Amschel Mayer had the manor house transformed into a villa in 1831, taking his cure from Frankfurt's patrician families. The gardens were expanded into an English landscaped park. Amschel Mayer enjoyed showing his many guests his gardens from »1001 Nights«: it was famous for its beautiful and rare plants and its tame deer.

date. In 1813 the new building of the Mayer Amschel Rothschild & Söhne Bank was completed. The address was no longer Judengasse, but Fahrgasse.

The house at the intersection of the former Judengasse and the city, built in the Frankfurt Classicist style of the day, stressed the Rothschilds' claim to be members of Frankfurt's bourgeois upper class. The building itself offered generous space for offices and residential rooms large enough to cater for big receptions.

Gutle Rothschild, mother of Amschel Mayer and his brothers, was always unenthusiastic about this »grand bourgeois« image her sons created. She remained until her death in 1849 in the original family house of Gruenes Schild.

For a short time, between 1811 and 1812, the Frankfurt Jews were granted rights equal to those of the city's Christian citizens. The visible expression of Amschel

Silver gilt vase.
Gift of the employees of the bank to Eva and Amschel Mayer von Rothschild on their 50th wedding anniversary in 1846

»One must not get on the wrong side of them.«
(Smidt, a diplomat from Bremen)

After the death of his father, the company founder, Amschel Mayer, took over at the helm of the Frankfurt bank in 1812. After 1816, the Meyer Amschel Rothschild & Söhne bank attained international importance via cooperation with its branches in London, Naples, Paris, and Vienna. It was the market leader in government bonds and also conducted the financial business of the German Confederation. As the seat of the German Federal Diet, after 1815 Frankfurt had become the centre of German politics. Diplomats also lived in the city, and many of them, such as Otto von Bismarck, had the Rothschilds manage their assets for them.

The Rothschilds' preeminent business position in the European financial world was duly honoured when in 1814 Amschel Mayer was made a Prussian Commercial Councillor, ennobled in 1816 by the Austrians and named Bavarian Consul General and Banker to the Bavarian Court in 1820. The family peerage also led to a change in the bank's name: »M. A. Rothschild & Söhne« became »M. A. von Rothschild & Söhne« in 1828.

Amschel Mayer's efforts to receive social recognition were initially only successful in the circles involved in the German Diet. It was contacts with members of the high aristocracy that first gave them an entry into Frankfurt society. Thus, in 1820, Smidt, a diplomat from Bremen wrote:

»Since arriving here, I have, to my great astonishment, found that people such as Bethmann, Gontard, Brentano etc. extend guest invitations to them (the Rothschilds) and are guests of the same, and, on hearing my surprise, others told me that one must keep on their good side and not get on the wrong side of them.«

The closed ranks of Frankfurt society was expressed above all in its associations. Here, bankers, merchants and senators met to debate, but also to play cards or billiards. The socially lower classes were precluded by the high membership fees and the Statutes proscribed membership for Jews. However, given the position they had attained, it was no longer possible to exclude the Rothschilds fully. In 1836 they were accepted into the »Casino« Association and in 1840 into the Frankfurt »Lesegesellschaft«.

In 1838 they were awarded another privilege. In that year, the Imperial Hall in Frankfurt's Römer City Hall was to be redesigned. A »Committee« with nationalist leanings called on members of different states, creeds and social strata to participate in a »truly national artistic enterprise.« Amschel Mayer was the only Jew tolerated among those giving donations. He financed two paintings: Lothar of Saxony, painted by Eduard Bendemann, and Otto IV of Brunswick, painted by Moritz Oppenheim.

Critical Times: The Year 1848

A recurrent motif in political controversies was the influence which the Rothschilds' financial empire exerted on politics by dint of its economic clout. Thus, as of the establishment of the German Diet in Frankfurt in 1816, Amschel Mayer and Salomon Mayer von Rothschild acted as the parliamentary representatives of Jewish interests.

In 1848 revolutionary groups took the connections between the Rothschilds and the powers that were as a reason to attack the family. The revolution consequently posed a threat to the banks in Paris and Vienna. In Frankfurt, rumours spread that Metternich, who had fled Vienna, was staying in the Rothschild palace on Bockenheimer Landstrasse. A large number of people assembled in front of the residence, although it did not come to violence. If one can believe the reports of Friedrich Stoltze, a local Frankfurt poet, then this had much to do with Amschel Mayer. As a generous donator to foundations and charities for the poor he had an almost unassailable position in the city.

In Memory of Amschel Mayer von Rothschild

Baron Amschel Mayer von Rothschild died in 1855. His friend Friedrich Stoltze described his life in a poem published on the title page of »Didaskalia«, a Frankfurt newspaper. Stoltze emphasized Amschel Mayer's charitable generosity, his traditional piety and his close relationship with his mother Gutle.

His father Meyer Amschel had been buried in the Old Jewish Cemetery on Battonnstrasse. The grave bore a traditional, plain gravestone with Hebrew lettering. Amschel Mayer's nephews, by contrast, had Eduard Schmidt of Launitz design a commemorative grave in the form of a large white marble sarcophagus which was then erected in the Jewish Cemetery on Rat-Beil-Strasse. The expensive material and the monumental shape of the grave expressed both wealth and power. The sarcophagus, 2.7 by 2.75 by 1.75 metres, covered with a tasseled carpet, towers over all the other graves and the wall to the adjoining Christian Central Cemetery. Witness was thus borne to Amschel Mayer's superior social position even after his death.

Tomb of Carl Mayer, Adelheid and Alexander von Rothschild and the tomb of Amschel Mayer von Rothschild

A Representative of Frankfurt
Mayer Carl von Rothschild (1820–86)

Amschel Mayer von Rothschild died in 1855, without a son to inherit him. In order to secure the succession at the bank, he had adopted his nephew Mayer Carl, who, after his uncle's death, together with his brother Wilhelm Carl took on management of the bank.

Training as a Banker

Various sources in the Frankfurt Municipal and University Library shed light on Mayer Carl's education. He and his brothers never attended a government school. Their father, Carl Mayer, head of the Naples branch of the Frankfurt bank, took care of all the details of their schooling, vocational training and education in social skills. He employed tutors who received detailed instructions on the lessons to be held. The curriculum included foreign languages, the natural sciences, art, philosophy and political science. In addition, the brothers received lessons in Hebrew and religion. As of his 13th birthday, Mayer Carl underwent training at the various Rothschild banks in Europe.

At the age of 17 Mayer Carl enrolled at Goettingen University. Studying there was a Frankfurt tradition. He read law, which included »General Political Science«, philosophy, philology, as well as political and historical studies. At the time, the famous historian Dahlmann taught at Goettingen, as did the linguists Jacob and Wilhelm Grimm and Ewald, the renowned Orientalist. As of 1838 Mayer Carl continued his studies – in Berlin. He attended lectures by the great historian Ranke, and the eminent legal scholar von Savigny. After university he took up his bank apprenticeship once more. He thus had the opportunity to make social contacts and experience the different European trading hubs.

On April 6, 1842 he married Louise de Rothschild, youngest daughter of his uncle Nathan Rothschild, at the synagogue at Dukes Place in London. In January, 1843, immediately after the birth of Adele, their first daughter, the couple moved back to Frankfurt. A marriage between cousins required special approval in Frankfurt at the time, and Mayer Carl had to pay 150 guilders for the certification. Now, under the tutelage of his uncle Amschel Mayer, he started work at the Frankfurt bank.

The couple acquired the house at Untermainkai 15, a prime Frankfurt residential location, from the widow of the banker Isaac Speyer. Diplomats, officers and bankers lived in the row of Classicist houses which had been built at the turn of the century when the Schneidwall on the Main had been torn down. The couple commissioned the architect Friedrich Rumpf, who had also been in charge of the remodelling of Amschel Mayer's palatial residence at Bockenheimer Landstrasse, to extend the house by seven windows in length and to design the interior in the Neo-Rococo and Neo-Renaissance style. Mayer Carl then acquired the Guenthersburg manor in the north east of the city as a summer house. He was emulating Frankfurt's upper crust, who often had country farm estates in the vicinity transformed into luxurious residences. He had the old building, erstwhile home of a patrician family, torn down and a palatial property built in the middle of an expansive English landscaped park. In the 1860s Mayer Carl had a farm estate established nearby, which was named »Luisenhof« after his wife.

»Herr von Rothschild succeeds in creating everything, except a political manifesto«
(Ex.: »Frankfurter Beobachter«, February 27, 1867)

By virtue of their leading position in trade in government bonds, in 1854 the Frankfurt branch of the Rothschilds were made Bankers to the Court of Prussia. The Duke of Parma appointed Mayer Carl consul in Frankfurt. The latter also acquired the titles of Consul of Bavaria, Austrian Consul General, was co-founder of Frankfurter Bank and of various insurance companies.

Mayer Carl first involved himself in politics in 1866. The same year, during the Austro-Prussian War, Frankfurt, which sympathized with the Austrian cause, was occupied by the victorious Prussians and forced to contribute 6 million guilders to the occupation costs. Mayer Carl and other bankers refused in the name of the Frankfurt commercial community to pay a further 25 million guilders demanded by the Prussian General Edwin von Manteuffel. In connection with this demand, the city sent a delegation, including Mayer Carl, to Berlin. Payment of the enormous amount was suspended after the preliminary peace reached between Prussia and Austria. Prussia was given a free hand in uniting the north German territories as far south as the Main river.

Frankfurt, until that time regarded as an object to be swapped against other states, was swallowed up by the State of Prussia in October, 1866. The city had to float a bond to pay its contribution to the occupation costs and other costs that had arisen through requisitioning. The Rothschild bank underwrote the largest sum, namely 200,000 guilders. When, in 1867, the City of Frankfurt was asked to nominate a representative to attend the North German Reichstag, tempers were still running high as the city have been seized by the Prussians.

At the same time, however, it was mooted that economic demands should be made of the Reichstag, such as repayment of the 6 million guilders contribution to occupation costs.

»Frankfurter Zeitung«, a newspaper owned by Leopold Sonnemann, was the first to venture the name of Mayer Carl von Rothschild in this context. The conservative banker admittedly did not fit in with the paper's liberal stance, but epitomized its ideas on economic policy. A financial expert with no political axe of his own to grind, Mayer Carl was the suitable compromise candidate for the middle class, which had no political party of its own. The electorate believed that he guaranteed to represent Frankfurt's interest in the North German Confederation best.

Only a little more than a third of the citizens enfranchised according to the electoral roll took part in the election of a representative for the North German Reichstag. Most of them refused to vote as a protest at the annexation of the city. Mayer Carl was almost unanimously voted in as Frankfurt's representative.

While, against an uncertain economic background, Mayer Carl was voted a member of this highest parliamentary body in 1867, he lost against Leopold Sonnemann in the elections to the All German Reichstag. Mayer Carl had again stood without a political manifesto. Leopold Sonnemann, by contrast, was the candidate of the Frankfurt Democratic Association and had espoused a federalist program. In order to keep the conservative financial expert in politics in Berlin, in 1871 the Prussian King made him the first Jew to a be member for life of the Prussian Upper House.

»Forget not, then, the poor, dear children«
Louise von Rothschild (1820–94)

Mayer Carl's wife Louise was born in London in 1820. She had great difficulty in adjusting to life in Frankfurt and English was the language spoken in her house. For Louise, a dedication to charity, the education of her children and their social obligations were all of equal importance. Her commitment to charity work was a reflection of her aristocratic lifestyle. In her book »Thoughts Suggested by Bible Texts. Addressed to my Children« she addressed questions of wealth and the obligation to provide welfare for others. In his Foreword to the German edition, the translator wrote:

Frankfurter!

Als der Baron von Rothschild im Juli 1866 vor dem General von Manteuffel stand und mannhaft seine Vaterstadt vertrat, war Leopold Sonnemann bereits seit 24 Stunden aus der Schußlinie nach Stuttgart gewichen.

Geben wir also lieber unsere Stimmen dem, der es weniger eilig hatte, dem

Baron Mayer Carl von Rothschild.

Der bekannte alte Frankfurter, mit gutem Gedächtniß.

5. Beilage Frankfurter Intelligenz-Blatt No. 65 Freitag den 17. März 1871.

Election appeal on behalf of Carl von Rothschild, 1871

»The remark by the Honourable Authoress is correct that these thoughts are written only for a certain social station, namely for children who live in wealth and free of any cares.« As of 1840 there was a general trend to publish morally instructive books, to »strengthen the spirit and the heart«, as it were.

Social etiquette forced women in the upper classes to limit themselves to the »feminine role« of being a mother, a wife and a housewife. Educational literature, which, particularly in the Jewish sphere, were often given a religious undertone, served as a point of orientation in giving one's life a meaning. Louise's elaborations on religion and morality were published and translated into many languages. Leopold Stein, the prominent Frankfurt reform rabbi, translated them into German.

During their youth, two of Louise's daughters also wrote books which focussed on the importance of the Jewish tradition. Clementine, who received lessons from Leopold Stein, compiled »Letters to a Christian Friend on the Essential Truths of Judaism«; Laura Thérèse wrote »Youthful Thoughts. From the Notebooks of a Young Girl«.

In keeping with Jewish tradition, which accords the wife the main responsibility for the education and upbringing of the girls of the family, Louise devoted much time to her seven daughters. Her ideal, namely of education and dedication to charity work, was adopted by her daughters.

Her daughters Adele Hannah, Emma Louise and Laura Thérèse all married English or French cousins. It was a family tradition that marital partners were chosen from among the family's ranks to strengthen ties within the family. Margarethe Alexandrine and Berta Clara, who married Christian nobles, trod a path of their own. Hannah Louise's life was quite extraordinary, in that she remained unmarried and

View of the Untermainkai. Coloured engraving by J. F. Mannskirsch, 1826

dedicated her whole life to charity in her home town of Frankfurt.

Mayer Carl von Rothschild died in 1886 and his wife Louise in 1894. In his will, Mayer Carl ordained that the Guenthersburg House was to be torn down. The surrounding park was then to be donated to the City of Frankfurt. The house at Untermainkai became the seat of the Freiherrlich Carl von Rothschild'schen Öffentlichen Bibliothek, the public library founded in his name.

The Family's Old House

The family's firm place in the history of the city becomes clear not least if one cast a glance at the building history of the family traditional house. In the final third of the 19th century the City decided to tear down the southern part of the Judengasse and to replace it with a broad street. In this part of what was now a completely dilapidated lane stood the Grünes Schild House, in which Gutle Rothschild, the five brothers' mother, lived until her death in 1849. She was already a legend in her lifetime.

The Grünes Schild House and the birthplace of Ludwig Börne had meanwhile become town attractions. Unlike the citizens' initiative to save Börne's old home, the Rothschilds succeeded in preventing their old family house and the neighbouring building from being torn down. After completion of construction work, various Rothschild rooms on the first floor of the Rothschilds' original home were open to the public: The room with the oriel

Stammhaus u. Familie
ROTHSCHILD
zu Frankfurt a. M.

Vater   Mutter

Maier Amschel Rothschild
(Gründer des Welthauses)

die fünf Söhne

Haus

Anselm Maier von Rothschild

Karl von Rothschild

Salomon von Rothschild

Nathan Maier Rothschild Esq.

Baron James von Rothschild

window, from which Gutle had watched the hustle and bustle of the Judengasse, an accounts room with a money chest.

The family used this carefully staged scenario to demonstrate its strong tradition as an old Frankfurt merchant company. Business success was presented here in a manner which everyone could recognize as the family's achievement. Pictures of the Grünes Schild House and the adjacent building were referred to in presentations of the family's history as the Rothschilds' original family house and offices. As one of the city's attractions, it ranked alongside even Goethe's birthplace. In 1938 the Nazis destroyed the interior. During World War II, Jews who were married to Christians were billeted in the house until is was razed to the ground during a bomb attack on March 18, 1944.

The Last Frankfurt Rothschild

Wilhelm Carl von Rothschild (1828–1901)

Wilhelm Carl presented himself in public in a manner that was the diametric opposite of that of his brother Mayer Carl. Wilhelm Carl devoted himself to banking and otherwise completely to religious study, going down in history as a shy man who lived a life out of the limelight.

Baron Willy – An Orthodox Rothschild

When, in 1886, Mayer Carl died, Wilhelm Carl became sole head of the bank. Baron Wilhelm Carl von Rothschild was a very devout Jew, who obeyed all the religious rules and laws. He followed his uncle, Amschel Mayer, in supporting the orthodox wing of the Jewish Community, which had formed after 1830 to oppose the liberal leaders of the same.

Given that the vast majority of the Community were in favour of a liberal leadership open to reform, a group of Jews who practiced the religion in traditional manner formed an association called the »Israelitische Religionsgemeinschaft«. They attempted to ensure that it was possible to still lead an orthodox life and to create an adequate religious and social framework for themselves. Like Amschel Mayer and Wilhelm Carl, the founders belonged to the most respected and affluent inhabitants of the city. The financial support provided by the Rothschilds enabled the Society to employ its own rabbi and build its own synagogue as well as a mikveh and school.

Samson Raphael Hirsch was appointed rabbi in 1851 and later became one of the best known advocates of so-called Neo-orthodox Judaism. He demanded, along the lines of the model life Wilhelm Carl led, that the halakhah (religious practice according to the rules of the Torah) be brought into harmony with modern bourgeois life. Wilhelm Carl's adherence to the traditions of his ancestors made him an example followed in traditional religious circles. Despite the sympathy he felt for Rabbi Hirsch and the »Israelitische Religionsgemeinschaft«,

Wilhelm Carl
von Rothschild

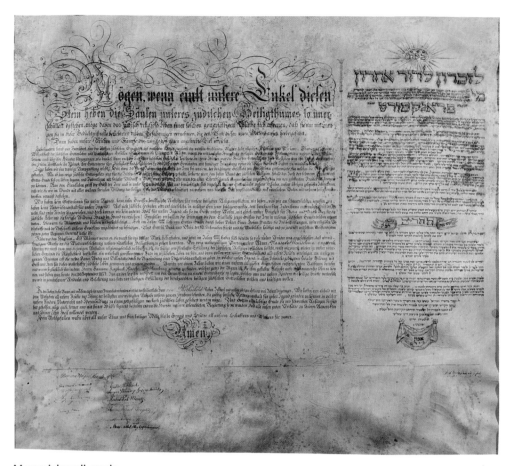

Memorial scroll, made on the occasion of the foundation stone being laid for the Israelite Religious Community synagogue in Schützenstrasse on September 30, 1852

in 1876 he did not follow when Hirsch called on orthodox members to quit the Jewish Community. An important reason was, as it was no doubt for many other members, the fact that the Jewish Community had the right to prohibit lapsed members from being buried at the communal cemetery.

Wilhelm Carl's religious lifestyle is extensively documented. We thus know that he never missed morning prayers, which took place at six in summer and at seven in winter at the palatial residence at Bockenheimer Landstrasse which he had inherited from Amschel Mayer. He then worked in the bank at the Fahrgasse from 11 a.m. till 8 p.m., stopping only for the afternoon prayer service. Each evening he devoted himself to study of the Talmud. Up until his death, the bank kept to the Sabbath.

Wilhelm Carl was also a model of conscientiousness with regard to the religious rule that one be charitable. Numerous people petitioned him and his wife Mathilde for support. Wilhelm Carl employed one staff member solely to appraise the petitions. He dutifully, in line with the Torah, paid a tenth of his income in charity.

In keeping with Jewish tradition, he insisted that he remain anonymous as the source of charity. After his death, his wife Mathilde kept up the charitable work.

An Artist and Devoted to Charity in Frankfurt – Hannah Mathilde von Rothschild (1832–1924)

Hannah Mathilde was the second oldest daughter of Anselm Salomon von Rothschild; her father was, in other words, Wilhelm Carl's cousin. She was born in Frankfurt in 1832 and married Wilhelm Carl in 1849. As with his brother Mayer Carl, owing to the fact that the couple were cousins, they had to have the marriage specially approved by the city authorities. Hannah Mathilde had been brought up in the orthodox Jewish tradition and remained a devout Jew until the end of her days. She was of one mind with her husband on the life they should lead. The couple led a very secluded life. They initially lived in a house on the Zeil, which, like all the Rothschild homes, was in a prime residential area. The building, designed in 1795 by Salons de Montfort, the star architect of the day, was the epitome of an up-market bourgeois residence.

The Grueneburg Villa was the family's Frankfurt summer residence, which they moved into in the 1860s. An avenue of chestnut trees led from the Grueneburgweg at the corner of Liebigstrasse to the porter's lodge and the estate buildings. The Grueneburg itself lay concealed in an English landscaped garden about 50 metres away. In later years, the couple lived in Koenigstein in the summer months, where they also had a villa built, again in large parklands, in the style of an English country manor. The Empress dowager Victoria and the Prince of Wales both attended the glorious opening ceremony. Hannah Mathilde was a close friend of Victoria, the widow of Emperor Frederick III. In 1888, following the death of her husband, Victoria had Castle Friedrichshof built in Kronberg im Taunus, a few kilometres away from the Villa Rothschild. Here, she became the focus of the Kronberg painting colony. Hannah Mathilde also joined this social circle. The visitor's book at the villa in Koenigstein contains drawings by various artists, but also dedications, for example from Emperor William II and other distinguished persons from inside and outside Germany.

Hannah Mathilde exploited these contacts in order to seek support for persecuted Jews. M. M. Mainz, a renowned banker who acted as a consultant to the foundation and assisted the couple remembers: »Anti-Semitic unrest had been reported in Corfu. One Friday midday, I

Hannah Mathilde
von Rothschild

The Villa Grüneburg

The Empress-dowager Victoria and Hannah Mathilde in Koenigstein. The two ladies, both clad in black, are standing at the edge of the wall on the left

visited the Baron at his house on the Zeil in order to request through the agency of that honourable gentleman that the Queen of Greece, who was to be his guest on the Saturday, intervene to stop the pogroms. The Baron promised me he would convey my request to his wife, who was in a better position to negotiate with the Queen, and our efforts bore full fruit.«

Hannah Mathilde's activities as a patron were guided not least by her artistic interests. As one of the wealthiest ladies in Frankfurt, she supported numerous scientific and artistic projects both in Frankfurt and elsewhere. Her musical talent was discovered at an early date. She received piano lessons from Frederic Chopin and also composed pieces herself. An album of pieces for the piano, an orchestrated waltz, and a large number of »lieder« composed by her have survived. Famous singers, such as Selma Kurz and Adelina Patti asked Hannah to write songs for them and many of these songs were brought out by the leading music publishers of the day. Her most famous composition was »Si vous n'avez rien à me dire«, a poem by Victor Hugo which she put to music.

Hannah Mathilde lived to the grand old age of 92. She had three daughters: Georgine Sara, who died young, Adelheid, who married her French cousin Edmond James, and Minna Caroline (Minka), who married the Frankfurt banker Maximilian Goldschmidt.

The End of the Frankfurt Bank

After the death of his brother Mayer Carl in 1886, Wilhelm Carl became sole head of the bank. Under Mayer Carl, the Frankfurt bank had already lost ground to the expanding joint stock banks. Under Wilhelm Carl the bank's operations contracted still further. The bank now focussed only on activities that bore no risk. It predominantly disbursed dividends and interest payments and managed the portfolios of a few particularly wealthy clients.

In 1901 Wilhelm Carl died, without leaving an heir to succeed him.

His son-in-law, Maximilian Goldschmidt, admittedly lived in Frankfurt, but owing to the Rothschild family tradition he was barred from continuing the bank's business. The other branches of the family discussed the possibility of Salomon Albert von Rothschild of Vienna taking over the bank, but decided in the event to close the bank down. A Berlin joint stock bank, Disconto-Gesellschaft, which had frequently cooperated with the Rothschilds in the years up to 1901, took on most of the Frankfurt bank's clients and staff. The bank's comprehensive archive was, with a few exceptions, destroyed at the family's behest.

The Name Lives On

The Goldschmidt-Rothschild Family

After the death of Wilhelm Carl and the related closure of the Frankfurt bank, Hannah Mathilde, his widow, was the last member of the Rothschild family proper left in Frankfurt. However, the family into which her youngest daughter, Minna Caroline, had married continued to use the name Rothschild as the second part of its surname. In 1878 Minna Caroline had married the banker Maximilian Benedict (Mayer Baruch) Goldschmidt, who came from a well-known Frankfurt banking family. The couple had three sons and two daughters. In 1903, shortly after the death of his wife, Maximilian was made a hereditary Prussian noble, so that he and his family were entitled to bear the name von Goldschmidt-Rothschild; in 1907 the family was granted a baronetcy.

The eldest son, Albert, married the cousin of his mother Miriam von Rothschild, of Paris. The marriage was short-lived and the couple had no children. He soon entered a second marriage, with Marion Schuster, who came from Switzerland, and the couple had three daughters and one son. As of the death of his grandmother Mathilde in 1924 Albert and his family moved into the Grueneburg. Albert and his younger brother Erich were partners in the von Goldschmidt-Rothschild & Co. Bank in Berlin, which for a few years maintained a branch office in Frankfurt. At the beginning of the 1930s the majority shareholders dissolved the bank in order to sell it.

When, confronted with the Nazis' anti-Semitic policies, Albert was trying to make preparations for the family to emigrate, he felt compelled to sell the Grueneburg. The City of Frankfurt was highly interested in acquiring the villa and the park, which it then purchased at highly favourable terms in 1935. In 1944 the

Minna Caroline Goldschmidt, daughter of Wilhelm Carl von Rothschild

building was destroyed by bombing. The park itself has by and large survived.

Rudolf, the second eldest son, first married Baroness Lambert, daughter of Zoé Lucie Betty née. von Rothschild: the couple had two sons. His second marriage, to Marie-Anne von Friedländer-Fuld, bore a further son. Having studied painting in Munich and London, he was a member of the Frankfurt Museum Association and collected modern art. He was a member of the Board of the Jewish Community, sat on many Frankfurt foundations and was a member of the Grand Council of Frankfurt University. After the death of his grandmother he and his family lived as of 1925 in the summer residence of Wilhelm Carl and Mathilde in Koenigstein. They were joined there by Albert and his family after the latter had been forced to sell the Grueneburg.

When, in the summer of 1938, Rudolf von Goldschmidt- Rothschild was no longer allowed to return to Germany from holidaying in Switzerland, the Third Reich's financial authorities immediately ordered the confiscation of the paintings in the Koenigstein Villa for purported tax still owing. Following the so-called »Night of the Crystals« in November, 1938 the contents of the building was seized and auctioned to pay »Reichsfluchtsteuer« (Tax Levied on Those Fleeing the Reich) and »Judenvermögensabgabe« (Jewish Assets Levy) that was outstanding. The villa and grounds were bought by Georg von Opel at a very low price. After conclusion of the reparations negotiations in the post-War period, the City of Koenigstein acquired the park and the villa, and the present Hotel »Sonnenhof« was opened there in 1956.

Maximilian von Goldschmidt-Rothschild, father of Albert and Rudolf, was also put under pressure to sell his residence at Bockenheimer Landstrasse 10 to the City of Frankfurt. According to the sales contract signed in September, 1938 the City had to grant the meanwhile 95 year-old permanent right to use the building and the grounds in return for rent, an agreement it did not honour. Shortly after the sale, and against the background of the November pogrom, Maximilian felt compelled to sell his precious art collection, also housed in the building, to the City far below price. The collection was placed under the aegis of the Museum of Applied Arts, which opened its rooms at Bockenheimer Landstrasse 10 to the public as Dept. II of the Museum.

Maximilian had to make do with one room in his house, until March 30, 1940, when he died. His sons Albert and Rudolf, were stripped of their German citizenship by the Nazi authorities. Albert committed suicide in exile in Switzerland in 1941; Rudolf died in 1962, also in Switzerland.

Foundations for Frankfurt

Frankfurt on Main was famous as a city of foundations. Up until the 1870s Frankfurt was the only large city in Germany which had succeeded in setting up a welfare network drawing almost exclusively on funds from foundations, i.e. without using tax money. However, this is not to forget that civil rights were only accorded to persons who could prove that they had the basis for a livelihood. This thus barred poorer segments of the population from moving into the city.

It was not until after the Freedom of Movement Act of 1867 that Frankfurt's population started to grow swiftly and the Supported Domicile Act of 1871, which accorded those in distress a right to communal assistance, that the funds from the foundations proved inadequate. Now, tax payers had to bear the brunt of the cost of welfare and social institutions.

In 1864 the Frankfurt Jews received equal civil rights and thus became citizens of Frankfurt. With the establishment of interdenominational foundations, the Jews wished to show that they were willing to shoulder their share of responsibility for the common weal and to contribute toward lessening social barriers. At the same time, by setting up Jewish foundations, they also stressed that they were Jews. Numerous Rothschild foundations provide striking examples of both approaches.

The Rothschilds' engagement for charitable work was of exceptional importance for Frankfurt. Hannah Mathilde and her son-in-law Maximilian, for example, donated one million marks towards the establishment of Frankfurt University, which was set up as a foundation.

The Rothschilds did not confine themselves just to spectacular projects such as the

Clementine Girls'
Hospital

university; there was no social domain in which they were not involved. The scope of their foundations ranged from orphanages and soup kitchens to old people's homes. The family insisted that a family member should always be appointed to the respective board of trustees or administrators of their foundations. They thus ensured that they maintained an influence on the foundations, until the Nazis put an end to this tradition.

The establishment and continuation of these institutions was the work of the female members of the family. Alongside their legal commitments and educating the children, discharging charitable duties played an important part in their lives. The foundations were generally named after deceased members of the family. The early death of Clementine, daughter of Mayer Carl and Louise, prompted the establishment of the interdenominational »Clementine Girls' Hospital« at Bornheimer Landwehr. The children's hospital still

exists today, having been combined with the Dr. Christschen Stiftung at Theobald-Christ-Strasse near the Frankfurt Zoo.

Hannah Louise, fifth daughter of Mayer Carl and Louise, remained single. On the death of her father, she inherited a large sum of money and set up two important foundations in Frankfurt. Like her mother Louise, who had provided the financing for the Central Swimming Baths, one of the first such baths in Germany, Hannah Louise also trod new ground with her foundations.

Interdenominational Foundations

When setting up the »Freiherrlich Carl von Rothschild'sche öffentliche Bibliothek«, originally at Bethmannstrasse and later in the palatial town house at Untermainkai, she followed the example of the English and American public free libraries, which afforded all segments of the population access to further education free of charge. With the »Carolinum« foundation (officially called the »Freiherr Carl von Rothschild'sche Stiftung Carolinum«) Hannah Louise introduced a new type of clinic to

Frankfurt: namely, a polyclinic with a dental care section. Frankfurt had meanwhile an adequate number of general hospital beds, but dental care was still underdeveloped. With the approval of the Rothschilds, in 1906 the Carolinum was transformed into a dedicated dental clinic. In 1910 the Carolinum participated as an independent foundation in the establishment of Frankfurt University. On Hannah Louise's sudden death in 1892, her mother ensured that the two foundations she had

set up were given a due legal basis, so that they still exist in Frankfurt today.

Those daughters of Mayer Carl and Louise who had married abroad still remained linked to Frankfurt. They played a large part in the foundations set up by their mother and sister and provided financial support. When, two years after Hannah Louise's death, her mother Louise also passed away, the sisters, who now bore the main burden of supervising the foundations, decreed that the library be moved to

The Carolinum Clinic
at Bürgerstrasse 7

the family house on the banks of the Main. The building there was accordingly redesigned, and today houses the Jewish Museum.

They also emphasized their loyalty to their home town by making considerable donations to the city. For example, Tischbein's famous painting »Goethe in the Campagna« was a given to the city by Adele Hannah.

Rothschild Library
ex libris
(1897–1911),
designed by
Katharina Ochs

Traditional Religious Foundations

While Louise and her daughter Hannah Louise above all set up non-denominational foundations, those institutions established by Hannah Mathilde, Louise's sister-in-law, were conducted according to orthodox Jewish rules.

This was also true of the first major Rothschild foundation, the »Georgine Sarah von Rothschild'sche Stiftung für erkrankte fremde Israeliten« (foundation for foreign Israelites who had fallen ill) established in 1870. The founding statutes of this hospital foundation specify: »It is our will that this institute shall for all eternity be run according to the religious rules of orthodox Judaism.« Hannah Mathilde and her daughters Adelheid and Minna Caroline followed the same policy when opening the »Freiherrlich Wilhelm und Freifrau Mathilde von Rothschild'sche Altersheim für Israelitische Frauen und Jungfrauen besserer Stände« (Old People's Home for Israelite Women and Spinsters of Better Families) in the family's house on the Zeil in 1903. The glorious interior of the family house was left almost intact for the inhabitants of the old people's home to enjoy.

In 1912, Adelheid donated the former bank building on Fahrgasse to the Jewish Community. The Museum of Jewish Antiquity, which housed the »von Rothschild Museum«, was set up there in 1922, with financial assistance from Hannah Mathilde and Adelheid. Exhibits from the family history, such as Oppenheim's portraits of Gutle and her five sons, were put on view in the offices of Mayer Carl and Wilhelm Carl, which were otherwise kept unchanged.

The daughters of Hannah Mathilde and Wilhelm Carl not only played an active part in the foundations their mother had set up, but also continued the tradition by esta-

1

Library in the »Baron William and Baroness Mathilde von Rothschild Old People's Home for Israelite Women and Spinsters of Better Families«

blishing foundations of their own. The statutes of the »Freiherrlich Wilhelm Carl von Rothschild'schen Stiftung für wohltätige und gemeinnützige Zwecke« (serving charitable purposes and the common good), set up by the youngest daughter Minna Caroline, read:

»As a symbol of the pious remembrance, in which I, Mrs. Max Goldschmidt, née Baroness von Rothschild, hold the city in which the original house of my family stands, I have decided to set up a foundation in memory of my blessed father, Baron Wilhelm Carl von Rothschild, in order to lend visual expression to my intentions.«

In 1910 the foundation built a hostel for single women at Huegelstrasse that exists to this day.

In total, the Rothschild family set up over 20 foundations in Frankfurt. No other family, be it Christian or Jewish, had done anything comparable on behalf of Frankfurt and its citizens.

The Rothschild Foundations during the Nazi Period

The Nazis' attempt to eliminate the Jews from economic and political life in Germany also impacted on the foundations. The Nazi government was bent on seizing control of all the mobile assets and real property belonging to the Jewish foundations.

The »Anselm Salomon von Rothschild'sche Stiftung zur Förderung des Kunstgewerbes« (for the promotion of the applied arts) was a »mixed«, i.e. interdenominational foundation, but was »Aryanized« and its assets merged with those of other foundations to form the Pestalozzi Foundation. The German »people« was to be spared having to receive support from Jews. Baron von Goldschmidt-Rothschild, the Jewish member of the Board of Trustees, was forced to retire from his office.

The foundations which, owing to the purpose for which they had been established, could not be »aryanized«, such as the »Freiherrlich Amschel Meyer von Rothschild'sche Stiftung für arme Israeliten in Frankfurt am Main« (for poor Israelites in Frankfurt) were forced to use their financial resources solely to support needy Jews and to further Jewish emigration.

It was, above all, the Rothschild old people's home on the Zeil which was a thorn in the Nazi Party's eye. An air-raid shelter had been built in the home and the population had purportedly complained »… that we are being made to enter the air-raid shelter of a Jewish house«.

In 1940, the foundation was, like almost all other Rothschild foundations, incorporated in the »Reichsvereinigung der Juden« (Reich Association of Jews, set up in 1939) on the proviso that the building on Zeil 92 was sold to the City of Frankfurt. There was no stopping the foundations being further stripped of their assets. The communication quoted above also states: »… some time ago the British ambassador in Berlin enquired as to the fate of the Rothschild foundations, clearly at the instigation of the English and French members of the Rothschild family, who stick closely together … In my opinion it is no longer necessary to take the English or French into consideration.«

The Nazis also endeavoured to elide the names of the Jews as patrons of the foundations from popular memory. Of all the Rothschild foundations in Frankfurt, only the Carolinum managed to weather the Nazi period without changing its name.

When called upon to amend the statutes to change the foundation's name such that its Jewish origins were no longer mentioned, the foundation's Board replied »that the name Carolinum is quite common locally and the public has no knowledge of its being connected with the Rothschild family.«

References

p. 17 Hessisches Staatsarchiv Marburg, Best. 17d Rothschild.

p. 22 Institut für Stadtgeschichte Frankfurt am Main (hereafter IfSt.), Ugb D 33 No. 53 Fasz. I No. 21.

p. 28sq. Paul Arnsberg, Die jüdischen Gemeinden in Hessen. Bilder – Dokumente, (Darmstadt 1973), p. 109.

p. 31 Archiv Schloß Fasanerie Eichenzell bei Fulda, Archiv. Kfst. Wilhelm I., Motiv: Hesp. geh. Kabinett Akten, Inv.-No. No. 1, Vol. I.

p. 44sq. Rachel Heuberger/Helga Krohn, Hinaus aus dem Ghetto ... Juden in Frankfurt am Main 1800–1950, (Frankfurt am Main, 1988), p. 24.

p. 45 Aron Freimann, Stammtafeln der Freiherrlichen Familie von Rothschild, Frankfurt am Main 1906, p. 52.

p. 58a Quoted from Richard Ehrenberg, Grosse Vermögen, (Jena, 1905), p 86.

p. 58b The Rothschild Archive, London, T 64/302.

p. 60a The Rothschild Archive, London, XI/109/8.

p. 60b The Rothschild Archive, London, XI/109/4/1/5.

p. 61 Wilhelm und Caroline von Humboldt in ihren Briefen, Bd. VI, 1817–1819, ed. by Anna von Sydow, (Berlin, 1913), p. 320.

p. 64 The Rothschild Archive, London, XI/109/ 63 file I.

p. 65 The Rothschild Archive, London, T64/109/9/302.

p. 67a Count Corti, vol. 2, pp. 28, 32, 35.

p. 67b see Count Corti, vol. 2, p. 23.

p. 73a Österreichisches Staatsarchiv/Haus-, Hof- und Staatsarchiv, Wien K 231 17 18.

p. 73b (Augsburger) Allgemeine Zeitung, Nov. 13, 1821.

p. 74 (Augsburger) Allgemeine Zeitung, Nov. 25, 1821.

p. 75a Adolf Trende, Im Schatten des Freimaurer- und Judentump. Ausgewählte Stücke aus dem Briefwechsel des Ministers und Chefs der preußischen Bankinstitute Christian von Rother, (Berlin, 1938), p. 94f.

p. 75b Maria Belli-Gontard, Lebens-Erinnerungen, (Frankfurt, 1872), p. 382.

p. 76f. Briefwechsel zwischen Friedrich von Gentz und Adam Heinrich Müller 1800–1829, Stuttgart 1857, p. 267-268, Letter dated Dezember 15, 1818.

p. 77 Freiherr von Handel, September 3, 1819, Österreichisches Staatsarchiv, Haus-, Hof- und Staatsarchiv Wien, Bestand Staatskanzlei, Diplomatische Korrespondenz, Frankfurt, Fasz. 23: Nichtpolitische Berichte und Weisungen.

p. 78 Allgemeine Zeitung des Judentums No. 34, Aug. 21, 1843, p. 504.

p. 79 Leopold Zunz, Die gottesdienstlichen Vorträge der Juden historisch entwickelt [1832], Vorrede, in: item, Gesammelte Schriften, (Hildesheim/New York 1976), repr. Berlin 1875 edition.

p. 83 Via Chiaia; the estate, called »Villa Pignatelli« is today a museum.

p. 84 Diaries of Sir Moses and Lady Montefiore, ed. by. Louis Loewe, (London, 1983), p. 52.

p. 94 Heinrich Heine, Augsburger Allgemeine Zeitung, May 5, 1843.

p. 95 Quoted from A. Mühlstein, James de Rothschild, (Paris 1981), p. 147.

p. 98 Constance Lady Battersea, Reminiscences, (London, 1922).

p. 100 Constance de Rothschild, in: The New Quarterly Magazine, January 10, 1876.

p. 105 See. Guy de Rothschild, Contre bonne fortune, (Paris, 1983), p. 23.

p. 107 Letter of Carl Mayer to his daughter Charlotte, The Rothschild Archive, London, T Fam. C 22.

p. 111 See Virginia Cowles, The Rothschilds. A Family of Fortune, S.173.

p. 112 See Anka Mühlstein. James de Rothschild, p. 8.

p. 119a Quoted from Anka Mühlstein, James de Rothschild, Paris 1981, p. 85.

p. 119b Quoted from Monika Richarz, Jüdisches Leben in Deutschland 1780-1871, 1976, p. 410.

p. 119sq. Heinemann Rosenthal, Kinheitserinnerungen, 1890, Quoted from Monika Richarz, Jüdisches Leben in Deutschland 1790–1871, 1976, p. 438.

p. 120a AZJ 1837, No. 24.

p. 120b AZJ 1839, No. 33.

p. 120c quoted from Jüdische Witze, ausgewählt von Salcia Landmann, 1962, p. 123.

p. 140 Moritz Busch, Tagebuchblätter, (Leipzig, 1899), Vol. 1, p. 317.

p. 161sq. Letter of the settlers to Edmond de Rothschild, Haifa, October 14, 1883. Central Zionist Archives, Jerusalem, J 15–5001.

p. 196a Quoted from a letter of the Lord Mayor of Frankfurt, Krebs, to the Gestapo, May 1940, IfSt Frankfurt am Main.

p. 196 Quoted from the book of the Carolinum minutes, 172, October 2, 1939, Archiv Zentrum der Zahn-, Mund- und Kieferheilkunde der Johann Wolfgang Goethe-Universität, Frankfurt am Main.

Bibliography on the History of the Rothschild Family

General reference works and monographs on the Rothschilds

Achterberg, Erich: Der Bankplatz Frankfurt am Main, Frankfurt am Main, 1955.

Arnsberg, Paul: Die Geschichte der Frankfurter Juden seit der Französischen Revolution. ed. by Kuratorium für Jüdische Geschichte e. V., Frankfurt am Main. Completed and revised by Hans-Otto Schembs, 3 vols., (Darmstadt, 1983).

Bergeron, Louis: Les Rothschild et les autres. La gloire des banquiers, Collection Histoire et Fortunes, (Paris, 1991).

Berghoeffer, Christian Wilhelm: Meyer Amschel Rothschild – der Gründer des Rothschildschen Bankhauses, Frankfurt am Main, 1922, 3rd ed., (Frankfurt am Main, 1924).

Bouvier, Jean: Les Rothschild, Paris 1967, 1983, [reprinted as] Les Rothschild. Histoire d'un capitalisme familial, (Paris, 1992).

Count Corti, Egon Caesar: [vol. 1:] The Rise of the House of Rothschild, [vol. 2:] The Reign of the House of Rothschild, transl. from the German by Brian and Beatrix Lunn, (London, 1928).

Cowles, Virginia: The Rothschilds. A Family of Furtune, (London, 1973).

Davis, Richard: The English Rothschilds, (London, 1983).

Ehrenberg, Richard: Grosse Vermögen – Ihre Entstehung und ihre Bedeutung, 1. vol.: Die Fugger – Rothschild – Krupp, (2nd rev. ed., Jena, 1905).

Gille, Bertrand: Histoire de la Maison Rothschild, vol I: Des Origines à 1848, vol II: 1848–1870, being: Travaux de Droit, d´Économie, de Sociologie et de Sciences Politiques 39, 56, (Geneva, 1965–1967).

Kracauer, Isidor: Geschichte der Juden in Frankfurt a. M. (1150-1824) (ed. by the Board of the Israelitische Gemeinde Frankfurt a. M.), 2 vols., (Frankfurt am Main, 1925-27).

Morton, Frédéric: The Rothschilds. A Family Portrait, first printed in New York, 1961, thereafter several new editions.

Mühlstein, Anka: James de Rothschild, (Paris, 1981).

Rothschild, Miriam: Dear Lord Rothschild. Birds, Butterflies and History, (London, 1983).

Wilson, Derek: The Rothschilds. A Story of Wealth and Power, (London, 1988), rev. ed. 1994.

In-depth literature on the main sections of the exhibition

Overture: A Magnificent Ambiente

Alcouffe, Daniel/Ennès, Pierre: Un ensemble exceptionnel de meubles et de porcelaines de Sèvres du XVIIIe siècle, in: La Revue du Louvre 1 (1991), pp.53–75.

Anthony Blunt (ed.), The James A. de Rothschild Collcetion at Waddesdon Manor, Gold boxes and miniatures of the 18th century prepared by Serge Grandjean, Fribourg (Switzerland) 1987.

Davies, Charles: Works of Art in the collection of Alfred de Rothschild, London 1884.

Grandjean, Serge: Catalogue des tabatières, boîtes et étuis du XVIIIe et XIXe siècle au Musée du Louvre, Paris 1981.

Hackenbroch, Yvonne: Reinhold Vasters, Goldsmith, in: Metropolitan Museum Journal 19/20 (1986), pp. 163–268.

Hoos, Hildegard: Profanes Silber vom 16.–20. Jahrhundert, Frankfurt am Main 1992

Jones, Alfred E.: Catalogue of the collection of old plate of Leopold de Rothschild, Esquire, London 1907.

– A catalogue of the objects in gold and silver and the Limoges enamels in the collection of the Baroness James de Rothschild, London 1912.

Koechlin, Raymond: Les donations de la famille de Rothschild, Paris 1909.

Luthmer, Ferdinand: Der Schatz des Freiherrn Karl von Rothschild. Meisterwerke alter Goldschmiedekunst aus dem 14.-18. Jahrhundert, 2 vols., Frankfurt am Main 1883–1885.

– Führer durch die Freiherrlich Karl von Rothschild'sche Kunstsammlung, Frankfurt am Main 1890.

Pechstein, Klaus: Der Merkelsche Tafelaufsatz von Wentzel Jamnitzer, in: Mitt. Verein für Gesch. Nürnberg 61 (1974), pp.90–121.

Schätze deutscher Goldschmiedekunst von 1500–1920 aus dem Germanischen Nationalmuseum Nürnberg, Berlin 1992.

Schestag, Franz: Katalog der Kunstsammlung des Freiherrn Anselm von Rothschild in Wien, 2 Bde, Vienna 1866-72.

Seelig, Lorenz: Der heilige Georg im Kampf mit dem Drachen, Bildführer No. 12, Bayerisches Nationalmuseum Munich, Munich 1987.

Seling, Helmut: Der Hanauer Ratspokal, in: Städel Jahrbuch N.F. 12 (1989) pp. 235–241.

Sotheby's, Catalogue of the celebrated collection of German, Dutch and other continental silber and silver-gilt, sold by the order of Victor Rothschild, Esq , London 1937.

Tait, Hugh: The Waddesdon Bequest. The Legacy of Baron Ferdinand Rothschild to the British Museum, London 1981.

– The Waddesdon Bequest, The Silver Plate, London 1988

– The Waddesdon Bequest, The Jewels, London 1986

Watson, Francis J.B.: Le Goût Rothschild, in: Apollo 101 (1975), pp. 334-5.

– Collectors contrasted: Baron Mayer Amschel de Rothschild and the 5th Earl of Rosebery at Mentmore and elsewere, in: Sotheby`s Art at auction 1976/77, pp. 12-30.

Wentzel Jamnitzer und die Nürnberger Goldschmiedekunst 1500 bis 1700, Munich 1985.

Meyer Amschel Rothschild – A Life in the Judengasse

Cohen, Salomon J.: Musterhaftes Leben des verewigten Herrn Bankiers Maier Amschel Rothschild. Als Denkmal für diesen allen Israeliten und allen Freunden der Tugend gewidmet, Frankfurt am Main 1813.

Dietz, Alexander: Stammbuch der Frankfurter Juden, Frankfurt am Main 1907.

Heilbrunn, Rudolf: Der Anfang des Hauses Rothschild. Wahrheit und Dichtung, in: Jahrbuch des Instituts für deutsche Geschichte, vol. 2 (1973), pp. 209–38.

Kracauer, Isidor: Die Geschichte der Judengasse in Frankfurt am Main, in: Festschrift zur Jahrhundertfeier der Realschule der israelitischen Gemeinde (Philanthropin) zu Frankfurt am Main 1804–1904, Frankfurt am Main 1904, pp. 303–464.

Freimann, Aron: Stammtafeln der Freiherrlichen Familie von Rothschild, Frankfurt am Main 1906.

Stern, Selma: The Court Jew. A Contribution to the History of the Period of Absolutism in Central Europe, Philadelphia 1950.

(see also Berghoeffer, Count Corti)

Wars, Princes and Business – The Career of a Court Jew

Arnsberg, Paul: Die jüdischen Gemeinden in Hessen. Bilder, Dokumente, Darmstadt 1973, pp. 108–27.

Aufklärung und Klassizismus in Hessen-Kassel unter Landgraf Friedrich II. 1760-1785, ed. von den Staatlichen Kunstsammlungen Kassel, exhibition catalogue, Kassel 1979.

Buderus von Carlshausen, Lothar: Carl Friedrich Buderus. Das Leben eines kurhessischen Beamten in schwerer Zeit, in: Hessenland. Monatsschrift für Landes- und Volkskunde, Kunst und Literatur Hessens 42 (1931), pp. 33–40, 65-71, 97–103.

Dietz, Alexander: Frankfurter Handelsgeschichte, vol. 4.2, Frankfurt am Main 1925, pp. 723–736.

Losch, Philipp: Kurfürst Wilhelm I. Landgraf von Hessen. Ein Fürstenbild aus der Zopfzeit, Marburg 1923.

Sauer, Josef: Finanzgeschäfte der Landgrafen von Hessen-Kassel. Ein Beitrag zur Geschichte des kurhessischen Haus- und Staatsschatzes und zur Entwicklungsgeschichte des Hauses Rothschild, Fulda 1930.

(see also Berghoeffer)

Nathans Crosses the Channel

Chapman, Stanley D.: The Foundation of the English Rothschilds: N.M. Rothschild as a Textile Merchant 1799–1811, in: Textile History VIII (1977), pp. 99–115.

Chapman, Stanley D: The International Houses: The Continental Contribution to British Commerce, 1800–1860, in: Journal of European Economic History 6 (1977), pp. 5–48.

Herries, Edward: Memoir of the public life of the right Hon. John Charles Herries, London 1880, vol. 1.

Lord Rothschild: The Shadow of a Great Man, London 1982.

Meyer Amschel Rothschild – Banker to the Court and Citizen

Brilling, Bernhard: Mayer Amschel Rothschild und die Abschaffung des Leibzolls in Bayern, in: Bulletin für die Mitglieder der Gesellschaft der Freunde der Leo-Baeck-Institute 7, 1964, Nr. 26, pp. 165–71

(see also Berghoeffer, Kracauer)

The Five Brothers: New Beginnings amongst Coninued Unity – The European Rothschild Bank

Ayer, J.: Century of Finance 1804 – 1904 – The House of Rothschild, London 1905.

Chapman, Stanley: The Rise of Merchant Banking, London 1984.

La communione israelitica di Napoli dal 1830 al 1890, Naples 1890.

Druon, Maurice: Ces Messieurs de Rothschild Frères, Paris 1967.

Endelmann, Todd M.: The Jews of Georgian England, 1714 – 1830. Tradition and Change in a Liberal Society, Philadelphia 1979.

Tagebücher von Friedrich von Gentz. Aus dem Nachlaß Varnhagen's von Ense, Leipzig 1873–74, 4 vols.

Gilam, Abraham: The Emancipation of the Jews in England, Diss, Washington 1979.

Graetz, Michael: Les Juifs en France au XIXe Siècle, Paris 1989.

Oppenheim, Moritz: Erinnerungen, ed. Alfred Oppenheim, Frankfurt a.M. 1924.

Otruba, Gustav: Die Wiener Rothschilds, in: Wiener Geschichtsblätter 41/4, 1986, pp. 149–169.

Ries, Hans: Zwischen Hausse und Baisse: Börse und Geld in der Karikatur, Stuttgart 1987.

Roth, Cecil: The Magnificent Rothschilds, London 1949.

Rothschild, Victor (Lord): The Shadow of a Great Man, London 1982.

Spellanzon, Cesare: Storia del Risorgimento e dell' unità d'Italia, vol. 1, Milan 1951.

Wolf, Lucien: Essays in Jewish History, ed. von Cecil Roth (The Jewish Historical Society of England) London 1954.

(see also Bergeron, Bouvier, Davis, Ehrenberg, Gille, Dietz, Mühlstein, Rothschild, Rubens)

The Price of Success

Andia, Béatrice (ed.), Antonin Carême, Paris 1984.

Boehn, Max von: Vom Kaiserreich zur Republik. Eine Kulturgeschichte Frankreichs im 19. Jahrhundert, Munich 1921.

Gruber, Alain: L'Argenterie de maison, du 16. au 19. siècle, Fribourg (Switzerland)1982.

Lady Morgan, Sophia: La France en 1829 et 1830, 2 Bde. Paris 1830.

Prevost-Marcilhacy, Pauline: James de Rothschild à Ferrières: les projets de Paxton et de Lami, Revue de l'Art 1992, pp. 58–73.

Ravage, Marcus Eli: Glanz und Niedergang des Hauses Rothschild, Hellerau [1930].

Rothschild, Dorothy de, The Rothschilds at Waddesdon Manor, New York/Paris/London 1979.

Rothschild, Guy de: Contre bonne fortune, Paris 1983.

Waddesdon Manor – The Rothschild Collection, in: Apollo, April 1994, pp. 4–63.

The Rothschilds' »Public« Face

Fuchs, Eduard: Die Juden in der Karikatur, Munich 1921.

Prawer, Siegbert S.: Israel at Vanity Fair. Jews and Judaism in the Writings of W. M. Thackeray, Leiden 1992.

Rubens, Alfred: The Rothschilds in Caricature, Transactions of the Jewish Historical Society of England 20, 1968/69.

Rütten, Raimund / Jung, Ruth / Schneider, Gerhard (eds.): Die Karikatur zwischen Republik und Zensur. Bildsatire in Frankreich 1830 bis 1880 – eine Sprache des Widerstands?, Marburg 1991.

(see also Berghoeffer, Cowles, Mühlstein)

The Advent of the Age of Industry

Brusatti, Alois: Unternehmensfinanzierung und Privatkredit im österreichischen Vormärz, in: Mitteilungen des österreichischen Staatsarchivs XIII (1960), pp. 331–379.

Cameron, Rondo E.: The Crédit Mobilier and the economic development of Europe, in: The Journal of Political Economy LXI (1953), pp. 461–88.

Chapman, Stanley D.: Rhodes and the City of London: another view of imperialism, in: Historical Journal 28/3 (1985), pp. 647–666.

The Rise of Merchant Banking, London 1984.

Drapala, R.: Hundert Jahre Eisenwerk Witkowitz (1828–1928).

Gille, Bertrand: La Banque en France au XIXe siècle. Geneva/Paris 1970.

– Lettres adressées à la maison Rothschild de Paris par son représentant à Bruxelles, 2 vols., Löwen/Paris 1961, 1963.

Handelskammer zu Frankfurt a.M. (ed.): Geschichte der Handelskammer zu Frankfurt a.M. 1707–1908. Beiträge zur Frankfurter Handelsgeschichte, Frankfurt am Main 1908.

Horn, Alfred: Die Kaiser-Ferdinands-Nordbahn, Vienna 1970 (= Die Bahnen Österreich-Ungarns, vol. 2)

Landes, David S.: The Spoilers Foiled: the Exclusion of Prussian Finance from the French Liberation Loan of 1871, in: Charles P. Kindleberger/Guido di Tella (eds.): Economics in the long view. Essays in Honour of W.W. Rostow, vol. 2: Applications and Cases, New York, London 1982, pp. 67–110.

März, Eduard: Die historischen Voraussetzungen des Credit-Mobilier-Bankwesens in Österreich, in: Schmollers Jahrbuch für Gesetzgebung, Verwaltung und Volkswirtschaft 79 (1959), pp. 573–87.

McKay, John P.: Baku Oil and Transcaucasian Pipelines, 1883: A Study in Tsarist Economic Policy, in: Slavic Review 43 (1984), pp. 604–23.

McKay, John P.: The House of Rothschild (Paris) as a multinational industrial enterprise 1875-1914, in: Alice Teichova et al. (eds.): Multinational enterprise in historical perspective, Cambridge 1989, pp. 74–86.

Ratcliffe, Barrie M.: Railway Imperialism: the example of the Pereires' Paris-Saint Germain Company, 1835-1846, in: Business History 1976, pp. 66–84.

Rothschild, Victor (Lord): »You have it, Madam« – The purchase, in 1875, of Suez Canal shares by Disraeli and Baron Lionel de Rothschild, London 1980.

Stern, Fritz: Gold und Eisen. Bismarck und sein Bankier Bleichröder, Frankfurt am Main/Berlin 1978.

Stürmer, Michael/Gabriele Teichmann/Wilhelm Treue: Wägen und Wagen. Sal. Oppenheim jr. & Cie. Geschichte einer Bank und einer Familie, Munich ²1989.

Turrell, Robert: Rhodes, De Beers and Monopoly, in: The Journal of Imperial and Commonwealth History 10/3 (1981/82), pp. 311–43.

Turrell, Robert / Jean-Jacques van Helten: The Rothschilds, the Exploration Company and Mining Finance, in: Business History 28 (1986), pp. 181–205.

Young, George F.W.: Anglo-German Banking Syndicates and the Issue of South American Government Loans in the Era of High Imperialism, 1885-1914, in: Bankhistorisches Archiv 16 (1990), pp. 3–38.

(see also Achterberg, Bergeron, Bouvier, Ehrenberg, Gille)

The Rothschilds in the Twentieth Century

Propaganda, Persecution and Relief Work

Friedman, Régine Mihal: L´image et son Juif. Le Juif dans le cinéma Nazi, Paris 1983.

Hollstein, Dorothea: »Jud Süß« und die Deutschen. Antisemitische Vorurteile im nationalsozialistischen Spielfilm, Frankfurt am Main 1983.

Rorimer, James J. in coll. with Gilbert Rabin: Survival – The Salvage and Protection of the Art in War, New York 1950.

Rothschild, Philippe: Vive la vie. Château Mouton, aufgezeichnet von Joan Littlewood, Munich 1984.

(see also Cowles, Guy de Rothschild)

Edmond de Rothschild and Palestine

Druck, David: L'oeuvre du Baron Edmond de Rothschild, Paris 1928.

Fraenkel, Josef: Herzl and the Rothschild Family, in: Herzl Year Book III, 1960, pp. 217–36.

Margalith, Israel: Le Baron Edmond de Rothschild et la Colonisation Juive en Palestine, Paris 1957.

Naiditch, Isaac: Edmond de Rothschild, Washington DC 1945.

Schama, Simon: Two Rothschilds and the Land of Israel, London 1978.

The Rothschilds in Frankfurt

Bibliographie zur Geschichte der Frankfurter Juden 1781 -1945, ed. by the Kommission zur Erforschung der Geschichte der Frankfurter Juden, Frankfurt am Main 1978.

Breuer, Mordechai: Jüdische Orthodoxie im Deutschen Reich 1871–1918, Frankfurt am Main 1986.

Schmidt, Isolde: Eduard Schmidt von der Launitz 1797–1869. Studien zur Frankfurter Geschichte 29) Frankfurt am Main 1992.

Stollberg, Jochen (Scholarly ed.): Die Rothschild´sche Bibliothek in Frankfurt am Main, ed. by the Gesellschaft der Freunde der Stadt- und Universitätsbibliothek Frankfurt am Main e.V., Frankfurt am Main 1988.

Schiebeler, Gerhard: Jüdische Stiftungen in Frankfurt am Main, Frankfurt am Main 1988.

Windecker, Dieter: 100 Jahre Freiherr Carl von Rothschildsche Stiftug Carolinum, Berlin 1990.

(see also Arnsberg, Corti, Kracauer)

Illustration and photo credits

Archives Nationales, Paris, p. 144

Bayerisches Nationalmuseum, München, aus der Slg. Baron Lionel Rothschild, London, p. 8 (a)

De Beers Consolidated Mines Limited, Kimberley, Südafrika, p. 146

The British Library, London, p. 97, p. 107

The British Museum, London, p. 116, The Waddesdon Bequest p. 8 (c)

Bundesarchiv, Außenstelle Berlin, p. 151, p. 152 (a), p. 152 (b), p. 153

Central Archives for the History of the Jewish People, Jerusalem, p. 52

Central Zionist Archives, Jerusalem, p. 159, p. 161, p. 162, p. 163, p. 164 p. 166

Else Claude, Frankfurt am Main, p. 183, p. 188 (b), p. 195

Clementine-Kinderkrankenhaus, Frankfurt am Main, p. 192

Colonia Versicherung AG, Köln, p. 138

Creditanstalt-Bankverein, Wien, p. 136

Deutsches Museum, München, Plansammlung Deutsches Museum, p. 129, p. 133

Freies Deutsches Hochstift, Frankfurt am Main, p. 44

Germania Judaica, Köln, p. 118

Gunnersbury Park Museum, p. 89 (b) (Photo: Janet Hall und Louanne Richards, London)

Hamburger Kunsthalle, p. 11 (Photo: Elke Walbeck), p. 85

Hessische Hausstiftung Museum Schloß Fasanerie Eichenzell bei Fulda, p. 26, p. 31

Hessisches Staatsarchiv Marburg, p. 29, p. 30, p. 32, p. 33 (b), p. 34

Historisches Museum Frankfurt am Main, p. 12, p. 14, p. 20, p. 21, p. 23, p. 35, p. 40, p. 43, p. 55, p. 72, p. 74, p. 88, p. 89 (a), p. 91, p. 99, p. 174, p. 178, p. 182

Historisches Museum der Stadt Wien, p. 76, p. 77, p. 78, p. 79, p. 117

The Industrial Dwellings Society (1885) Ltd., London, p. 126

Institut für Stadtgeschichte Frankfurt am Main, p. 45, p. 157 (b), p. 181

The Israel Museum, Jerusalem, p. 70 (a), p. 70 (b)

The Jewish Museum, London, p. 64 (a)

Jüdisches Museum Frankfurt am Main, p. 3 Photo Maria Obermaier, Frankfurt a.M, p. 13, p. 15, p. 25, p. 32 (a), p. 86 (a), p. 101, p. 110 (Photo M. Obermaier, p. o.), p. 124, p. 175, p. 184

Kunsthistorisches Museum Wien, Gewidmet von Baronin Clarisse de Rothschild zum Gedächtnis von Baron Alphonse de Rothschild, 1948, p. 8 (b), p. 9

Leo Baeck-Institut, London, p. 186

Manchester Central Library, p. 36, p. 37

Musée du Château de Sceaux, p. 105 (Photo: M. Lemaitre, Paris)

Museen der Stadt Hanau, Slg. Mayer Carl v. Rothschild, Frankfurt am Main, p. 7

The Museum of London, p. 59

Museum of Modern Art, New York, p. 154

The Museum of Rischon Lezion, p. 160

Contributors to the Exhibition

The Jewish Museum wishes to thank the following museums, public collections, private collectors and institutions for making objects and exhibits available to the exhibition.

Amsterdam:
Rijksmuseum

Afalterbach:
Museum für Geldgeschichte

Basel:
Museum Haus zum Kirschgarten

Berck-sur-Mer:
Stadtverwaltung

Berlin:
Bundesarchiv
Deutsches Historisches Museum
Sammlung Haney

Bexhill-on-Sea:
Jack Spier

Cologne:
Colonia Versicherung AG
Kölnische Rückversicherungs-Gesellschaft AG
Sammlung Germania Judaica

Darmstadt:
Werner Abel
Hessisches Staatsarchiv

Düsseldorf:
Heinrich Heine Institut

Ecouen:
Musée National de la Renaissance

Eichenzell bei Fulda:
Hessische Hausstiftung, Archiv und Museum Schloß Fasanerie

Exbury:
Mr. Edmund L. de Rothschild

Frankfurt am Main:
Szymon Ajnwojner
BHF-Bank
Bundesarchiv Koblenz, Außenstelle Frankfurt am Main

Else Claude
Clementine Kinderkrankenhaus
Deutsches Institut für Filmkunde
Deutsches Postmuseum
Historisches Museum
Historisches Portfolio-Handelsgesellschaft für Historische Wertpapiere mbH.
Forschungsinstitut Senckenberg
Institut für Stadtgeschichte
Christine Lenger
Museum für Kunsthandwerk
Theater der Stadt Frankfurt
J.P. Schneider Kunsthandlung
Städelsches Kunstinstitut
Stadt- und Universitätsbibliothek
Zentrum der Zahn-, Mund- und Kieferheilkunde (Carolinum)

Graz:
Akademische Druck- und Verlagsanstalt

Hamburg:
Museum für Kunst und Gewerbe

Hanau:
Matthäus Steiger
Museen der Stadt Hanau

Hofheim:
Irmgard Zehner

Jerusalem:
Central Archives for the History of the Jewish People.
Central Zionist Archives
Arthur Fried
Yad Hanadiv
The Israel Museum
The Jewish National and University Library

Kelkheim:
Dietrich Kleipa

Königstein:
Stadtarchiv

London:
The Board of Trustees of the Victoria & Albert Museum
The British Museum
The Jewish Museum
The Museum of London

David Pearlman
Tate Gallery
N M Rothschild & Sons Limited
Lord Jacob Rothschild
Rothschild Archive
Rainer Zietz Limited

Mainz:
Universitätsbibliothek

Marburg:
Hessisches Staatsarchiv
Universitätsbibliothek

Munich:
Bayerisches Hauptstaatsarchiv
Bayerisches Nationalmuseum
Helene Habermann
Staatliche Münzsammlung

Nottingham:
Stanley Chapman

New York:
Leo Baeck Institute
The Jewish Museum
B. Zucker Foundation

Nuremberg:
Germanisches Nationalmuseum

Ostrava:
Vítcovice akciová spolecnost

Paris:
Archives Nationales
Gilbert de Goldschmidt-Rothschild
J. Kugel Antiquaires
Musée d'Orsay
Musée Carnevalet
Musée du Louvre
Musée National du Moyen-Age, Thermes de
    Cluny
Baron David de Rothschild
Baron Elie de Rothschild
Baron Eric de Rothschild
Hubert Thierry
La vie du Rail SNCF

Peterborough:
Miriam Rothschild

Pregny:
Baron Edmond de Rothschild

Ramat Gan:
Avraham Frank

Rechovot:
The Weizmann Archives

Regensburg:
Museum der Stadt Regensburg

Rüsselsheim:
Museum der Stadt Rüsselsheim

Sèvres:
Musée National de Céramique de Sèvres

Utrecht:
Centraal Museum

Vienna:
Bezirksmuseum Döbling
Historisches Museum
Jüdisches Museum
Kunsthistorisches Museum
MAK – Österreichisches Museum für Angewandte
    Kunst
Österreichisches Staatsarchiv, Archiv der Repu-
    blik
Österreichisches Staatsarchiv, Allgemeines Ver-
    waltungsarchiv
Österreichisches Staatsarchiv, Haus-, Hof- und
    Staatsarchiv
Österreichisches Staatsarchiv, Verwaltungsar-
    chiv-Verkehrsarchiv
Technisches Museum
Universitätsbibliothek der Technischen Univer-
    sität

Wiesbaden:
Hessisches Hauptstaatsarchiv

and the many private contributors who wish to
remain anonymous.
We also thank all those institutions and persons
named in the credits for providing information
and visual material and permission to reproduce
them.

Five generations of the Rothschild family, portrayed graphically

Meyer, Amschel
(1743/4–1812)
=1770
Gutle Schnapper
(1753–1849)

Jeanette (1771–1859)

Amschel Mayer (1773–1855) Frankfurt

Salomon Mayer (1774–1855) Wien
- Anselm Salomon
  - Mayer Anselm Leon
  - Caroline Julie Anselme
  - Hannah Mathilde
  - Sara Louise
  - Nathaniel Mayer
  - Ferdinand James Anselme
  - Salomon Albert Anselm
    - Georg Anselm Alphonse
    - Alphonse Mayer
    - Louis Nathaniel
    - Eugène Daniel
    - Charlotte Esther
    - Valentine Noémi
    - Oscar Ruben
  - Alice Charlotte
- Betty

Nathan Mayer (1777–1836) London
- Charlotte
- Lionel Nathan
  - Leonora
  - Evelina
  - Nathan(iel) Mayer
    - Lionel Walter
    - Charlotte Louise
    - Nathaniel Charles
  - Alfred Charles
  - Leopold
    - Lionel Nathan
    - Evelyn Achille
    - Anthony Gustav
- Anthony Nathan
- Nathaniel
  - Constance
  - Annie
- Hannah Mayer
- Mayer Amschel
- Louise

Isabella (1781–1861)

Babette (1784–1869)
- Nathalie
- Nathan James Edouard
  - Henri James Nathaniel
  - Jeanne Charlotte L.
- Mayer Albert
- Arthur
- Hannah

Carl Mayer (1788–1855) Neapel
- Charlotte
- Mayer Carl
- Adolph Carl
- Wilhelm Carl
- A. Alexander, Carl
  - Adèle Hannah Charlotte
  - Emma Louise
  - Clementine Henriette
  - Laura Thérèse
  - Hannah Louise
  - Magaretha Alexandrine
  - Bertha Clara
  - Georgine Sara
  - Adelheid
  - Minna Caroline

Julie (1790–1815)

Henriette (1791–1866)

James Mayer (1792–1868) Paris
- Bettina Caroline
- Lionel James Mayer
- Charlotte Béatrice
- Edouard Alphonse J.
  - Alphonse Edouard Emile
  - Guy Edouard Alphonse
  - Jaqueline Rebecca L.
  - Bethsabée
- Charlotte
- Mayer Alphonse
- Gustav S. James
- Salomon James
- Edmond James
  - Octave
  - Zoé Lucie Betty
  - Aline Caroline
  - Bertha Juliette
  - André
  - Robert Philippe G.
    - Diane Cécile
    - James Gustave Jules
    - Cécile Léonie
    - Elie Robert
  - Hélène Betty
  - James Armand Edmond
    - Edmond Adolphe
  - Maurice Edmond Charles
  - Miriam Caroline Alexandrine

Der Name Rothschild hat in Europa noch heute einen besonderen, wenn nicht einzigartigen Klang. Mit ihren vielfältigen Aktivitäten hat die Familie Rothschild die Geschichte Europas in den letzten zwei Jahrhunderten mitgeprägt. Insbesondere in der dunkelsten Zeit der deutschen Geschichte hat sie jedoch von Deutschen zugleich unermeßliches Leid erfahren. Die Historie dieser wahrhaft europäischen Familie ist somit auch ein Teil unserer eigenen Geschichte.

Ausgehend von der Wechselstube in der bedrückenden Enge des Frankfurter Judenghettos des 18. Jahrhunderts entwickelten sich die Rothschilds zum führenden europäischen Bankhaus des 19. Jahrhunderts. Den Grundstein legte bereits Meyer Amschel Rothschild. Diskretion, Vorsicht, Weitblick und Beharrlichkeit machten ihn zum Prototypus des internationalen Bankkaufmanns. Gewinnerwirtschaftung, Sicherheit und Liquidität waren die Eckpfeiler seiner Unternehmungen; sie sind noch heute für das Bankwesen unerläßlich. Zwar zeichneten sich die Rothschilds auch durch Kühnheit aus, zugleich aber haben sie auf manches zu riskant erscheinende Geschäft verzichtet.

Die fünf Söhne Meyer Amschels bauten das Haus Rothschild zu einer internationalen Großbank mit Niederlassungen an den damals wichtigsten Finanzplätzen Europas aus. Obwohl jede Filiale selbständig agierte, blieb doch der innere Zusammenhang bestehen. Dies ermöglichte nicht nur eine Begrenzung des Risikos. Großtransaktionen, wie sie bei den Rothschilds vorherrschten, konnten auch von einer anderen als der nationalen Warte betrachtet und beurteilt werden. Der Nachrichten- und Gedankenaustausch ermöglichte zugleich, Kriege und Krisen besser zu überstehen. In einer sich wandelnden Welt, für die ein gut funktionierendes Bankwesen immer wichtiger wurde, setzte das Haus Rothschild damit Maßstäbe.

Die Familie Rothschild hat viel dazu beigetragen, daß Frankfurt im 19. Jahrhundert zu einem der wichtigsten Finanzplätze Europas wurde. In diesem Jahr feiern wir nicht nur den 250. Geburtstag Meyer Amschel Rothschilds, sondern auch die 1200jährige Stadtgeschichte Frankfurts. Es ist sicherlich positiv und zukunftweisend für die Stadt, wenn in diesem Jahr das Europäische Währunginstitut seine Arbeit in Frankfurt aufnimmt. Frankfurt kann damit seine europäische Perspektive sichtbar erweitern, eine Perspektive, zu der Meyer Amschel Rothschild vor über 200 Jahren bereits wesentlich beigetragen hat.

Über die Ausstellung »Die Rothschilds – eine europäische Familie« freue ich mich. Mit der Ausstellung stattet Frankfurt auch ein wenig Dank ab an eine große Familie. Ich wünsche der Veranstaltung viel Erfolg.

Dr. Dr. h.c. Hans Tietmeyer
Präsident der
Deutschen Bundesbank

Danke, Herr von Rothschild!

Schon als Gründungsmitglied unserer Bank anno 1835 haben Sie, Baron Carl von Rothschild, echte Pionierarbeit geleistet. Das hat sich gelohnt: Bereits sechs Jahre später konnten wir uns mit unserer Mobiliar-Feuer-Versicherungsgesell- schaft im Frank- furter Raum nie- derlassen. Später expandierten dann das Bankgeschäft und unser Börsenbüro. Heute gehört die Filiale Frankfurt zu unseren wichtigsten und erfolgreichsten Außenstellen. Die Stadt Frankfurt als klassischer Handels- und Warenumschlagplatz hat dazu ebenso beigetragen wie das Frankfurter Bankhaus Rothschild. Und das wissen wir zu schätzen.

Die HYPO. Eine Bank – ein Wort.

Es gehört für mich zu den wichtigsten Projekten, die in Frankfurt aus Anlaß des zwölfhundertsten Stadtgeburtstags realisiert werden, wenn das Jüdische Museum die Geschichte der Familie Rothschild aufarbeitet. Hier werden in der Tat exemplarisch Linien gezogen, die nicht nur Geschichte – in allen Facetten – lebendig halten, sondern die in zwei wesentlichen Bereichen auch in die Zukunft weisen.

Fraglos markiert der Name Rothschild – in Verbindung mit Frankfurt – den Beginn der Bedeutung Frankfurts als Bankenmetropole. Zugleich aber verbindet sich dieser Aspekt sofort mit einer europäischen, einer weltweiten Bedeutungsdimension. Hier wird die Vergangenheit Ausgangspunkt für Gegenwart, für Zukunft.

Für ein Kreditinstitut, das von der Gründung an sehr bewußt den Namen seiner Vaterstadt im Firmennamen trägt, möchte ich an etwas erinnern, was wohl wenig präsent ist. Aus der Arbeit am Friedrich-Stoltze-Museum, das die Frankfurter Sparkasse seit über fünfzehn Jahren betreibt, weiß ich um die enge, auch fördernde Freundschaft, die Meyer Amschel Rothschild mit Friedrich Stoltze verband, dem (satirisch-freiheitlich) schreibenden Urfrankfurter. Sie ist Ausdruck gemeinsamen Frankfurter Bürgersinns: weltoffen und heimatverbunden.

In vielen noch heute erzählten Anekdoten wird an Meyer Amschel Rothschild als Frankfurter erinnert – und er wird wohl dabei anerkennend verehrt. Es wird an den Frankfurter erinnert, der dem Schreiber Stoltze ein Etui mit silbernen Löffeln als Dank für ein Auftragsgedicht mit der Bemerkung überreichte, Stoltze solle ihm nicht böse seien, er habe seinen Namen eingravieren lassen. Als der Beschenkte ihm versicherte, dies sei ihm sehr angenehm, mußte er sich belehren lassen: »Angenehm ist, wenn nichts draufsteht und man es verkaufen oder versetzen kann ohne viel Umständ'.«

Die Aufarbeitung rothschildscher Geschichte nimmt ihren Ausgangspunkt dort, wo der weitsichtige Bankier und Frankfurter Bürger eins waren. Auch dies weist als verpflichtende Aufgabe in die Zukunft, um in ihr zu sichern, was in der Vergangenheit einmal untrennbar war.

Klaus Wächter
Sprecher des Vorstandes der
Frankfurter Sparkasse

Im Strom ... der Geschichte.

Historisches Museum Frankfurt am Main

AD 20 RWGK.

Landesbank Hessen-Thüringen.

Weltoffenheit und unternehme-
risches Handeln in der Ver-
antwortung gegenüber Staat und
Gesellschaft – Merkmale, die sich
mit dem Namen Rothschild verbin-
den. Sie haben die Geschichte der
Stadt Frankfurt bis in die heutige
Zeit geprägt. In diesem Strom der
Geschichte als gestaltende Kraft
sichtbar zu werden, verstehen wir
als Vermächtnis und Aufgabe zugleich.

Helaba Frankfurt
LANDESBANK HESSEN-THÜRINGEN

Landesbank Hessen-Thüringen Girozentrale
Frankfurt/Erfurt
Amsterdam, Berlin, Budapest, Darmstadt, Dublin,
Düsseldorf, Kassel, Leipzig, London, Luxemburg,
New York, Prag, Stuttgart, Warschau und Zürich.

Helaba Frankfurt.
Die Bank mit den guten Verbindungen.

 Finanzgruppe

Der Name Rothschild ist eng verbunden mit dem Aufstieg des Bankplatzes Frankfurt am Main im 18. und 19. Jahrhundert. Von der Frankfurter Judengasse aus legte der Gründer der Dynastie, Meyer Amschel Rothschild (1744–1812), die Grundlagen für das spätere internationale Finanzsystem der Familie. Die Rothschilds waren die Financiers der Herrscher Europas und nahmen bis 1870 auf dem europäischen Markt für Staatsanleihen eine dominierende Stellung ein.

Mit dem Aufstieg der kapitalstarken Aktienbanken in den siebziger Jahren des 19. Jahrhunderts begann in Deutschland der Niedergang der Privatbankiers. Auch das Bankhaus Rothschild blieb davon nicht verschont. Zudem wurde Berlin nach der Reichsgründung 1871 das politische, wirtschaftliche und finanzielle Zentrum Deutschlands und überflügelte Frankfurt, den bisher führenden deutschen Bankplatz. Ein Symbol für diesen Funktionsverlust war die Liquidation des Frankfurter Stammhauses der Rothschilds im Jahre 1901, nachdem der letzte Inhaber ohne männliche Nachkommen gestorben war. Der Geschäftsbetrieb und der größte Teil der Mitarbeiter der Rothschild-Bank wurden von der Disconto-Gesellschaft, Berlin, übernommen und bildeten die Basis für deren Frankfurter Filiale.

Die Disconto-Gesellschaft fusionierte 1929 mit der Deutschen Bank und errichtete damit ihre Frankfurter Filiale.

Nach dem Zweiten Weltkrieg wurde Frankfurt am Main wieder der führende Bankplatz in Deutschland, an dem alle bedeutenden Banken ihren Sitz nahmen. Im Jahre 1989 kamen auch die Rothschilds zurück an den Main: die Londoner und die Züricher Rothschild-Bank errichteten eine Repräsentanz in der Mainmetropole.

Ich begrüße es sehr, daß durch diese Ausstellung im Rahmen des Stadtjubiläums einer breiten Öffentlichkeit das Wirken der Rothschilds in Frankfurt bewußt gemacht wird.

Hilmar Kopper

Mitglied des Vorstandes der
Deutschen Bank AG

„DIE HANDLUNG IST DIE SEELE DIESER REICHEN STADT."

■ So charakterisierte Goethes Großonkel Johann Michael von Loen anno 1741 seine Vaterstadt. „Unter den Kaufleuten selbst sind große und ehrwürdige Männer", fuhr er fort, „sie haben meistens in ihrer Jugend schöne Reisen gethan, verstehen die vornehmsten europäischen Sprachen, lesen gute Bücher und zeigen in ihrem ganzen Umgang eine edle Lebensart."

■ Handel und Wandel bestimmten von jeher die Geschichte Frankfurts. Die Orientierung nach draußen hat in der Main-Metropole eine lange Tradition. Frankfurt gibt ein gutes Beispiel dafür, daß grenzüberschreitende Verbindungen nicht erst seit der Industrialisierung lebensnotwendig sind. Weltoffenheit und Toleranz, die Bereitschaft, Fremde in den Stadtmauern aufzunehmen, und das Verständnis für andere gehören neben dem Leistungswillen der Menschen seit alters zu den Stärken dieser Stadt.

■ Mit den Rothschilds betrat 1763 eine nachmals wahrhaft europäische Familie die große Bühne Frankfurt: Mayer Amschel Rothschild und seine vier Söhne.

Sie orientierten sich über die Mauern der Stadt, die Grenzen der Herzog- und Fürstentümer hinweg und nutzten den Wandel in der Wirtschaft und der Gesellschaft Europas für ihren Aufstieg.

■ Aus dem Münzhandel, dem Handel mit Juwelen, Antiquitäten und Waren aller Art schufen sich die Rothschilds einen neuen Beruf, den des Bankiers. Mit sicherem Gespür für die Möglichkeiten der Zukunft wandten sie sich den jeweils neuesten und ertragreichsten Geschäftspartnern zu und schufen damit die Grundlagen ihres guten Rufs innerhalb und außerhalb des Kontinents.

■ Als eine der großen Frankfurter Banken mit eigener Tradition begrüßen wir diese einzigartige Gesamtschau zur Geschichte einer berühmten europäischen Familie aus Frankfurt im Jüdischen Museum. Die Ausstellung – so wünschen wir uns – möge dazu beitragen, die Erinnerung an eine große Gründerfamilie wachzuhalten und zugleich das Verständnis für die Herkunft und Zukunft des modernen Bankwesens zu fördern.

Die DG BANK ist das Spitzenkreditinstitut der deutschen Genossenschaftsorganisation. 1895 als „Preußenkasse" in Berlin gegründet, zog sie 1949 an den Bankenplatz Frankfurt am Main, wo sie seit 1976 als Deutsche Genossenschaftsbank firmiert.

FRANKFURTER HYPO

Die Frankfurter Hypothekenbank freut sich, einen Beitrag zur Rothschild-Ausstellung leisten zu können.

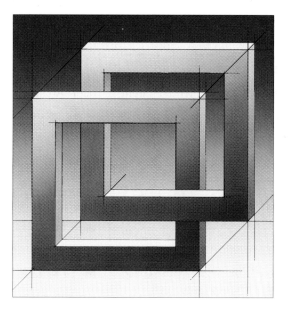

Als älteste reine private Hypothekenbank zählt die 1862 gegründete Frankfurter Hypo zu den führenden deutschen Spezialinstituten für Immobilienfinanzierungen und Finanzierungen der öffentlichen Hand. Ihre Darlehensmittel beschafft sich die Bank durch den Verkauf von Pfandbriefen. Pfandbriefe der Frankfurter Hypo werden von Standard & Poor's mit „AAA" bewertet.

Frankfurter Hypothekenbank

Junghofstraße 5–7 · 60311 Frankfurt am Main

Congratulations to the City of Frankfurt on its 1200th Anniversary

Rothschild GmbH
Ulmenstrasse 22, 60325 Frankfurt am Main

N M Rothschild & Sons Limited
New Court, St. Swithin's Lane
London EC4P 4DU

Rothschild & Cie Banque
17 Avenue Matignon
75008 Paris

Rothschild Bank AG
Zollikerstrasse 181, 8034 Zurich